WORKBOOK

CAROL NUTTALL AND AMANDA FRENCH

ADVANCED
OUTCOMES

NATIONAL
GEOGRAPHIC
L E A R N I N G

Australia · Brazil · Mexico · Singapore · United Kingdom · United States

ngl.cengage.com/outcomes

PASSWORD   outcomes!C4#

NATIONAL GEOGRAPHIC
L E A R N I N G

Outcomes *Advanced Workbook*
Carol Nuttall and Amanda French

Publisher: Gavin McLean

Publishing Consultant: Karen Spiller

Development Editor: Steve Longworth

Editorial Manager: Scott Newport

Head of Strategic Marketing, ELT: Charlotte Ellis

Senior Content Project Manager: Nick Ventullo

Senior Production Controller: Eyvett Davis

Cover Design: eMC Design

Text Design: Studio April

Compositor: Q2A Media Services Pvt. Ltd.

National Geographic Liaison: Leila Hismeh

For product information and technology assistance, contact us at
Cengage Learning Customer & Sales Support, cengage.com/contact

For permission to use material from this text or product,
submit all requests online at **cengage.com/permissions**
Further permissions questions can be emailed to
permissionrequest@cengage.com

ISBN: 978-1-305-10228-6

National Geographic Learning
Cheriton House, North Way, Andover, Hampshire, SP10 5BE, United Kingdom

National Geographic Learning, a Cengage Learning Company, has a mission to bring the world to the classroom and the classroom to life. With our English language programs, students learn about their world by experiencing it. Through our partnerships with National Geographic and TED Talks, they develop the language and skills they need to be successful global citizens and leaders.

Locate your local office at **international.cengage.com/region**

Visit National Geographic Learning online at **NGL.Cengage.com/ELT**
Visit our corporate website at **www.cengage.com**

CREDITS

Although every effort has been made to contact copyright holders before publication, this has not always been possible. If notified, the publisher will undertake to rectify any errors or omissions at the earliest opportunity.

Text

The publisher would like to thank the following sources for permission to reproduce their copyright protected statistical data:

Page 26: United Kingdom: http://www.statistics.gov.uk/STATBASE/Expodata/Spreadsheets/D5204.xls Copyright © UK Statistics authority. *Reproduced under the terms of the Click-Use Licence.* New Zealand:

http://www.socialreport.msd.govt.nz/civil-political-rights/representation-women-government.html Copyright © Ministry of Social Development, NZ Government.

Photos

The publisher would like to thank the following sources for permission to use their copyright protected images:

4 (tl) © microimages/Fotolia.com; 4 (tr) © AndreasWeber/iStockphoto; 4 (b) © Dorling Kindersley ltd/Alamy Stock Photo; 5 (t) © Justin Horrocks/iStockphoto; 5 (b) © Robert Mayne/iStockphoto; 7 (t) © Herve Collart/Sygma/Corbis; 7 (b) © fabianohugen/Fotolia.com; 8 © Dustie/Shutterstock.com; 9 © Tatyana Pavlova/Fotolia.com; 11 © Aldo Murillo/iStockphoto; 12 © GlobalStock/iStockphoto; 13 © Pictorial Press Ltd/Alamy Stock Photo; 14 © wavebreakmedia/Shutterstock.com; 16 (t) © Barry Vincent/Alamy Stock Photo; 16 (m) © Renato Bordoni/Alamy Stock Photo; 16 (b) © eclypse78/Fotolia.com; 17 © Rawpixel/Shutterstock.com; 18 © charles taylor/Shutterstock.com; 19 (t) © nico_blue/iStockphoto; 19 (m) © phildate/iStockphoto; 19 (b) © anandkrish16/iStockphoto; 20 (l) © Christa Brunt/iStockphoto; 20 (r) © Nikada/Getty Images; 23 (t) © FrankyDeMeyer/iStockphoto; 23 (b) © kreicher/iStockphoto; 25 © Lionel Healing/AFP/Getty Images; 27 © rrmf13/iStockphoto; 28 © nuno/iStockphoto; 29 © Dirk Freder/iStockphoto; 30 © Francesco Ocello/Shutterstock.com; 31 © AP Photo/Alden Pellett; 32 (tl) © bikeriderlondon/Shutterstock.com; 32 (tr) © lisafx/Bigstock.com; 32 (ml) © Rich Legg/iStockphoto; 32 (mr) © Jennifer_Sharp/iStockphoto; 32 (b) © duncan1890/iStockphoto; 33 © Spanic/iStockphoto; 34 © Yuri_Arcurs/Bigstock.com; 35 © Rahul Sengupta/iStockphoto; 37 © jclark/Bigstock.com; 39 (tl) © LanceB/iStockphoto; 39 (tr) © FANDER09/iStockphoto; 39 (bl) © Edgar Monkey/Fotolia.com; 39 (br) © tamzinm/Shutterstock.com; 40 Sheffield Hallam University; 41 (t) © DNY59/iStockphoto; 41 (b) © LuVo/iStockphoto; 42 © REX Shutterstock; 44 © djgunner/iStockphoto; 46 © Greg Epperson/Shutterstock.com; 47 © mseidelch/iStockphoto; 49 (t) © Florilegius/Alamy Stock Photo; 49 (b) © pukrufus/iStockphoto; 50 (t) © Axrock/iStockphoto; 53 © monkeybusinessimages/iStockphoto; 55 © zoranm/iStockphoto; 57 © Juice Images/Fotolia.com; 58 © dmbaker/iStockphoto; 59 © stevecoleimages/iStockphoto; 62 © morchella/Fotolia.com; 64 © Neil Tingle/Alamy Stock Photo; 65 © boryak/iStockphoto; 67 © imageBROKER/Alamy Stock Photo; 68 (t) © Vehbi Koca/Alamy Stock Photo; 68 (b) © Terry Harris/Alamy Stock Photo; 71 (t) © CrazyD/iStockphoto; 71 (b) © Andreas Karelias/Alamy Stock Photo; 72 (t) © Konstantin Yolshin/Shutterstock.com; 72 (b) © wynnter/iStockphoto; 73 (t, b) © Mary Evans Picture Library/Alamy Stock Photo; 74 © Bettmann/Corbis; 76 © Yuri Arcurs/Fotolia.com; 77 © Danil Melekhin/iStockphoto; 80 (tl) © Paul Glendell/Alamy Stock Photo; 80 (tr) © jwilkinson/iStockphoto; 80 (bl) © Zak Waters/Alamy Stock Photo; 80 (br) © Les Gibbon/Alamy Stock Photo; 82 © diego cervo/Fotolia.com; 83 © ricardoinfante/iStockphoto; 85 (l) © Lise Gagne/iStockphoto; 85 (r) © LUke1138/iStockphoto; 86 © Blend Images/Alamy Stock Photo; 88 (l) © Asia Images Group Pte Ltd/Alamy Stock Photo; 88 (r) © Peter Horree/Alamy Stock Photo; 89 © mbbirdy/iStockphoto; 90 (l) © phildate/iStockphoto; 90 (r) © Golden Pixels LLC/Shutterstock.com; 91 (l) © Randy Faris/Corbis; 91 (r) © Stock Foundry Images/Alamy Stock Photo; 93 © Kevin Foy/Alamy; 95 (t) © Mutlu Kurtbas/iStockphoto; 95 (b) © Heng Sinith/epa/Corbis; 96 (t) © ImageryMajestic/Shutterstock.com; 96 (b) © Sebastian Wasek/Alamy Stock Photo; 97 (t) © OrlowskiDesigns/iStockphoto; 97 (b) © Stephen Frink Collection/Alamy Stock Photo; 98 © Ade_Deployed/iStockphoto.

Cover: © Henry Sudarman/500px;

Illustrations by Mark Draisey and Clive Goddard

Printed in China by RR Donnelley
Print Number: 06   Print Year: 2020

CONTENTS

01 CITIES

VOCABULARY City life

1 Complete the sentences with the words in the box.

congested	run down	spotless
sprawling	vibrant	well-run

1 At rush hour in Bangkok, thousands of motorcycles hit the streets. The centre's really ....

2 There was no rubbish anywhere in the city centre. It was completely ....

3 Istanbul is a big, ... city. It seems to go on for miles and miles.

4 The area is very .... , with many buildings in poor condition or completely derelict.

5 We have a very .... bus service. Over 95% of all buses arrive on time.

6 Reykjavik's nightlife is really .... , with lots of great bars and nightclubs.

2 Match the descriptions (1–8) with the words and phrases (a–h).

1 The atmosphere is awful! I sometimes feel like I'm choking!

2 Pick that up! Do you want to get a fine?

3 They come on time, and everything runs really smoothly.

4 The crime rate's quite high, so I worry about being attacked if I'm out after dark.

5 She's always got to have the last word in fashion – the latest shoes, watch, smartphone ... You name it.

6 Most of the buildings in the area are condemned, and there are plans to redevelop it.

7 We were just crawling along for two hours! So I was late for my meeting.

8 There are new bars and restaurants springing up in the area. It's really livened up.

a muggings and shootings

b slum

c network of buses and trams

d traffic

e smog and fumes

f buzz

g dropping litter

h conspicuous consumption

LISTENING

3 🔊 1.1 Listen to part of a radio programme in which two students give their opinions of a city. Which city (a–c) are they talking about?

4 Listen again. Who is more positive about the aspects of life in the city: Aytak (A) or Eileen (E)? Or neither (–) or both (A+E)?

1 the climate ....
2 the city centre ....
3 the cleanliness ....
4 the local accent ....
5 the local people ....
6 the safety ....
7 the nightclubs ....

Learner tip

Understanding a speaker's tone can often help you work out their opinion or attitude. For example, is the speaker's voice neutral or emotional? Do they sound bored, angry, enthusiastic or sarcastic?

DEVELOPING WRITING
An informal email – writing a reply

5 **Read the email. Write questions from the prompts (a–d) and use them to complete the gaps (1–4).**

a for / you / when / best / be / ?

....

b do / how / you / ?

....

c there / anything / on / good / be / ?

....

d what / be / like / it / ?

....

To	Arlene
From	Sushant
Subject	Holidays!

¹....... I'm studying like crazy here, because it's my finals next week. So apologies if this is just a quick message. I've been thinking a lot about your invite to come and stay, and yes, I'd love to! My exams finish on Friday, so I could get on a train any time after then. ².......

I've never seen your hometown, so I'm really looking forward to it! ³....... I'd really like to explore, and maybe go to some local events too. ⁴.......

Anyway, I'd better get back to my revision. Speak soon!

Sushant

6 **Read the reply on the right. Which topics does Arlene mention?**

nightlife	what's on
architecture	atmosphere
countryside	language
food	shopping

7 **Choose the correct words to complete Arlene's reply.**

8 **Find words and expressions in Arlene's email which mean the same as 1–4.**

1 go into town for a night out ....

2 have a big selection ....

3 a popular destination ....

4 collect (someone) in a car ....

To	Sushant
From	Arlene
Subject	Re: Holidays!

Hi Sushant,

That's great news! I'm studying for my exams at the moment too, but I'll have finished by next Saturday, so why don't you come then? I know what you mean about the need to get ¹*out and about / up and around*. I'm sick and ²*tired / bored* of these four walls! Let's hit the town on your visit. Belfast's got a wild clubbing scene, so we'll be spoilt for choice. Restaurants are really pricey, though, so we'll give them a ³*miss / loss*!

Anyway, you'll love Belfast. It's a friendly, cosmopolitan city, with a really vibrant feel to it. In the last few years there've been a lot of changes. It used to be a bit ⁴*run down / affluent* in places, but it's all been ⁵*done / made* up, and now it's a tourist hot-spot! There are some very trendy boutiques, if you're into that kind of thing. I think the Music Festival's going to be on that week so we could check ⁶*out / up* some bands, if you're up for that?

Let me know when your train gets in, and I'll come and pick you up.

Take care,
Arlene

9 **Imagine that Sushant sent his email to you. Write a reply (150–190 words) to Sushant, answering his questions and giving information about your town or city. Include three or four of the topics from exercise 6.**

01

VOCABULARY
Emphasising and exaggerating

1 Rewrite the sentences in a more emphatic way, using the words in brackets.

1 It was like the Arctic in there. (really, really)
   The room was ....

2 The view was panoramic, like being on top of the world. (miles and miles)
   You could see ....

3 The people are crazy drivers; it's like being on a race track. (totally)
   The way people drive ....

4 It was very hot in the restaurant and I had to get out. (unbearably)
   I had to leave ....

DEVELOPING CONVERSATIONS
Reinforcing and exemplifying a point

2 Complete the dialogues with suitable words and phrases from the box. You do not need to use all of them.

spotless	literally	miles and miles	unbearably
completely	packed	totally	really, really
loads and loads	lively	absolutely	

A: It looked like a bomb had hit it the next morning.
B: Yeah?
A: Honestly. There were ¹..................... of empty cans and plastic plates all over the floor, and the place ²..................... stank of beer.

C: The cinema was absolutely ³.....................
D: Really?
C: Seriously. The queue outside beforehand stretched for ⁴.....................; right round the block! It was ⁵..................... insane!

E: The hotel was ⁶..................... up-market.
F: Oh, yes?
E: Really. It was like the Ritz. The rooms were ⁷..................... huge, and the service was impeccable. The whole place was ⁸..................... too, everywhere was so clean it looked brand new.

PRONUNCIATION
Intonation for emphasis

Language note stress

- -

English speakers use stress to focus the listener's attention on what is important. Extreme words often have a strong stress.

3 Practise saying these sentences. Then underline the syllables you think should be stressed the most.

1 I swear, the shop was filthy inside!
2 The woman in the baker's was incredibly helpful.
3 Honestly, the stench was unbearable!
4 It was really, really great to see you again!
5 Seriously, he drove like crazy to get here!
6 Getting across town was a nightmare!

4 ⬤ 1.2 Listen and check. Practise again and try to imitate the intonation.

READING

5 Quickly read the article opposite. In what order do you learn about these things? Write 1–6.

population increase	....
a method to deal with waste	....
protest against changes	....
the creation of green spaces	....
concerns for the future	....
an idea to improve travel	....

6 Read the article again. Are the statements true (T) or false (F)?

1 Curitiba's difficulties are unusual when compared to other large cities.
2 In Curitiba, people are rewarded for collecting waste.
3 Lawnmowers are used to maintain all the grassy areas in the city.
4 Lerner invested more money in buses than trains because buses were faster.
5 A number of children prevented motorists from entering the new pedestrian centre.
6 Retail companies suffered as a result of Lerner's initiatives.
7 Curitiba is now a more affluent city.
8 The bus system is less popular now than it was initially.

7 Complete the sentences with *one* particle in each gap. The expressions are all taken from the article.

1 What is the government doing to deal .... the problem of urban unemployment?
2 The tenants have come .... with a plan to do up the tower block.
3 The council keeps the lawns .... good trim.
4 At first, residents opposed plans for a new city skate park, but the skaters eventually won them ....
5 Commuters are .... in arms about the new parking regulations.
6 The cost of the new stadium has put the council's finances .... enormous strain.

All Change in Curitiba!

Ticket

38125 166 45   26/08

Retain ticket for inspection

Like many other major world cities, Curitiba in southern Brazil has had to deal with issues such as pollution, poverty, and limited public funding. However, the architect and three-times mayor of the city, Jaime Lerner, has introduced some innovative solutions.

As part of his 'Master Plan', Lerner hoped to make the city more environmentally friendly. He initiated a recycling scheme based on an 'incentives' system. In return for delivering recyclable rubbish to specified processing points, residents receive a bag of vegetables or bus tokens. As a result, Curitiba now has one of the highest recycling rates in the world. Lerner also ordered the creation of 26 urban parks. As well as curbing pollution, these control flooding. They also make an unusual sight for tourists – as a low-cost method to keep the lawns in trim, sheep are allowed to graze there!

Easing traffic congestion presented a challenge as resources were limited, but Lerner came up with the idea of a rapid transit bus system, with extra long buses and special 'pod' shaped bus stops all over the city. It runs as swiftly as an underground railway but for a tenth of the cost. Commuters were delighted.

Lerner did not win over all the city's residents immediately, however. When his plans to pedestrianise part of the centre were passed, local businesses were up in arms, fearing a reduction in profits. Realising he needed to act quickly, Lerner had the transformation of six blocks completed

within three days. When a group of stubborn motorists attempted to drive through the new pedestrian area, Lerner arranged for local primary schools to hold a painting workshop on the streets. The drivers were forced to turn back. Luckily for Lerner, this rebellion was short-lived. The ensuing increase in turnover rapidly persuaded shop owners to change their minds. What's more, the incident also effectively demonstrated that Lerner was a mayor who could get things done.

Lerner's pragmatism and determination helped shape the Curitiba of today. The average income per capita has risen from a level that was below the Brazilian average in the 1970s to 66% above the average, and surveys indicate high levels of resident satisfaction.

So, is it all just one big success story? In some respects, Curitiba may have been too successful for its own good. People and businesses have flocked to the city, which now has more than 1.8 million residents. This has put the city under enormous strain. Forty years ago, buses transported 54,000 passengers a day. Now the number is 2.3 million. According to some experts, the transport system has reached its maximum efficiency capacity. Following a surge in complaints about the noisy and packed buses, the service is in decline. What's more, the city is struggling to provide sufficient housing, employment and school places for all its new residents.

How long Curitiba can retain its image as a model sustainable city depends on what planners will do next – one thing's for certain, the city will keep on changing.

Glossary

graze: eat grass
flock to: go to (a place) in large numbers
sustainable: capable of being continued with minimum long-term damage to the environment

VOCABULARY Recovery and change

1 Complete the text with the correct form of the words in the box.

decline	flourish	neglect	initiate	pour
demolish	soar	undergo		

The city of New Orleans is now almost as well known for its hurricane as for its colourful carnival.

In 2005, Hurricane Katrina, as it came to be known, devastated the city, leaving large areas underwater and rendering many buildings so severely damaged that they had to be ¹..................... . The task of ²..................... plans for recovery seemed immense.

However, the disaster presented the city with a unique opportunity for improving areas which had long been in ³..................... . Several run-down, ⁴..................... buildings were replaced by new schools that soon proved highly successful, the number of pupils ⁵..................... within the first two years of them opening. Furthermore, the nature of the disaster meant that large parts of the city had to ⁶..................... major reconstruction. As a result, the local building industry has ⁷..................... in recent years, becoming the area's main source of employment. Meanwhile, entrepreneurs have ⁸..................... funds into researching new methods of flood prevention, and this in turn has helped to regenerate local business.

New Orleans may still have a way to go toards full recovery, but at this year's carnival it will definitely have something to celebrate again.

GRAMMAR Perfect forms

2 Find and correct *six* mistakes in the sentences.

1 She said she hasn't been to Buenos Aires before last year.
2 My family has lived in Milan until 1994.
3 I'm sure there's a reason why he didn't turn up. He may have thought you meant half past eight.
4 The town hall was reopened last year, had been completely rebuilt after the fire.
5 It is believed that the number of university graduates will had doubled by 2020.
6 By the time we got there, the concert finished.
7 Where had you been? We've been waiting here for hours and hours!
8 Having visited the city several times, Kasia was starting to feel at home there.

3 Complete the sentences with the correct form of the verbs in brackets.

1 It was the third time the city .... by an earthquake. (destroy)
2 For the last two years, the city council .... the centre. (develop)
3 He .... a town planner ever since 2010. (be)
4 The city may .... from the recession, but it's still facing problems with crime. (recover)
5 At the time I met them, they .... from city to city for many years, never making a permanent home. (travel)
6 The improved transport network is thought to .... an influx of new entrepreneurs to the area. (encourage)
7 .... up as part of the council's 'clean up the city' campaign, the area is now more popular with affluent families. (do)
8 The new motorway .... by this time next month. (complete)

Language note participle clauses

Participle clauses are often used in written English as a more concise form of expression. We can use a perfect participle clause to talk about consecutive past events. *Having left town, I called home.* (The speaker had already left town by the time they called home.)

VOCABULARY Binomials

4 Match the binomials (1–6) with their meanings (a–f).

1 first and foremost   a fed up
2 peace and quiet   b in some places
3 on and off   c relaxing, calm situation
4 long and hard   d most importantly
5 sick and tired   e carefully
6 here and there   f for short periods over time

5 Complete the sentences with the correct binomials from exercise 4.

1 I've been working with the company .... for about five years now.
2 James went to live in a village because he was .... of all the traffic in town. He'd had enough.
3 I work in the city centre all week, and retreat to the .... of the village at weekends.
4 The new mall will be .... a shopping centre, but will also boast an entertainment complex, with cinemas and a bowling alley.
5 There are high rise blocks everywhere, but .... you can still see the occasional town house.
6 You need to think .... before you buy the flat. It's very expensive.

6 Complete the sentences with *one* word in each gap.

1 The only place I can find a bit of peace and .... is the park.
2 We looked .... and hard for a suitable café, but nowhere looked very inviting.
3 I bought a few bits and .... at the shops.
4 We've lived here on and .... for most of our lives.
5 I don't see her much any more, but every .... and then, she gives me a call.
6 The research centre where I work has so many rules and .... regarding health and safety!

Vocabulary Builder Quiz 1

Download the Vocabulary Builder for Unit 1 and try the quiz below. Write your answers in your notebook. Then check them and record your score.

1 Complete the sentences.

1 It's a big decision. I want you to think long and .... before you commit yourself.
2 The local council has .... plans to pedestrianise the main shopping area.
3 I don't go into the centre every day, but I enjoy shopping there .... and then.
4 She felt .... to protest against the parking restrictions outside the hospital.
5 I'm .... and tired of commuting to work, so I'm moving to the city.
6 She freaked .... when she saw the damage.

2 Choose the noun which *can't* follow the adjective.

1 affluent   *suburb / career / woman / lifestyle*
2 raise   *questions / hopes / plans / doubts*
3 spotless   *tip / house / image / reputation*
4 reverse   *a trend / a service / a policy / a decision*
5 spark   *outrage / protest / interest / nerves*
6 impose   *a crowd / a ban / restrictions / a fine*

3 Complete the sentences with the correct form of the words in brackets.

1 Police cracked down after a series of .... (mug).
2 Conspicuous .... (consume) is fuelled by the media.
3 The streets are choked by traffic .... (congest).
4 The exhibition, ... (title) 'Urban Truths' is coming to the Tate next month.
5 The city is surrounded by .... (sprawl) suburbs.
6 I was .... (thrill) to see my old friend again.
7 .... (demolish) of the inner-city slums will take place next week.

4 Complete the words.

1 The centre .... went major reconstruction.
2 The global .... turn has caused increasing unemployment.
3 It was a very run-.................... old building.
4 The street was spot.................... clean.
5 We welcomed the .... turn in the economy.
6 After the earthquake, residents were temporarily re-.................... in a hotel apartment complex.

Score ____ /25

Wait a couple of weeks and try the quiz again.
Compare your scores.

VOCABULARY Describing people

1 Complete the descriptions with the words in the box. There are two extra words that you don't need to use. Then match the descriptions (1–6) with the pictures (a–f).

pain	bitchy	charming
incompetent	laid-back	principled
snob	stubborn	

1 You're always boasting about meeting royalty.
  You're such a .... !   ....
2 You haven't got a clue what you're doing.
  You're ....
3 You say some really nasty things about people.
  You're so mean and ....
4 I admire you for being so .... You always
  stand up for the things you think are right.   ....
5 You're such a ....'. . Go away and let me
  work!   ....
6 You're so .... Don't you ever get stressed? ....

2 Choose the best options to complete the definitions of the underlined words.

1 Someone who <u>takes things in his stride</u>
   a gets stressed out easily.   b always remains calm.
2 If you <u>undermine</u> someone, you
   a make them feel less confident.
   b encourage them.
3 Very <u>principled</u> people
   a have strong values.
   b aren't sure what to believe in.
4 Someone who <u>sucks up to the boss</u>
   a is not interested in his work.
   b wants to get a promotion.
5 When someone <u>exaggerates</u>, you should
   a listen to them carefully.
   b not take them seriously.

LISTENING

3 🔊 2.1 Listen to three people talking about working with relatives. What is the relationship between the speakers and the people they are discussing?
For example: *brother and sister*
Speaker 1 ....
Speaker 2 ....
Speaker 3 ....

> **Learner tip**
> Don't choose an answer just because you hear a key word – it could be misleading! Try to work out the meaning from key words *and* their context.

4 Listen again and match the speakers (1–3) with the statements (a–g). One statement matches two speakers.
This speaker
a appreciates the value of criticism.   ....
b has the same role at work as a relative.   ....
c believes it is important to have some personal space.   ....
d admires a relative's work.   ....
e believes it is possible to solve most problems.   ....
f is about to leave a job.   ....
g keeps work and home life separate.   ....

DEVELOPING CONVERSATIONS
Giving your impression

5 Complete the conversation. Choose the correct words or phrases.

A: So, what do you ¹*get / make* of Holly, then?

B: Hmm, I'll tell you when I've decided.

A: I think she's great. What's not to like?

B: Well, I agree she comes ²*up / across* as a really lively person and fun to be with. But I get ³*over that / the feeling* she could have a bitchy side.

A: Really? I didn't ⁴*get / make* that impression of her. What makes you think that?

B: Oh, nothing I could put my finger on, exactly. But yesterday, Raoul made a nasty joke at Sarah's expense and Holly really ⁵*seemed to / looked to* enjoy it. It bothered me a bit, that's all.

A: Hmm, well I've seen quite a bit of her and she ⁶*strikes / seems* me as a really friendly girl. You could be wrong, you know.

B: I hope so.

DEVELOPING WRITING
An online comment – giving advice

6 Read the post below, which appeared in an online forum. What do you think the main topic of the forum is?

....

Posted by: AmyLou29
Level: Bronze user
Time: 20:15

I got divorced two years ago, after five years of marriage. I was devastated, and I thought I could never trust anyone again. Then a year ago I met a wonderful man. He came across as a really decent person, honest and reliable. I fell head over heels in love. But a month ago he suddenly stopped calling, without any explanations. I didn't hear from him until last week. He said he'd had a lot going on, but he was sorry and he wanted to start again where we left off. Should I trust him?

7 Quickly read Sammi's comment in exercise 8, ignoring the gaps. Which adjectives in the box best describe her response?

balanced	bitchy	compassionate
forceful	indifferent	outraged
patronising	unsympathetic	

8 Now complete Sammi's reply with the correct form of the verbs in brackets.

Posted by: Sammi_Martyn
Level: Platinum user
Time: 21:09

Hi AmyLou,
I'm sorry ¹................... (tell) you that this guy is bad news. There's no doubt in my mind that he's using you. He ²................... (should / treat) you like that. He's not interested in a steady relationship with you or he ³................... (call) you *last* month. If you ⁴................... (ask) me, he's acted really selfishly. Are you willing to put up with that kind of behaviour, or ⁵................... you .... (rather have) a more fulfilling relationship? Ask yourself how much you really care about him. If I ⁶................... (be) you, I ⁷................... (refuse) to see him for a while and see what happens. If he's interested, he'll do everything he can to win you back. If not, you ⁸................... (have better / end) it now, before you ⁹................... (hurt) again. ¹⁰................... (stay) with this guy would be the worst thing you could do.

9 Read Emmanuel's post. Write a comment (150–190 words) replying to Emmanuel and giving advice.

Posted by: Emmanuel_W
Level: Newbie
Time: 21:23

I've been seeing this girl for about three months now and I really like her. I thought we were becoming really close, but in the last couple of weeks she's made excuses several times when I've asked her out. I've noticed that she spends a lot of time talking to my best friend and flirts with him a lot. It's started to bother me. What should I do?

VOCABULARY Phrasal verbs

1 Complete the sentences with the correct particles.

1 We're going .... in August, so please will you water our plants?
2 You need to put your foot .... and stop letting him behave like that.
3 If you ask me, he's going .... a difficult patch at work.
4 Well, she's getting .... a bit now. She'll be 90 next June!
5 He made a lot of business plans, but nothing came .... any of them.
6 All her frustration got channelled .... pottery, and the results were amazing!
7 I can't understand why he, of all of us, got singled .... for promotion.
8 I don't know how you put .... with the arrogance of that guy!
9 We had a fantastic time, and ended .... getting home at three in the morning.
10 Jane's seen 15 candidates this morning, and has narrowed it .... to three for a second interview.

> **Language note** phrasal verbs
>
> We frequently use phrasal verbs, such as *go out with*, *split up*, *settle down* and *break up*, when discussing relationships.

PRONUNCIATION Contracted forms

2 Underline the words which are usually contracted in spoken English.

1 I would have thought you would have been delighted!
2 He will have finished it by tomorrow.
3 She said there would be rain later, but I do not know if there will.
4 She could not have known who would be there.
5 I would not have helped you, even if I could.
6 These are mine, but I do not know whose those are.

3 ✿ 2.2 Listen and check. Practise saying the sentences.

READING

4 Quickly read the essay opposite. Which is the best summary (a–c) of the writer's view?

a *Cinderella* needs to be updated to make it more relevant to today's readers.
b *Cinderella* presents some complex moral problems which are not easily resolved.
c *Cinderella* teaches readers some useful lessons about life and ethics.

5 Read the essay again. According to the writer, are the statements true (T) or false (F)?

1 The enduring popularity of *Cinderella* is surprising to some.
2 The main themes of the story are unique.
3 Cinderella is in charge of her own destiny.
4 It is sometimes argued that the story includes negative stereotypes.
5 Some experts believe that that the story has different layers of meaning.
6 The story teaches children that parents are always fair.
7 Recent adaptations of *Cinderella* have greatly improved the story.
8 The story is more important than the characters in it.

6 Choose the correct words.

1 You're missing the *point* / *tip* of what I'm saying. That isn't what I meant at all!
2 Her timidity *put* / *set* her apart from her more outgoing sisters.
3 He strove in *effort* / *vain* to convince her. She simply wouldn't listen.
4 I was really struggling, but Max came to the *help* / *rescue* and sorted everything out.
5 Suddenly, we were *headed* / *faced* with a very real problem.
6 His eventual arrest was an example of justice in *action* / *performance*.

Making a case for *Cinderella*

Cinderella is a classic fairy tale about a young girl who is mistreated by her stepmother and stepsisters. She is eventually rescued by a fairy godmother who helps her to marry a prince and live happily ever after. There are more than 700 versions of the tale.

Reviled by both feminists and educators alike, *Cinderella* has acquired a negative reputation for being outdated, sexist romanticism. So its detractors might understandably be bewildered by the fact that the story has been revised so many times and still adorns children's bookshelves around the world today. So what is it about this particular fairy tale that continues to attract readers? Are the critics right, or are they simply missing the point?

Folk literature abounds with tales of the poor underdog who makes good, and *Cinderella* echoes this well-established theme. What sets *Cinderella* apart, however, is the way in which family relationships are foregrounded. Cinderella is victimised by a cruel stepmother and stepsisters, whom she strives in vain to please. In the story, Cinderella is a passive heroine – she does not defeat her persecutors herself but requires outside intervention to escape. This is offered by the all-good fairy godmother, who comes to the rescue, giving Cinderella the freedom to realise her dreams.

Critics of the tale often condemn the depiction of the stepmother, arguing that she sends a particularly unpleasant message to children (i.e. that stepmothers are evil). However, several psychologists advise against our interpreting the story too literally.

On another, deeper level, the stepmother and the fairy godmother can both be considered 'mother' figures. As such, they symbolise the good and bad aspects of any parent's character in a way that is intuitively accessible to young minds. Children often feel helpless when faced with a strict parent. They may feel they are being treated unjustly, particularly when sibling rivalry is involved, as in the story. The message conveyed by the fairy godmother is that there is always hope. Undoubtedly, this is a very optimistic view. Nevertheless, folk tales should not be read as realistic stories but rather as tales which appeal directly to the unconscious. This tale resonates with children because of the underlying positivity of its message.

Some modern versions of the tale have tried to address the problem of unconvincing characterisation. In Cameron Dokey's *Before Midnight: A Retelling of 'Cinderella'*, published in 2007, the stepmother and stepsisters have well-developed, multi-dimensional personalities. Although such contemporary renditions seem more up-to-date and 'natural', they lose something in the re-telling and perhaps misunderstand the purpose of fairy tales. Through reading traditional tales, children gain initial contact with social concepts such as fairness and jealousy, punishment and forgiveness – concepts which are articulated through plot rather than characterisation.

Herein lies the secret of *Cinderella*'s success. Perhaps more than any other fairy tale, it presents a highly satisfying example of justice in action. That renders it a powerful tool for developmental learning.

Glossary

fairy tale: a story, usually for children, about events of a fantastical nature
stepmother: the wife of your father by a subsequent marriage
underdog: person in a position of inferiority or adversity

GRAMMAR *Would*

1 Match the sentence halves.

1 I wouldn't have asked for your help
2 She wouldn't change her mind
3 He assured me everything would be OK
4 Would you mind not
5 She would never arrive on time for a date
6 Frankly, I would've thought you'd
7 I'd feel happier about going
8 He *would* do something
9 I wouldn't tell her about it
10 I knew this would happen, but

a or apologise for being late.
b if I knew someone else there.
c had enough of his behaviour by now.
d like that! It's so typical of him.
e if I'd known you'd go to so much trouble!
f raising your voice like that?
g there's no telling some people, is there?
h even though I begged her to reconsider.
i or you might upset her.
j but of course it wasn't.

2 Match the sentences (1–10) in exercise 1 with the functions (a–f).

a to make requests, offers or comments more polite
b to talk about past habits or actions that happened regularly
c to talk about hypothetical consequences in conditional sentences
d to give advice
e to express an opinion or make a comment
f to talk about the future in the past

3 Complete the sentences with *would / wouldn't* and *one* of the verbs in brackets.

1 Her ex-husband .... any maintenance. (pay / give)
2 .... you .... me a hand with the shopping? (offer / give)
3 She was so lazy, she .... a finger around the house. (put / lift)
4 He tried to reason with her, but she .... down. (back / come)
5 She's really hard work as she hardly says a word. I wish she .... up a little. (lighten / stand)
6 I .... more time for her if she weren't so bitchy. (spend / have)

4 Rewrite the sentences using *would* and the word in brackets.

1 He never minced his words when commenting on their behaviour. (mince)
....
2 I think she did that on purpose. (say)
....
3 Please help me with this application form. (mind)
....
4 She's always getting upset over such trivial things! (get)
....
5 Surely Peter knows all about that! (thought)
....
6 She threatened to leave if he didn't stop yelling. (warned)
....
7 I'm sorry I shouted, but you kept interrupting me. (if)
....
8 You should go and talk to her and try to patch things up. (were)
....

VOCABULARY Relationships

5 Decide whether the statements are true (T) or false (F).

1 If someone keeps himself to himself he is sociable.
2 When you confide something to someone you admit hidden feelings to them.
3 Parents who push their kids hard are ambitious for them.
4 Someone gets back on the straight and narrow if he recovers from an illness.
5 If someone sends you mixed messages he sends you the wrong information.
6 If we find someone in remarkably good health we are surprised about it.

6 Complete the dialogues with the correct form of the words and phrases in the box.

a scene	get on	be on speaking terms
end up	get on each other's nerves	
through a bit of a rough patch		

A: So, how are you and Joe?
B: We've been going [1]..................., as it happens.
A: Oh, no! How come?
B: Well, little things really. We just seem to [2].................. .
It all started with my mother coming to stay. As you
know, she and Martin don't [3].................... very well
at the best of times. But this time, Mum brought
her new dog with her, and Martin refused to have it
in the house. He caused [4].................... over it in fact,
and my mother [5].................... leaving under a cloud.
They haven't [6].................... ever since, and I'm caught
in the middle!

back down	confrontation	his weight
collaborate	friction	see eye to eye

C: We were [7]....................with a team from the Art
department, and Sahid and Zenia just didn't
[8].................... on anything. Neither of them was
willing to [9]...................., and naturally this caused
[10].................... among the rest of us. Eventually, their
bickering led to a ridiculous [11]...................., with
Zenia accusing Sahid of not pulling [12]....................
and refusing to work with him any longer.
D: So, what happened?
C: We lost the project to Mike's team.

spark her interest	make it so awkward
come as a real shock	on first name terms
when it comes down to it	

E: So you know him?
F: Not well, but we're [13]...................., share the odd
drink in the club bar, that sort of thing ... And that's
what [14].................... . If I'd known she was his wife, I'd
never have flirted with her. [15]...................., I'm quite
old-fashioned about such things. It [16].................... to
learn that she was married, and then to find out
that I knew the husband ...
E: I would imagine she'd be more embarrassed
than you.
F: That's the funny thing. It seems to have
[17].................... even more ....

come to his aid	put him at his ease
keep an eye on him	

G: What's happened to that boy you told me about?
H: Who, David? I've been [18]...................., and he seems
to be getting on a bit better. He got into a spot of
trouble the other day, but a boy from his class
[19].................... . They've become friends since then,
and this seems to have [20].................... somewhat.

Vocabulary Builder Quiz 2

Download the Vocabulary Builder for Unit 2 and try the quiz below. Write your answers in your notebook. Then check them and record your score.

1 Complete the sentences with the correct particles.
1 Show your mother some respect and stop answering
.... !
2 She really drags you .... She's awful!
3 They sounded .... the boss about their product idea.
4 They had a dreadful row, but don't worry – it'll soon blow
....
5 They look .... on her just because she didn't go to
private school. What snobs!
6 To my surprise, things turned .... well.
7 Always stand .... for what you believe in.

2 Complete the sentences with the correct form of the word in brackets.
1 That was an awful thing to say to her! Don't be so .... !
(bitch)
2 I'm sick and tired of covering for his .... He's just not
up it. (incompetent)
3 He got all .... about staying in a hostel, and said he'd
prefer a hotel. (snob)
4 I'm sorry but it's a principle I'm not .... to compromise
on. (will)
5 What got me was the .... of her outburst. She was so
angry! (intense)

3 Choose the correct verb to complete the sentences.
1 He was *contested / subjected* to a number of awkward
questions by the police.
2 There were a huge number of applicants, but we *narrowed /
dragged* it down to 10 for an interview.
3 I *detected / determined* the final cost of the project.
4 She doesn't really *push / pull* her weight at work.
5 He has *contributed / confided* his concerns about his job to me.
6 He's so lazy. He's always *slacking / siding* off.
7 I think we can *draw / get* some valuable lessons from this
experience.

4 Are the sentences true (T) or false (F)?
1 If you need to lighten up, you're too relaxed.
2 Toddlers usually have to attend school.
3 You're going through a rough patch when things are difficult.
4 Making a scene usually involves an argument.
5 Your counterpart is your opponent or rival.
6 Your colleagues will be unhappy if you suck up to the boss.

Score ___ /25

**Wait a couple of weeks and try the quiz again.
Compare your scores.**

03 CULTURE AND IDENTITY

VOCABULARY Society and culture

1 Choose the best option to complete the definitions.

1 A bureaucratic society is one in which
  a there are a lot of rules and regulations.
  b religion plays a powerful role.
  c there is a fair amount of social mobility.

2 A culture known for its hospitality is
  a unfriendly.   b welcoming.   c narrow-minded.

3 If you conform to certain standards of behaviour, you
  a ignore them.   b challenge them.   c obey them.

4 A secular organisation is one which
  a follows a particular religion.
  b does not have a religious nature.
  c respects many different religions.

5 If life is tough, it is
  a hard.   b wild.   c relaxing.

6 If you take the mickey out of someone, you
  a criticise them.   b bully them.   c tease them.

2 Complete the sentences with *one* word in each gap.

1 Many second generation immigrants have lost .... with the traditions and habits of their own culture.

2 People in the community are polite and friendly on a .... level, but feelings of resentment run deep.

3 In the village, community life .... around the church, as there are few facilities available.

4 I was struck by the positive .... of most of the town's inhabitants, despite the bleak weather.

5 Generally, they're very liberal there, and have a live and .... live attitude.

6 It's a ....-dominated society, with few women in government.

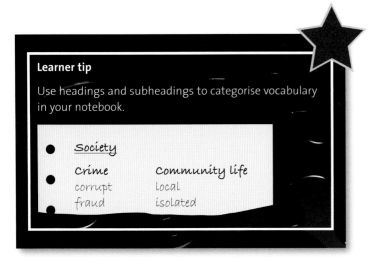

Learner tip

Use headings and subheadings to categorise vocabulary in your notebook.

- Society
- Crime   Community life
  corrupt   local
  fraud   isolated

LISTENING

3 🎧 **3.1 Listen to three speakers talking about celebrations. Match the celebrations (1–3) with the pictures (a–c).**

1 Martisor
2 Chalandamarz
3 Hinamatsuri

4 Listen again and write the correct letter: M for Martisor, C for Chalandamarz or H for Hinamatsuri.

Which celebration

1 can be expensive?   ....
2 can be noisy?   ....
3 involves a weather-related superstition?   ....
4 is a religious festival?   ....
5 lasts several days?   ....
6 is not very old?   ....

5 What do the festivals have in common? Choose *two* of the following.

1 They take place in springtime.
2 Certain colours are particularly important.
3 Children play an important role.
4 People believe they may bring good luck.

DEVELOPING CONVERSATIONS
Challenging overgeneralisations

6 Choose the correct words.

1 I don't know *of / about* that. After all, we're living in a secular society.
2 I wouldn't go that *distant / far*. Writers should be allowed to speak their minds.
3 Isn't that a bit of an *exaggeration / excess*? Not all criminals are violent.
4 That's one *method / way* of looking at things, but children could learn about different beliefs at home.
5 I really don't *consider / see* it like that myself. Nobody should be forced to join the army if they don't want to.
6 That's a bit *hard / harsh*, isn't it? I agree we need to crack down on crime, but there's got to be a better way.
7 That's a bit of an *over-analysis / overstatement*, isn't it? What about freedom of expression?
8 I'm not *firm / sure* about that. We can build patriotism and community spirit in other ways.

7 Match the responses (1–8) in exercise 6 with the opinions (a–d).

a We should teach religion in schools.
b All offenders must go to prison – they're a danger to society.
c All books should be censored.
d Compulsory military service is the best way to teach respect for society.

PRONUNCIATION
Intonation when agreeing or disagreeing

8 ◈ 3.2 Listen to the conversations and answer the question.

Does the voice go up or down at the end of a sentence when we
1 agree with someone?   ....
2 disagree with someone?   ....

A: It's important to respect religious beliefs.
B: Yes, I think that's essential.

A: We should teach religion in schools.
B: Oh, I don't know about that.

9 Practise saying the opinions and responses.

A: All offenders should go to prison.
B: Well, I'm not sure about that.

A: Racism is never justifiable.
B: I completely agree.

A: Most government officials are corrupt.
B: That's a bit of an overstatement, isn't it?

A: We need to invest more in the arts.
B: Yes, they're hardly thriving at the moment.

A: Wars can be good for the economy.
B: That's one way of looking at things, but I'm not sure I agree.

GRAMMAR Cleft sentences

10 Put the words in the correct order.

1 me / was / what / of / the / number / bothered / homeless people on the streets.
2 found / thing / the / incredible / of / was / the / one / lack / I / crime.
3 me / amount / that / worries / the / thing / is / the / money / of / politicians are wasting.
4 what / annoys / that / the / most / me / is / no one seems to be listening.
5 one / mad / is / thing / drives / me / that / all the red tape.

11 Find and correct *four* mistakes in the sentences.

1 What found I difficult to cope with were the crowded streets.
2 The thing that amazes me the most are the strict censorship laws.
3 A thing that I couldn't get used to was the bureaucracy.
4 What annoyed me the most was the lack of respect.
5 One thing I hated was that the fact that the officials were so corrupt.
6 The thing that me disturbs the most is the fact that everyone seems scared.

VOCABULARY Household objects

1 Complete the sentences with the words in the box. There are five extra words that you don't need to use.

bucket	cloth	dishwasher	drill
glue	needle	oven	pan
pin	sink	string	tap
toilet			

1 I need to mend a tear in my jacket. Have you got a .... and thread?
2 That was a great meal, Sam! Right, I'll clear the table, and you can load the ....
3 Use a .... to make some holes for the screws.
4 The lamb's roasting in the .... – it should be ready by one.
5 After you've wiped up the mess, wring out the .... over the sink, please.
6 Let the .... run for a bit and the water will get warm.
7 We need a plumber. The .... blocks every time anyone flushes it.
8 Help me put this poster up, will you? Can you stick a .... in just there?

2 Choose the correct words.

1 This floor needs sweeping. Pass me the *mop / brush*.
2 Knot the *rope / string* tightly so that the bikes don't fall off while we're driving.
3 The clock isn't broken, you just need to change the battery. Give it here, and I'll take out the *nails / screws* from the back.
4 My gran's just moved to a bungalow as she can't climb the *ladders / stairs* in her old terrace any more.
5 You need to wear knee *pads / bandages* when you're skateboarding.
6 There are usually two or three *cables / wires* inside a plug.
7 The wood's not very thick, so just hit the nail lightly with the *drill / hammer*.
8 Make sure you rinse the glasses after you've washed them – last time, the wine ended up tasting of *washing-up liquid / soap*!

READING

3 Quickly read the web page opposite. Match the descriptions (1–3) with the people in the web page (A–C).

This person
1 reluctantly changed their citizenship. ....
2 has no regrets about changing their citizenship. ....
3 has not changed their citizenship. ....

Language note legal English

- -

We often use special technical language when discussing laws and regulations, such as to **hold** or **grant** citizenship rather than to **have** or **give** citizenship.

4 Seven sentences from the web page have been removed. Write the correct letter (a–h) in the gaps in the web page. There is one extra sentence that you don't need to use.

a With their encouragement, I've prospered, and I'm grateful to the country that made this possible.
b My parents saw it as a betrayal.
c I'm not ready for such drastic measures yet.
d This is very frustrating, and frankly I could do without the red tape.
e On the other hand, I wasn't prepared to reject my national heritage.
f I compromised by getting a permanent residence permit.
g But my future lies here.
h My national roots run deep, it seems.

5 Match the verbs from the web page (1–6) with the definitions (a–f).

1	come up (text A)	a	move to a new place
2	seek (text A)	b	officially accept
3	relocate (text B)	c	become clear
4	abandon (text B)	d	give up, lose
5	take on (text B)	e	try to get
6	transpire (text C)	f	happen

Citizenship: a question of belonging?

| Home page | Why change citizenship? | About us | Contact us |

Why change citizenship?

▶ Citizenship: FAQs
▶ Personal stories

What does it mean to become a citizen of a different country to the one you were born in? Read about some personal experiences below.

A Geert (the Netherlands / Australia)

I made Australia my home 25 years ago and I've never regretted it. The wonderful thing about this country is that it's genuinely multicultural, and 'equal opportunities' isn't just a pretty phrase. I managed to set up my own business here, and have received support from local authorities to do so. ¹.................... When the possibility of dual citizenship came up, I grabbed at the chance.

As an Australian citizen, I have the right to vote, work in public service and even seek election to Parliament, if I want to! Of course, there's nothing stopping me from going back to the Netherlands if I ever change my mind, but I can't see that happening. I'm proud of my native homeland and I'll remember it fondly. ².................... I feel like an Aussie now, through and through.

B Lesley Ann (Canada / Germany)

I met my husband while we were working for a German-owned company in Canada and we were married within the year. Four years ago the company relocated us to Germany, and we've been living here ever since. I've been made to feel very welcome in Germany, but I'm still Canadian at heart. Mathi thinks I'm crazy, but I get homesick for wild forests, ice hockey – even the cold! ³.................... And I'm not ready to abandon them just yet. I'm not eligible for dual citizenship here, so if I wanted to hold German citizenship, I would have to renounce my Canadian status.

⁴.................... This meant I could legally live and work in Germany indefinitely, without losing my Canadian citizenship. By rejecting the country of your birth to become the citizen of another country you are effectively taking on a new identity. ⁵....................

C Kamran (India, the USA)

I first came to the States as a student and then found work with an international company. My work required me to travel overseas a lot and it was difficult to obtain a visa each time with my Indian passport. It therefore seemed sensible to apply for US citizenship.

Unfortunately, it soon transpired that if I went down this road I would be re-classified as an Overseas Indian Citizen, not a full Indian national. I was heartbroken. ⁶.................... They hardly spoke to me for months. And I felt as though I was rejecting my heritage.

After some painful soul-searching, I filled in the forms and was granted the citizenship, and I can now travel with relative ease. Yet whenever I return to India for longer stays, I have to register with an office of foreign nationals. ⁷.................... But if I want to keep everyone happy – including myself – then it's a compromise I need to accept.

Glossary

dual citizenship: citizenship of two or more countries
renounce: say formally that you no longer want to be connected with something
register: formally record your details

VOCABULARY Words and phrases

1 Complete the conversation with the phrases in the box.

a chance would be a fine thing
b just not the done thing
c no big thing
d one thing led to another
e the furthest thing from my mind
f the sort of thing
g with one thing and another

A: I really enjoyed doing voluntary work overseas. You know, seeing how hard it is for people in some parts of the world to simply survive, well, it's ¹.................... that makes you appreciate what you've got! I swear I'll never moan again about not having enough clothes!

B: So, how did you get involved?

A: I met this girl in college who'd done it, and we talked about it, and ².................... I didn't really plan it.

B: I really admire you for it. It must have been difficult at times.

A: No, it's ³.................... , really. I just signed up, packed my bags and went.

B: I'd love to do it.

A: Then why don't you? It's easy.

B: Huh! ⁴.................... ! I could never take the time off work!

A: Then quit! You're always talking about taking a year off to travel!

B: What? And jeopardise my career? It's ⁵.................... in my family, I'm afraid! My parents don't approve of people going round the world when they could be at home earning money.

A: That's true! I suppose once you've got a job, it's difficult.

B: Yes, and I've just bought a flat, too. So, what ⁶.................... , travel is ⁷.................... at the moment. I've got too many other things to worry about!

A: Oh well! Maybe later …

DEVELOPING WRITING
A description – adding interest

2 Quickly read the description below. Tick (✓) the things that the writer is doing.
1 giving information only ....
2 including personal opinions ....
3 using mainly formal language ....
4 adding details and examples ....
5 using adjectives and adverbs ....
6 using passive structures ....

Holi, the Festival of Colour

Holi, the Festival of Colour, is one of the most exuberant and colourful festivals in the Nepalese calendar. For any springtime visitors to the country, it's an event ¹everyone should see.

The festival is usually spread over two days or more at the beginning of March. On the first evening, huge bonfires ²are lit. These commemorate the death of the evil spirit, Holika, and symbolise the end of winter. The high point of the festival happens on the second day, called Dhulundi. The atmosphere is ³very exciting. Everyone abandons social conventions and throws coloured powders and water over each other, celebrating life and the triumph of good over evil. People ⁴have lots of fun in the streets and they party ⁵in a very enthusiastic way.

To me, Holi is special because it's a time when people forget their differences and become united in a general feeling of goodwill. It truly is an expression of hope and joy, and it never fails to ⁶make me happy.

3 Add interest to the description by replacing the underlined phrases with the words and phrases in the box.

bring a smile to my face	electric
go wild	light up the skies
like there's no tomorrow	not to be missed

Learner tip

Add details to make your descriptions more interesting. In addition to adjectives, adverbs and strong verbs, you can include similes and metaphors, but use these sparingly or your writing could sound over the top!

4 Choose the correct words.
1 The locals gave us a *hot / warm* reception, offering us refreshments and a place to sit.
2 I don't like big parties as a *rule / fashion*, but this was an exception. It was wild!
3 I knew the city like the *back / front* of my hand. I knew every street and alley.
4 Her speech at the Culture Festival provided plenty of *food / material* for thought. We were discussing it for weeks.
5 He *rained / showered* us with gifts at Christmas. We felt very spoilt!
6 The festival programme ran like *clockwork / machinery*, without any delays or mistakes.

5 Find words and phrases in exercise 4 to match definitions a–f below.
a extremely efficiently
b welcoming
c very well
d usually
e very generously gave us lots of
f provided much to think about

6 Write a description (150–190 words) of a festival or celebration you have been to. Use vivid language to add interest.

Vocabulary Builder Quiz 3

Download the Vocabulary Builder for Unit 3 and try the quiz below. Write your answers in your notebook. Then check them and record your score.

1 Match to form collocations.

1	flush	a	the cloth
2	rip	b	a glass
3	sweep	c	the toilet
4	wring out	d	a needle
5	thread	e	the floor
6	rinse	f	your shirt

2 Choose the correct verbs.
1 Life *relates / revolves* around the village square.
2 She wishes to *assume / retain* her French citizenship when she moves to Germany.
3 I'm busy today, so I've a chicken to just *stick / fill* in the oven.
4 It can be funny when tourists *encounter / misinterpret* hand gestures made by locals.
5 She got down on her knees and *soaked / scrubbed* the floor clean.
6 It's important to respect the country's customs and *conform / interfere* to its rules.
7 I've *ripped / stained* my top with wine.

3 Correct the sentences by placing the words in bold in the correct sentence.
1 The people are known for their **normality**. Visitors receive a warm welcome.
2 I love all the gadgets and **roots** you can find in Karen's kitchen.
3 Generally, the people there have a positive **assumption** on life.
4 She had lived in Paris for years, but wanted to go back to her rural **appliances**.
5 Your **outlook** that the British are always cold is misguided, to say the least.
6 After trekking across Asia, she wondered how she would accept the **hospitality** of a nine to five job again.

4 Are the definitions for the underlined words correct (C) or incorrect (I)?
1 A <u>secular</u> society is one with a dominant religion.
2 A <u>hypocrite</u> is someone who doesn't really believe what they claim to.
3 <u>Bizarre</u> customs are ones that seem weird to you.
4 An <u>elite</u> group usually holds a privileged position in a society.
5 <u>Diverse</u> interests are very similar.
6 A <u>draughty</u> room is a warm one.

Score ___ /25

Wait a couple of weeks and try the quiz again. Compare your scores.

04 POLITICS

VOCABULARY Politicians

1 Complete the profile with the words in the box.

flexibility	compromise
self-confidence	honesty
ruthlessness	passion
charisma	communication
compassion	bravery

Posted by PoliticalDreamer @ 8:45

Profile of the ideal politician

My idea of the perfect politician would be someone who is known for the [1]................... and understanding they show towards the people in the community they represent. They would be charmingly [2]................... and have excellent [3]................... skills to argue for their cause, as well as the [4]................... to persuade people of all ages and social levels. They'd be [5]................... enough to not be affected by criticism, and have the [6]................... to stand up for their beliefs in the face of opposition. That said, they would also instinctively know when it's necessary to back down, and have the ability to [7]................... in order to reach a solution that suits everyone. Ideally, they would also be known for their [8]................... , but unfortunately, I don't think it's always possible tell the complete truth in the political arena.

Comments 1

Civilcynic65
Dream on, PoliticalDreamer! The only politicians I know of are characterised by their [9]................... for their own political gain, and their [10]................... in stamping on anyone who gets in their way!

PRONUNCIATION Sound and spelling: \ʃ\, \tʃ\ and \z\

2 Choose the word with a different sound.

1 /tʃ/   **ch**arisma, **ch**arming, **ch**ange, **ch**aritable
2 /ʃ/   compa**ss**ion, ruthle**ss**ness, pre**ss**ure, obse**ss**ion
3 /z/   wi**s**dom, plea**s**ant, ha**s**ty, di**s**aster
4 /ʃ/   ma**ch**ine, **ch**arming, bro**ch**ure, **ch**ef
5 /tʃ/   na**tu**re, down**tu**rn, sta**tu**e, for**tu**nate
6 /z/   po**ss**essive, i**ss**ue, di**ss**olve, sci**ss**ors

3 🔊 4.1 Listen and check. Practise saying the words.

DEVELOPING CONVERSATIONS Giving opinions

4 Match the topics (a–c) with the opinions (1–6).
a reducing the number of MPs in Parliament   ....
b keeping animals in captivity   ....
c becoming a cashless society   ....

1 I'm generally in favour, but I have .... with regard to old people. They find credit cards difficult to handle.
2 I'm .... to the idea. It's cruel because they suffer from captivity-related stress.
3 I'm .... the idea. We have too many bureaucrats running our world, so I'd take it a step further and reduce them by 20%.
4 It's .... , just not in practice. I think people will still want to use coins and notes for small, daily transactions.
5 I'm .... it. The last thing we need is to make the Commons even less representative of the electorate.
6 I think the negatives .... the positives. They can breed in a protected environment but they'll go crazy in a confined space.

5 Complete the opinions in exercise 4 with the phrases in the box.

a good idea in theory	completely opposed
far outweigh	some slight reservations
totally against	totally in favour of

6 Complete the second sentence so that it has a similar meaning to the first.
1 I totally support the idea.
   I'm a huge fan .... the idea.
2 I don't know what I think about the matter.
   I don't know where .... the matter.
3 I'm totally against vivisection.
   I'm completely opposed .... vivisection.
4 I think the negatives far outweigh the positives.
   I have some major .... it.
5 It's a good idea in theory, just not in practice.
   It's OK .... principle. I just .... unworkable.
6 I'm generally in favour. I just have some slight reservations.
   It has some problems but on .... I like it.

GRAMMAR Conditionals 1

7 Choose the best options.

1 They .... taxes if they get into power, you can be certain of that.
   a could raise
   b raise
   c are going to raise

2 If the party lost the election, it really .... be the end of the world.
   a wouldn't
   b mightn't
   c couldn't

3 If the vote goes against him tomorrow, he .... have to stand down. We'll see.
   a 's going to
   b would
   c might

4 If scientists came up with a practical solution, the politicians .... listen to them, for sure.
   a might
   b could
   c would

5 If the police go in there, there .... trouble, you mark my words.
   a will be
   b would be
   c is

6 If they make wage cuts, it .... a general strike, or it might cause protests.
   a 's triggering
   b could trigger
   c will trigger

8 Find and correct *six* mistakes.

1 If you'd be elected, what would you do about housing?
2 You're going to get the sack if you'll be late again!
3 If you hear anything, could you tell him straight away?
4 If they asked for a raise tomorrow, he definitely won't give it to them.
5 What if you were unemployed, though, what will you do then?
6 I consider running for office, if I were you.
7 If the scandal might break, he would lose the election.
8 You can't worry about gossip, if you want to become a politician!

VOCABULARY Consequences

9 Choose the correct words.

1 The government's decision to liquidate the company *triggered / boosted* an angry protest.
2 The move could *devastate / discourage* new businesses from investing in the area.
3 This latest scandal could *boost / compound* existing problems within the party.
4 The policy threatens to *undermine / bankrupt* education and put teachers' jobs at risk.
5 The new community centre will *boost / benefit* young people in the area.
6 This new law aims to *reduce / undermine* petty crime and reduce arrests.

10 Complete the sentences with the words in the box. There is one extra word that you don't need to use.

bankrupt	boost	compound	reduce	devastated	lead
triggered	undermine				

1 It is hoped the negotiations will .... to further sanctions being lifted.
2 We're launching a new advertising campaign to .... sales of our product.
3 The police raid on the inner city neighbourhood last night .... a riot that may last for several days.
4 The city was .... by the earthquake and it will take years to rebuild it.
5 The rise in prices will only serve to .... the problem of unemployment among the poor.
6 The breakout of rebel fighting in the east is likely to further .... relations between the two nations, which were already fragile.
7 The government's new tax policies will .... many small businesses.

LISTENING

1 🎧 **4.2 Listen to the first part of a radio programme. Which global issue is going to be the main topic?**

a political reform   c the developing world

b conservation   d globalisation

2 🎧 **4.3 Listen to an extract from the second part of the programme. Complete the sentences with *one* or *two* words. Write *exactly* what you hear.**

1 Some politicians believe the issue of biodiversity loss has been ....

2 Sara thinks that the most worrying thing about biodiversity loss is that it's ....

3 The presenter is concerned about Sara's ....

4 Lyle currently makes his living as a ....

5 Lyle is concerned that Sara's approach would have negative consequences for ....

6 Thanks to income from the cassava crop, Brazilian villagers have already built new housing and a ....

7 Encouraging farmers to grow sustainable crops would be more difficult in Europe as countries there are ....

8 Sara believes that the issue of biodiversity loss is more important than ....

3 **Match 1–6 with a–f to make compound expressions. Check the audioscript on pages 103–104 if necessary.**

1	third	a	species
2	global	b	friendly
3	environmentally	c	care
4	policy	d	world
5	endangered	e	warming
6	health	f	makers

VOCABULARY 'Ways of' verb groups

4 **Choose one word which does not fit in each sentence.**

1 He *strolled / crept / giggled / raced / staggered* along the street.

2 Sara *gazed / raced / stared / glared / looked* at Paul.

3 Anna *screamed / muttered / gasped / said / crept / mumbled*: 'It wasn't me.'

4 He *clutched / grabbed / chattered / held* her arm.

5 Sammy *gazed / laughed / giggled / chuckled* when he saw Mark's funny outfit.

5 **Complete the sentences with the correct form of a word from exercise 4.**

1 Furious at being ignored, he left the room .... something about taking his ideas elsewhere.

2 After being attacked, John .... home unsteadily along the dark, narrow street.

3 She .... longingly at the cream cake, cursing her decision to go on a diet.

4 The children .... when the party clown tickled them with his feather stick.

5 Andy .... the thief as he ran past, and pushed him to the ground.

6 They .... lazily along the sea front, enjoying the gentle afternoon breeze.

READING

6 **Quickly read the article opposite, ignoring the gaps. Who is or are 'tipping the balance of power'?**

....

Learner tip

When you complete a gapped text you need to think about the way the text is organised. Look carefully at any pronouns (*he, these,* etc.) or linkers (*however, what's more,* etc.) as well as the words before and after the gap. These could give you useful clues.

7 **What do these numbers in the article refer to?**

1 56 (line 2)   ....

2 ⅓ (line 4)   ....

3 800,000 (line 11)   ....

4 70 (line 12)   ....

5 30 (line 25)   ....

8 **Seven sentences have been removed from the article. Write the correct letter (a–h) in the gap. There is one extra letter which you don't need to use.**

a However, none have been as ambitious or as successful as the Rwandan parliament.

b To this end, he reformed the political constitution and supported a series of equality measures.

c The most important of these are felt to be improvements in family legislation and anti-discrimination measures to protect minority groups within the nation.

d Nevertheless, having a quota system goes a long way to ensuring that their voices are heard.

e Not only was this remarkable for Rwanda, it was remarkable as a world achievement.

f A number of political commentators have claimed that the quota system doesn't work.

g This has led to accusations of unfairness and bias.

h In spite of this imbalance, however, the country was still legally and politically male-dominated.

Tipping the balance of power

The relatively small African nation of Rwanda is a pioneer in world politics. In 2008 women held 56% of parliamentary seats in the Lower House, including the Speaker's chair, and a third of all cabinet positions,
5 notably that of Foreign Minister and the Minister for Education. [1]...... This is the first ever time that a national parliament boasted a female majority.

So, why is a country like Rwanda ahead? One contributing factor has definitely been the support of
10 President Paul Kagame. The genocide of 1994 devastated the country. More than 800,000 Rwandans died, with the remaining population being 70% female. [2].................... Archaic legislation gave women an inferior place in society – something which Kagame was determined to
15 redress in the 21st century.

[3].................... Among the new government's early achievements was the passing of several bills aimed at ending domestic violence and child abuse. A special committee for women's affairs was also set up, resulting
20 in the abolition of discriminatory laws such as those preventing women from inheriting land.

Several neighbouring African countries have adopted similar quota systems geared towards facilitating women's entry to parliament. In South Africa and
25 Mozambique, for example, women hold over 30% of the seats in parliament and have also made admirable strides in bringing about social reform in their countries. [4]....................

The system has not been without its detractors.
30 [5].................... They argue that simply increasing the number of seats in parliament does not guarantee that women will be making decisions that matter. Various restrictions imposed on parliamentary decision-making often seriously hamper the voting power members
35 can exert. What's more, some have argued that the system prevents women from being taken seriously as politicians and results instead in their being seen as token figures.

[6].................... In a society where it is still difficult for
40 women to gain access to good quality education, the fact that women form the majority in parliament shows just how determined they are to bring about change.

Even the country's male population agrees that overall the nation has benefited from the increased presence
45 of women in government. Open opposition is limited, and many men welcome the change, saying that it has brought about numerous improvements. [7]....................

Obviously, there is still a lot of scope for improvement, but the Rwandan model sets an impressive precedent.
50 It's one which the rest of the world will be watching with interest.

Glossary

cabinet: group of politicians in a government who make most of the executive decisions

quota system: a voting system that gives preference to a certain group of people, such as people of a particular gender or race

9 Find words in the article which mean the same as 1–6.

Paragraphs 2–3

1 murder of a whole race of people ....

2 old and out-of-date ....

3 the act of completely ending something ....

Paragraphs 4–5

4 helping, making something easier ....

5 critics ....

6 restrict, make something more difficult ....

DEVELOPING WRITING
A report – evaluating data

1 Look at the chart and read the report. Does the writer interpret the statistics in the chart in a positive or negative way?

....

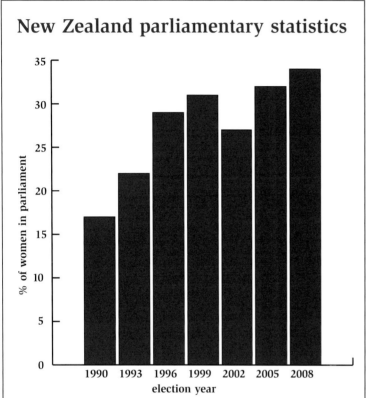

New Zealand parliamentary statistics

This chart ¹*suggests / presents* the percentage of women in parliament in New Zealand in the election years between 1990 and 2008. As shown in the chart, ²*overall / throughout* there has been a steady increase in the representation of women in parliament during this time.

In 1990 women held only 17% of the total number of seats. In the ³*following / coming* election, that figure rose to 22%, a climb of 5%. In 1996 there was another leap ⁴*forward / onward*, with the number of female parliamentarians increasing by 7%.

Change after 1996 is comparatively slower. Between 1999 and 2008, the number of seats held by women only ⁵*raises / grows* by 3%. Progress is not continuous. The year 2002 is unusual because it indicates a ⁶*drop / descent* in the number of seats, with 4% fewer women in Parliament than in 1999. ⁷*Moreover / However*, this dip is not repeated.

To ⁸*sum / conclude* up, although the pace of change has slowed in recent years, the statistics show that there has been a definite progression towards greater representation for women in the New Zealand parliament.

2 Choose the correct words to complete the report.

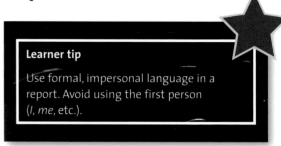

> **Learner tip**
>
> Use formal, impersonal language in a report. Avoid using the first person (*I*, *me*, etc.).

3 Complete the sentences with the correct form of the words in the box. You may need to add extra words.

difficult	long	ruthless	small
so	such	unhappy	

1 The increase was so .... as to be insignificant.
2 He was .... than other politicians and always got his own way.
3 This is .... year of all to interpret, as not all figures were available for that year.
4 The .... she's been in power, the .... her citizens have become, and the more they've clamoured for change.
5 The parliamentary building was .... small, and it was .... a hot place, that few MPs wanted to linger there for long.

4 Summarise the information in the chart below in a report (150–190 words). Select and report the main figures, and make comparisons where relevant.

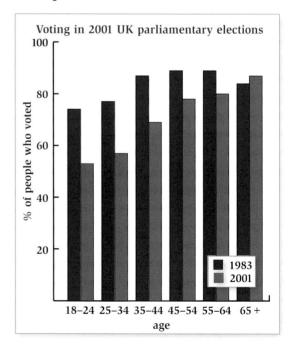

VOCABULARY Elections and politics

5 Choose the best options.

Students at Brighton College of Art have ¹*arrived / reached* a consensus and demanded a re-election of the President of the Students' Union. This decision followed the discovery of an attempt to ²*cover up / trigger* a scandal surrounding Oliver Smith's controversial ³*broad / landslide* victory last week. Smith is the son of Marjory Smith, a well-known ⁴*outspoken / unanimous* Labour MP. It has been alleged that friends of Smith had ⁵*ensured / rigged* the voting in the elections. According to a poll ⁶*conducted / cast* among students a month ago, Penny Walker had a 40% lead. Walker is a ⁷*standing / prominent* figure in the debating society, while Smith does not belong to any student organisations. Students are threatening to ⁸*strike / lobby* and miss classes if their demand is not met.

GRAMMAR Conditionals 2

6 Rewrite the sentences, starting with *If*.

1 We'd never have won without their support.
  If ....
2 She was in a meeting, otherwise she'd have seen you.
  If ....
3 I'd stop and talk, but I have to finish this report.
  If ....
4 This would never have happened with us in power.
  If ....
5 She didn't campaign for long enough, and that's why she isn't in office now.
  If ....

Vocabulary Builder Quiz 4

Download the Vocabulary Builder for Unit 4 and try the quiz below. Write your answers in your notebook. Then check them and record your score.

1 Cross out the word which does NOT collocate with the word on the right.
1 *carry on a / conduct a / call a / the latest* referendum
2 *stand as an / cover up an / lobby an / an outspoken* MP
3 *reach a / a broad / set up a / an emerging* consensus
4 *a landslide / a hollow / a narrow / an emerging* victory
5 *rig an / call an / establish an / the run-up to the* election
6 *a broad / a sex / expose a bribery / cover up a* scandal
7 *a prominent / an alleged / an influential / a political* figure
8 *cast a / a unanimous / a narrow / a protest* vote

2 Complete the sentences with the correct form of the words in brackets.
1 She resigned amid .... (allege) of corruption.
2 The advantages of this proposal far .... (weigh) the disadvantages.
3 She made .... (satire) jokes about the MP.
4 Women still fail to have fair .... (represent) in many parliaments in the world.
5 He is a staunch supporter of the .... (opposite) party.
6 What's your .... (stand) on the question of nuclear disarmament?
7 He wrote a .... (satire) play which mocked the workings of the Houses of Parliament.

3 Are the definitions of the <u>underlined</u> words true (T) or false (F)?
1 A <u>petition</u> is a kind of survey to find out people's opinion.
2 A <u>hollow</u> victory is worthless.
3 To <u>compound</u> a problem is to find a solution to it.
4 If you hold a <u>referendum</u>, you vote to make a decision about an issue.
5 A <u>ballot</u> lets people vote in secret.

4 Add the missing prepositions.
1 The company decided to bid .... the contract.
2 She expressed some reservations .... the proposal.
3 The press officer yelled .... the journalists.
4 He decided to stand .... election to the party leadership.
5 The government has allocated extra funds .... emergency relief services.

Score ___/25

Wait a couple of weeks and try the quiz again.
Compare your scores.

VOCABULARY Nights out

1 Match the two halves of the anecdotes.

1 They caused quite a scene, actually.
2 It just didn't live up to the hype.
3 Honestly, we were in stitches.
4 I couldn't stop yawning throughout the presentation.
5 It was terrible. She was in floods of tears.
6 When I realised, I was utterly mortified.

a It was absolutely hilarious!
b I've never been so bored in my life!
c It was quite awkward, as everyone was looking.
d I was so embarrassed, I just wanted the ground to swallow me whole.
e A real disappointment after those rave reviews.
f The news really left her in bits.

2 Complete the conversation with the correct form of the phrases in the box.

be in bits	be mortified	burst into tears
feel a bit rough	cause a scene	live up to the hype

A: So, how was the restaurant last night? I've heard wonderful things about it.

B: I know, but quite frankly, it didn't ¹.................... .

A: Really? Why not?

B: Well, the food was rather tasteless, I thought. But the company was even worse! Xavier overdid it with the wine and eventually ².................... . He started shouting at the waiter and we were asked to leave. I ³.................... . It was so embarrassing. His girlfriend, Sally, was so upset that she ⁴.................... . They ended up arguing, and she told Xavier that she never wanted to see him again. So, then Xavier ⁵.................... . Paul and I didn't know what to do with him.

A: It must have been awful!

B: It was rather! We spent most of the night consoling Xavier, and I finally crawled into bed at 4.30. So, thanks to him, I ⁶.................... . today. You haven't got a painkiller, have you?

DEVELOPING WRITING
A review – emphasising your ideas

3 Quickly read the review. Which rating do you think the writer will give this film?

a ★ disappointing
b ★★ mixed reactions
c ★★★ worth a view
d ★★★★ outstanding

REVIEW *How to Train Your Dragon*

A ¹*winning / stilted* combination of vivid imagery, ²*cracking / wooden* dialogue and a ³*disjointed / powerful* storyline makes *How to Train Your Dragon* one of the most ⁴*successful / thriving* animated films ever made.

The film portrays an isolated village which is under attack from dragons. All the villagers become dragon-killers to protect themselves, apart from the shy, awkward teenager Hiccup. His macho father Stoick, the head man of the village, is both embarrassed by his son and afraid for his safety. But Hiccup has a secret: he once managed to wound a ⁵*fearful / fearsome*, fire-breathing dragon, but instead of killing it, he befriended it.

As the film develops, its anti-violence message is made clear with ⁶*admirable / spine-tingling* wit and insight. The story is carried along by a mixture of sharp humour and tenderness. The dragon is irresistible, and its character skilfully developed. The 3D effects and design create ⁷*handsome / stunning* scenes, and there are some truly ⁸*attractive / exhilarating* flying sequences.

This film may have been made primarily for kids, but it is bound to entertain people of all ages. Don't miss it!

4 Choose the best options to complete the review.

Learner tip

In a review, use descriptive words to emphasise your opinion but think carefully about the context. Many adjectives which have similar meanings are used in different ways, such as a *handsome* actor but a *stunning* or *spectacular* set.

5 Replace the underlined words with the adjectives in the box.

| devastating | disjointed | irresistible | |
| spectacular | spine-tingling | stilted | wooden |

1 The acting was <u>not very convincing</u>.
2 The special effects were <u>very pretty</u>.
3 The storyline <u>was confusing</u>.
4 The cute dragon was <u>easy to like</u>.
5 The dialogue was <u>not very natural</u>.
6 The tragic ending was <u>very sad</u>.
7 The escape scene in the cave was <u>scary</u>.

6 A film website has asked users to send in reviews of films they have seen in the past year. Write a review (150–190 words) giving the name of the film and saying what you liked or didn't like about it. Make a recommendation for other users.

Learner tip

When you write a review of a film or book, *do*
- include a brief outline
- comment on its strengths and weaknesses
- include personal opinions and a recommendation

but *don't*
- give a complete summary of the plot
- include too many background details
- give away the ending!

DEVELOPING CONVERSATIONS
Commenting on what is said

7 Complete each of the replies with your own words and a word from the box.

| ~~devastated~~ | rough | awkward | serious |
| pleasant | burst | | |

1 A: Anyway, he just came out and told me she'd died in the crash.
   B: I bet you ....*were devastated.*....
2 A: So, there we were, nice and cosy, holding hands, and my ex-girlfriend appeared!
   B: I imagine ....
3 A: The food was fantastic. I had second helpings of everything.
   B: You must ....
4 A: I had to have six stitches in my chin, without anaesthetic!
   B: That can't .... !
5 A: I didn't get home until 6 this morning.
   B: You must ....
6 A: I told him I'm leaving him and going to Africa as a volunteer.
   B: You can't .... !

PRONUNCIATION Intonation in responses

Language note intonation

Use intonation to emphasise your interest in what the other person is saying. A flat intonation can make you sound bored, especially to native speakers.

8 Practise saying the sentences. Underline the stressed syllables.
1 You must be getting quite good at it.
2 It must've been amazing.
3 I bet that was awful.
4 I imagine she was quite relieved.
5 I bet she was mortified.
6 You must be getting pretty tired of it.

9 🔊 5.1 Listen and check. Practise again and try to imitate the intonation.

VOCABULARY Noun + *of*

1 Choose the correct words.

1 I might be a bit late, as I've got a *supply / bunch / swarm* of stuff to do first.

2 I can't quite remember his name. It's on the *onset / tip / fraction* of my tongue.

3 Can we look forward to the *pleasure / supply / creation* of your company tonight?

4 She was attacked by a *flood / bunch / swarm* of wasps and almost died.

5 Due to migration to the cities, there is a shortage in the *creation / supply / bunch* of manual labour in rural areas.

6 I searched the whole house but there was no *set / supply / sign* of life.

7 The council received *bundles / floods / swarms* of complaints about the roadworks.

8 The new factory will mean the *pleasure / creation / onset* of more jobs in the area.

2 Complete the sentences with the words in the box.

manner	front	record	production
awkwardness	pack	fraction	thrill

1 I managed to make a cheap booking online for a .... of the normal cost.

2 There were all .... of people at the exhibition, from well-known art critics to ordinary schoolchildren.

3 I'll meet you in .... of the cinema at 7 o'clock, OK?

4 Having got over the .... of bumping into my ex-boss, I soon relaxed and enjoyed the evening.

5 The book is a wonderful .... of the artist's early life in France.

6 Have you been to see the latest .... of Macbeth at the New Globe theatre yet?

7 There's nothing to compare with the .... of watching your favourite band perform live.

8 I know a great trick. Has anyone got a .... of cards?

READING

3 Quickly read the text opposite. What kind of text is it?

a a journal article

b a blog report

c a proposal

d a competition entry

4 Match the headings (a–f) with the gaps in the text (1–5). There is one extra heading that you don't need to use.

a Social interaction

b Skills development

c Attracting younger members

d Summing up the benefits

e A need for promotion

f Mental health benefits

5 *Six* of the following points are made in the text. Number the points 1–6 in the order they appear.

.... Chess improves ability in certain subjects.

.... Membership is inexpensive.

.... It's better for you than some sports.

.... The club is conveniently located.

.... Playing helps people to relax.

.... It allows people to meet players from different countries.

.... The club could create money for the council.

.... Chess helps develop prediction skills.

6 Complete the words with the correct prefixes.

1 It's impossible to .... wit this genius. She's too smart!

2 There were .... numerable fans – millions of them!

3 As a result of her .... ability she uses a wheelchair.

4 This .... national sport is played around the globe.

5 I need to .... wind and relax after work.

6 I refer you back to the .... mentioned study.

Evening Chess Club

 1.......

For the last two years, membership of the evening chess club has been in decline, especially among younger members. Advertising is essential if it is to survive and thrive. The campaign should highlight the following practical details. Firstly, the club is easily accessible by car or public transport. Secondly, the membership is affordable for everyone, with discounts available for the elderly, students and those claiming disability or other benefits. Thirdly, this is a family club and parents are encouraged to bring their children. Advertising literature should also give prominence to these key selling points:

 2.......

Although online chess has become increasingly popular, meeting fellow players face-to-face adds an extra dimension to the game. Potential members need to be made aware that there is an on-site coffee shop, and snacks such as fresh sandwiches and patties are also made available. Regular tournaments stimulate friendly competition and allow members to meet players from different local clubs. If sufficient interest is generated by an advertising campaign, there might be an opportunity to extend the scope of the club. It is hoped that in the future it will be possible for members to participate in evening and weekend tournaments at an international level.

 3.......

The latest medical research should also be emphasised. Studies have shown that chess improves both memory and concentration, as players need to focus not only on their own strategy but also on anticipating their opponent's moves in order to gain an advantage. Studies have shown that chess may even offset the risks of such diseases as Alzheimer's in older players. Finally, chess is excellent at stress reduction. As this is an evening club, it could be promoted as the perfect way to unwind after a hard day's work.

 4.......

In addition to the benefits already mentioned, chess promotes imagination and creativity, as players seek to outwit each other. Players develop problem-solving skills and the capacity to foresee the consequences of their actions. Chess also develops vital social skills among younger players, such as learning about the value of fairness and respect for their opponent. Players gain confidence as they improve their skills. Some studies have suggested that regular participation in a skills-based hobby such as chess can improve ability at maths and logic as well as overall performance at school. I would recommend that separate flyers be targeted at teachers and parents in the area, drawing particular attention to these many advantages.

 5.......

For the aforementioned reasons, I strongly recommend that the council invest in further advertising to promote the club. Evening Chess Club provides local people with an enjoyable and rewarding evening activity to complement the existing sports and social programmes in the area. Increased membership would bring innumerable benefits to the community, as well as raise some much-needed additional revenue for the council's leisure programme.

> **Glossary**
>
> **claim benefits:** get financial help from the government
> **patties:** pies filled with meat and potato
> **Alzheimer's:** a progressive neurological disease which leads to loss of mental ability

GRAMMAR Noun phrases

1 Match the <u>underlined</u> words and phrases in 1–6 with the grammar words and phrases (a–e). Use one of the grammar words or phrases twice.

1 Ice Is Nice's new single features lyrics <u>unsuitable</u> for day-time radio.
2 Julian Vaughn has written a spine-chilling thriller which explores the boundary <u>between good and evil</u>.
3 Kelly Malone stars in the historical drama *The Good Housekeeper*, <u>based on the novel of the same name</u>.
4 A <u>crowd</u> of celebrities attended the premiere of Ron Miles's film *The Holocaust*.
5 <u>Having just returned from the Amazon,</u> naturalist Sir Bob Henley is giving a talk on Exotic Frogs at the Geographical Society.
6 Alice Downey, <u>whose performance in the comedy *Caring for Candice* won her two awards</u>, will be hosting the show.

a adjective
b noun
c prepositional phrase
d relative clause
e participle clause

2 Rewrite the sentences. Include the extra information in brackets and your own words if necessary.

1 The film stars the actress. (Australian / 37 / year / old)
The film stars the 37-year-old Australian actress.
2 Ken Wilson's talk was very popular. (thunderous applause / receiving)
....
3 *Macbeth* is a gloomy play. (written / Shakespeare)
....
4 Look at the actress. (designer dress / with)
....
5 The National Theatre Company is producing new plays. (number)
....
6 The Frankies gave a concert. (superb / watched / millions)
....

LISTENING

3 ⏺ 5.2 Listen to two conversations about evening activities. Match the conversations with two of the pictures (a–d).
Conversation 1 .... Conversation 2 ....

4 Listen again. Are the statements true (T) or false (F)?

1 Amy hadn't been to a party the night before.
2 She played the game because she had seen it in adverts.
3 She liked the game immediately.
4 She's going to play the game again.
5 John never goes into town on Friday nights.
6 He thinks that watching DVDs is better than going to the cinema.
7 John and his friends organised the club after a friend lost her job.
8 He usually prefers horror films.

Language note colloquialisms

Many English colloquialisms are based on common words or phrases which have been put together in a different way. For example, an *all-nighter* is a time when you spend 'all night' doing something. Use the context to help you work out the meaning.

VOCABULARY Describing books

5 Choose the best option to complete the sentences.

1 Vikram Chandra weaves a complex .... in his novel *Sacred Games*.
   a plot   b argument   c speech
2 The novel .... the history of the war.
   a carries   b finds   c traces
3 *Angela's Ashes* is an astonishing .... of a poverty-stricken childhood.
   a memory   b memorial   c memoir
4 The story tells of a young boy's .... to overcome dyslexia.
   a struggle   b conflict   c combat
5 The dialogue between the six main .... in the novel is hilarious at times.
   a narrators   b protagonists   c commentators
6 The book .... some sensitive issues, such as drug addiction and abuse.
   a sorts   b tackles   c discovers

6 Add the missing prepositions.

1 The book revolves .... the lives of four women living in a small Irish village.
2 A historical novel, it is set .... the 1800s.
3 McCall Smith has a wonderful talent for bringing his characters .... life.
4 The plot is .... turns tragic and funny.
5 The story is told .... the first person.
6 The murder .... which the book is based took place in 1860.

Language note prepositions

When a verb + preposition occurs in a relative clause, note the different word order:
The novel is set in Cuba. → *The place in which the novel is set is Cuba.*

Vocabulary Builder Quiz 5

Download the Vocabulary Builder for Unit 5 and try the quiz below. Write your answers in your notebook. Then check them and record your score.

1 Choose the correct words.

1 He told us a *tale / memoir* about fairies.
2 The novel *centres / turns* on the relationship between a patient and her psychiatrist.
3 We were all in *bits / stitches* at his hilarious jokes.
4 He gave her a lovely *supply / bunch* of flowers on her birthday.
5 It was so boring I couldn't stop *yawning / crawling*.

2 Which words relate to books?

1 dialogue   2 issues
3 narrator   4 trace
5 flaw   6 memoir

3 Complete the sentences with the correct form of the words in brackets.

1 Michael Jackson is .... (synonym) with disco music.
2 The film explores themes of .... (accept) for your religious and political beliefs.
3 The plot centres on the locals' struggle to free themselves from .... (oppress).
4 CGI has enabled the .... (create) of epic fantasy films like *The Hobbit*.

4 Complete the sentences with the correct particles.

1 We need to factor .... the hidden costs.
2 The protagonist is .... turns violent, reflective and sensitive.
3 The film gives us an insight .... his work.
4 No one can deny the universal appeal .... the cinema.
5 Ouch! You're treading .... my toes.
6 .... the rear of the main house, there is a wonderful rose garden.
7 When I travel, I prefer going .... the beaten track, and exploring the less touristy areas.

5 Complete the sentences with suitable nouns.

1 She was attacked by a .... of wasps yesterday, and had to be taken to hospital.
2 J&B distillaries would like the .... of your company on Saturday, 15th December, to celebrate their centenary.
3 The .... before the release of the latest Star Wars film was incredible.

Score ___/25

Wait a couple of weeks and try the quiz again. Compare your scores.

LISTENING

1 🔊 **6.1 Listen to three people describing conflicts. Match the speakers (1–3) with the people involved in the conflicts (a–d). There is an extra option that you don't need to use.**

a   an employee and a manager
b   a parent and a son
c   two students
d   a television presenter and a guest

2 **Listen again. Why were the speakers unhappy? Match the speakers (1–3) with the reasons (a–f). There are three extra reasons that you don't need to use.**

This speaker thinks that the person they're describing

a   was being selfish.   ....
b   was inefficient.   ....
c   hadn't told the truth.   ....
d   was being lazy.   ....
e   shouldn't have shouted.   ....
f   had treated him unfairly. ....

3 **Choose the correct speaker.**

Which speaker

a   lost his/her temper?   ....
b   still speaks to the person he/she disagreed with?   ....
c   eventually pretended to agree with the
    other person?   ....
d   felt humiliated by the other person?   ....
e   didn't speak to the other person for a short
    period?   ....
f   shocked other people who were watching?   ....

VOCABULARY
Arguments and discussions

4 **Match the statements (1–8) to the follow-on sentences (a–h).**

1   No, I didn't mean that at all!
2   OK, I heard you, and I've got the message.
3   Sorry, that came out all wrong.
4   Look, we're getting nowhere here.
5   You're definitely angry about something.
6   It was only a small scratch, so just calm down!
7   Hey! There's no need to raise your voice.
8   Wait a minute! You misunderstood me.

a   So, I think we should clear the air.
b   I can hear you perfectly well from here.
c   We keep going round in circles.
d   Can you pretend I didn't say it?
e   It's not the end of the world.
f   You're twisting my words.
g   I think we've got our wires crossed.
h   Now can we just move on?

5 **Complete the sentences with the words and phrases in the box.**

prove	are missing	of taking	take
are trying to	in discussing		

1   What's the point you .... make?
2   I just don't see the point .... the matter further.
3   There's no point .... it any longer.
4   Doesn't what you're saying .... my point?
5   OK, I .... your point.
6   I think you .... the point here.

6 **Rewrite the sentences using the words provided and phrases from exercises 4 and 5.**

1   Look. I could have phrased that better.
    Sorry, that ....
2   It's no use talking about it now. Wait until she's calmed down.
    There's no .... Wait until she's calmed down.
3   I certainly did not mean that! You're putting words in my mouth!
    Don't .... and make out I meant something else.
4   Alright, I can see what you're saying.
    OK, I take ....
5   Let's talk about it and get things straight.
    I think we should ....
6   There seems to be some sort of misunderstanding.
    I think we've ....

GRAMMAR *Wish* and *if only*

7 Find and correct *four* mistakes.

1 I wish I know the answer to these questions.
2 I wish he wouldn't keep texting when we're talking.
3 I wish we'd never gone camping with them.
4 I wish you can come to support me when I see the boss later.
5 If only I would be better at remembering facts when I'm arguing with someone.
6 I wish I didn't go to class yesterday.

8 Complete Dave's letter to his girlfriend with the correct form of the words in brackets.

> Dear Penelope,
>
> I'm so sorry about everything. If only
> ¹..................... (*you / let*) me explain. I
> wish ²..................... (*I / take*) it all back,
> but I can't. I shouldn't have taken your
> car, but I was so angry with you. If
> only ³..................... (*we / not fight*) like
> that yesterday, then I wouldn't have
> got drunk and crashed it. If only that
> ⁴..................... (*tree / not be*) there! I wish
> ⁵..................... (*I / not yell*) at the police
> officer, either. Then I might not be
> sitting in this cell.
> You know I love you.
> I just wish ⁶.....................
> (*you / find*) it in your
> heart to forgive me.
>
> Love always,
> Dave

Language note *I hope* versus *I wish*

Use *I hope* if you want something that is possible.
I hope I can come to your party. (I'll try my best and if possible I'll come)
Use *I wish* if something isn't possible.
I wish I could come to your party. (but unfortunately I can't)

9 Rewrite the sentences beginning with the words given.

1 My phone never works properly. It's so annoying!
  I wish my ....
2 You're always late and it gets on my nerves!
  I wish you ....
3 I agreed to help my brother move house. That was a mistake.
  If only I ....
4 I have to go to work today. I don't want to.
  I wish ....
5 I want to come to your party but I can't.
  If only ....
6 There are too many commercials on TV.
  If only ....

DEVELOPING CONVERSATIONS
Defending and excusing

10 Match comments (1–6) with the responses (a–f).

1 I can't believe you left the address on your desk!
2 There's no need to snap at me like that.
3 Why on earth did you buy such a huge home cinema?
4 Why can't you ask Joe? It's not as though he's got anything better to do.
5 I told you we shouldn't have come. I'm so bored!
6 I wish you'd stop going on about it.

a I know. It's just that he's not as tactful as you.
b I wouldn't have if you hadn't been yelling at me to hurry up.
c So you keep saying. I wish you would drop it.
d It's just that I'm not sure what to do, that's all.
e OK. I'm sorry. It's just that you keep interrupting me.
f Why not? It's not as if we can't afford it.

PRONUNCIATION Soft and hard *c* and *g*

11 Look at the <u>underlined</u> letters in the words in the box and write the words under the correct heading in the table.

asso<u>c</u>iated	ne<u>g</u>otiation	<u>c</u>asualty	ra<u>g</u>e
le<u>g</u>itimate	<u>c</u>easefire	nu<u>c</u>lear	a<u>g</u>reement

1 /s/ re<u>c</u>eive	3 /dʒ/ intelli<u>g</u>ent
2 /k/ <u>c</u>areful	4 /g/ <u>g</u>o

12 🔊 6.2 Listen and check. Practise saying the words.
13 Match the sentence halves to complete the rules.

1 We usually pronounce *c* as /s/ and *g* as /dʒ/
2 We usually pronounce *c* as /k/ and *g* as /g/

a after the letters *e*, *i* or *y*.
b after other letters.

VOCABULARY Conflict and resolution

1 Choose the correct words.

Film of the Week

Blood Diamond (2006) *showing on Channel 5, Wednesday at 9pm*

Sierra Leone 1999, a country ravaged by the ¹*coup / conflict* between government ²*casualties / troops* and rebel forces. In the opening scene, the Revolutionary United Front (RUF) ³*invades / defends* a small village, capturing a fisherman called Solomon Vandy, and forcing his son Dia to become a child soldier. Solomon is forced to dig for diamonds, the rebels' main source of funding. He finds a large pink diamond, and manages to hide it, but the rebel officer in charge, Captain Poison, sees him do so. However, fighting suddenly ⁴*breaks down / breaks out* between the army and the rebels resulting in the latter being ⁵*defeated / withdrawn*. Both Solomon and Captain Poison are imprisoned, and with them is Danny Archer, an ex-mercenary turned diamond smuggler. He overhears Captain Poison yelling at Solomon about the diamond and sees an opportunity. After ⁶*negotiating / establishing* Solomon's release, Archer agrees to help him ⁷*gain / track down* his family in exchange for the diamond.

The two men ⁸*suffer sanctions / join forces* with an American journalist called Maddy Bowen, who wants to help Solomon. On discovering Archer's true motives, however, she refuses to continue unless he agrees to help her expose the atrocities and human rights ⁹*violations / negotiations* surrounding the blood diamond trade in Sierra Leone. Archer agrees, and they use the press convoy to travel across country. Maddy leaves the country, and the men finally succeed in finding the mining camp, where they find not only Solomon's son, but also Captain Poison. The ¹⁰*resolution / tension* rises as Dia refuses to acknowledge his father, and Archer and Solomon ¹¹*gain ground / are surrounded* by Captain Poison and his men, but an air strike by South African mercenaries enables Solomon to kill Poison. Their troubles aren't over, however, as the leader of the South African mercenaries now wants the diamond for himself. Archer manages to ¹²*achieve a resolution / seize control* by killing him and his men, but gets badly injured. Realising he is dying, he gives the diamond to Solomon and tells him to take his son and go. He delays the soldiers chasing them to give Solomon and Dia time to escape. His final act before he dies is to phone Maddy to ask her to help Solomon and his family get to safety.

READING

2 Quickly read the article. What is the main topic?

a the differences between human and animal behaviour

b the effects of war and why it is so destructive

c whether future wars are inevitable

d the groups of people who are more likely to be violent

3 Read the article again. For statements 1–9, decide whether the writer agrees (✓), disagrees (✗) or doesn't comment (DC).

1 It is surprising what students believe about war. ....

2 The press should pay far less attention to war stories. ....

3 The number of wars seems to have increased recently. ....

4 Primates are more likely than humans to engage in conflict. ....

5 Certain countries have made progress in considering a more peaceful approach. ....

6 People shouldn't share what they have if their reasons for doing so are selfish. ....

7 We don't need to reduce the number of children we have. ....

8 The ratio of men to women in government should be equal. ....

9 It may be possible for humans to stop acting aggressively towards one another. ....

4 Find words or phrases in the article which mean

1 ordinary people in a war situation, not soldiers (paragraph 1) ....

2 the number of people who died in war (paragraph 1) ....

3 making peace (paragraph 3) ....

4 punishment (paragraph 3) ....

5 agreements between two groups, with both sides getting part of what they want (paragraph 5) ....

6 defeat (paragraph 5) ....

Evolution and war

Will there ever be an end to war? The majority of the attendees on my current anthropology course answered a fatalistic 'No'. Their response was largely predictable, given that we are relentlessly bombarded with images of the military, its machinery and weapons, war-torn cities and grieving civilians. The media grimly reminds us of the sheer number of ongoing conflicts around the world; about the huge casualty rate in countries which we would probably struggle to locate on a map. There seems to be a general impression that there is no chance of a peaceful life on the planet, so long as there is human life.

It's certainly true that conflict appears to have escalated in the last decade. Some anthropologists claim that this is natural, insofar as it is an intrinsic part of human nature to be aggressive. Primates, our closest living relatives, also have a tendency towards violence. Therefore it is easy to draw the conclusion that humans fight because it is an ineradicable part of our genetic heritage. However, are we wrong to make this assumption?

While primates can display exceptional levels of brutality towards outsiders, they are also capable of reconciliation (mainly through grooming and mating) and can even avoid conflict when they perceive that there is a strategic advantage in doing so. Put more simply, apes and monkeys will only fight if they believe they can win or escape retribution. Surely, then, humans have the capacity to avoid hostility too. There is already some evidence that the world's major powers have realised the lose-lose scenario that would follow nuclear conflict, as many governments are currently discussing disarmament and arms reduction programmes.

So are there more proactive ways to avoid conflict? The more instinctively peaceful primates are the ones with access to plentiful food, and this should tell us something basic about human conflict. If human populations were more willing to distribute their food, fuel and other natural resources more equitably, there would be less reason to fight. Even if our motive for sharing is technically self-centred, this is irrelevant because in the long term it simply makes sense for us to do so.

Historically, whenever there has been more demand than supply for food, fuel or land, conflict has arisen. Therefore, in order to share these resources, it is vital that population growth is limited. One way to achieve this is through the schooling of women; statistics show that in countries where women are more educated, the birth rate tends to be lower. And with greater education, women are also able to participate more in decision-making at all levels of society, including government. While I hesitate to label women as the more peaceful gender, they have a different set of negotiation skills than men. And we need the skills of both to help find the kind of compromises required to avoid large-scale conflict. Evolution may have instilled within us the instinct to fight, but we can also evolve to overcome it.

DEVELOPING WRITING
A formal email – complaining

1 Quickly read the email. Why is James writing?

....

To   admin@dvdonline.co.nz
From   Johnson, James
Subject   DVD rental club

Dear Sir or Madam,

I ¹.................. signed up for membership of your online DVD rental club. ².................. , the experience has been rather disappointing.

I chose your club ³.................. <u>due to</u> the promises made in your advertisement. This claimed that the DVDs would be delivered within two days of ordering, and that each DVD was guaranteed to be of a high quality. However, neither of these selling points has turned out to be true.

I waited over a week for the first DVD to arrive. I rang your customer assistance number on several occasions, but <u>despite</u> leaving multiple messages ⁴.................. asking for information, my calls were never returned. After nine days, the DVD eventually arrived in a torn envelope. I could not play it <u>as</u> it had ⁵.................. been damaged. I returned the DVD to your company and attached a note with an explanation of what had happened. Nevertheless, this month's fee was still debited from my bank account.

I feel that this is an example of ⁶.................. poor service, and I would like to request a full refund. Furthermore I would like to cancel my subscription with immediate effect.

James Johnson

2 Complete the email with the words in the box.

desperately	evidently	extremely
largely	recently	unfortunately

3 Look at the <u>underlined</u> linkers in the email. Choose the correct options.

due to
1 means
   a *because of*   b *in order to*
2 is followed by
   a a noun or noun phrase
   b a subject + verb + object clause

despite / in spite of
3 mean
   a *although*   b *in contrast*
4 are followed by
   a an *-ing* form
   b a subject + verb + object clause

as
5 means
   a *because*   b *so*
6 is followed by
   a a noun or noun phrase
   b a subject + verb + object clause

> **Language note** *despite / in spite of*
> -
> *Despite* and *in spite of* can also be followed by a noun.
> *Despite this problem, I have generally been satisfied with your service.*

4 Rewrite the sentences using linkers from exercise 3. Use each linker at least once.

1 Although he promised to call us back, he never did.
....

2 It was because of the wrong instructions that we couldn't use the product.
....

3 There was a fault in the camera so we couldn't take any photos.
....

4 The casing was cracked, which is why the game didn't work.
....

5 I asked for a red model but I was sent a yellow one.
....

6 I wish to return this camcorder because the lens is scratched.
....

5 Imagine you have bought one of the items or services in the pictures. Write a letter of complaint (150–190 words) explaining why you are dissatisfied with the item or service and saying what you would like to happen next.

VOCABULARY Extended metaphors

6 Complete the dialogue with the correct form of words and phrases in the box.

invade	target	bombard	aggression	gun
launch	defend	capture	challenge	combat

A: Have you seen their new ad? It's unbelievable! Cowden have ¹................... a marketing campaign that directly ²................... our customers. Houseman will be out for blood this morning.

B: I know. She's called me to see her in her office in ten minutes.

A: Have you got your ³................... ready? Because she'll come at you with ⁴................... blazing for not having anticipated this.

B: But how could I possibly have predicted it?

A: You're Marketing Manager! She'll say you should have been aware that they were developing a new product, so that we could do something to ⁵................... any negative impact it might have on our own. She'll see this as a strategic move to ⁶................... our corner of the market, and will ⁷................... you with accusations of negligence and complacency, so you'd better think of a counter-attack, and fast.

B: How? I'm going to get fired, aren't I?

A: Not if you're clever. Look, Cowden have ⁸................... our territory. You need to go in there and convince Houseman that we can rise to the ⁹................... and retaliate with an ¹⁰................... advertising campaign of our own. Tell her you're already working on it, and you'll have a proposal for her by the end of today.

B: OK, you're right. Thanks.

7 Write your own poem with one of the following titles or your own idea, using war as an extended metaphor. Remember that it doesn't need to rhyme.

'Life is a battle'	'Hostile Health'
'Corporate Combat'	'Sport means War'

Vocabulary Builder Quiz 6

Download the Vocabulary Builder for Unit 6 and try the quiz below. Write your answers in your notebook. Then check them and record your score.

1 Complete the sentences with the correct form of the words in brackets.
1 The .... (continue) of random bomb attacks has caused widespread public outrage.
2 He was extremely .... (aggression), which didn't gain him any sympathy.
3 There was a .... (note) lack of violence or vandalism at yesterday's match.
4 The .... (complex) of the reasons for the dispute is hampering efforts to find a solution.
5 Sexual .... (harass) in the workplace is unacceptable.
6 There is considerable .... (hostile) between them.
7 There were three .... (fatal) after the shooting.

2 Match 1–6 with a–f to make common collocations.
1	lasting	a	of weapons
2	group	b	casualties
3	surrender	c	of wills
4	suffer	d	peace
5	settle	e	dynamics
6	battle	f	a dispute

3 Are the words verbs (V), nouns (N) or both (V+N)?
1 march ....
2 seize ....
3 scan ....
4 trial ....
5 grip ....

4 Complete the sentences with suitable verbs.
1 She .... amends after destroying his painting.
2 After the new wave of attacks, tension .... throughout the town.
3 The rebels wanted to .... a ceasefire to tend to the wounded.
4 Their marriage .... down and they got divorced.
5 There's no need to .... offence at a simple comment!
6 They .... a coup and took control of the presidential residence.
7 We need to .... our troops from the war immediately. It's time our soldiers came home.

Score ___ /25

Wait a couple of weeks and try the quiz again. Compare your scores.

VOCABULARY Talking about science

1 Complete the text with the correct form of the words in the box.

breakthrough	create	due to	negative
pave the way	reproduce	undertake	

Researchers at Sheffield Hallam University have ¹.................... the world's first environmentally friendly wedding dress. It is believed to be a ².................... in the quest to create more sustainable fashion in the UK. The wedding dress is the ultimate symbol of the ³.................... aspects of throwaway fashion, as it is an expensive item that is only worn once.

Fashion and engineering students ⁴.................... the project in order to further their understanding of materials. The fabric they developed can dissolve harmlessly in water. This is ⁵.................... the presence of a biodegradable substance, polyvinyl alcohol, which the students added to the existing material. The fabric can be ⁶.................... for other designs and it is hoped the discovery will ⁷ .... for further developments in ethical fashion.

2 Choose the correct words.

1 Seven people were tested for lead poisoning, but fortunately the results were all *adverse / negative*.
2 Oliver lay in a critical *condition / disorder* for two weeks after the accident.
3 We're *down to / due to* our last bottle of milk. Remind me to buy some tomorrow.
4 He dug down through the soil to the hard, *root / underlying* rock.
5 They have *reproduced / devised* a new method for extracting the mineral.
6 She agreed to *undertake / carry out* responsibility for the Biology Department.

DEVELOPING CONVERSATIONS
Expressing surprise and disbelief

3 Write responses to the statements using *on earth* and the correct form of the words in brackets.

1 I'm planning on becoming a surgeon. (why / want / that)
   Why on earth do you want to do that?
2 In the 19th century some men created a mermaid, with an animal's head and a fish's tail. (how / manage / that)
   ....
3 Did you know that some rats can swim as far as half a mile in open water? (how / achieve)
   ....
4 In 1999 scientists discovered a highly unusual fossil. (what / be)
   ....
5 I'm planning on going tornado chasing. (why / do)
   ....
6 I think the crop circles in Wiltshire have been made by humans. (but how / make)
   ....
7 Heinz is planning to go and study fish in the Bahamas. (how / afford)
   ....

PRONUNCIATION
Expressing opinion and attitude

4 Underline the phrases which express the opinions or attitudes of the speakers.

1 Why on earth do you want to do that?
2 Believe me, you're making a mistake.
3 On the whole, it went very well.
4 It was a disaster, to say the least.
5 What in the world were you thinking of?
6 Funnily enough, the experiment was unsuccessful.

5 ♦ 7.1 Listen to the pronunciation, paying attention to whether the phrases have a falling tone (↘) or rising tone (↗) at the end. Practise saying the sentences.

DEVELOPING WRITING
A report – making recommendations

6 Write suitable subheadings for the paragraphs (A–D) of the report.

Report on the declining popularity of science at Wollangang College, Australia

A ....
The [1]purpose of this report is to [2]examine the possible reasons why there has been a decline in the number of students electing to study science at Wollangang College. The report will focus on two key areas of dissatisfaction and make recommendations for improvement.

B ....
It has been suggested by numerous students that the content of courses is unsatisfactory. A [3]considerable proportion have expressed some criticism of existing course books, commenting that most do not reflect the latest developments. Many felt they could learn more from the internet or television programmes.

C ....
[4]With regard to science facilities, opinions [5]differed. Some students thought that facilities were acceptable, while others said that they found the laboratories off-putting and dull in appearance. A number of science students said that they would like to be able to go on field trips, in addition to learning in the classroom.

D ....
[6]Overall, it was felt that science subjects could be made more appealing by [7]updating the course content and improving facilities. The use of televisual and online media in the classroom could make the subject seem more relevant. Furthermore, renovation of the laboratories would [8]enhance their appeal, and regular field trips would add variety. In this way, more students might be encouraged to participate in science courses.

7 Match the synonyms (a–h) with the underlined words in the report (1–8).

a large number   ....
b varied   ....
c make them more attractive ....
d consider; investigate ....
e in general; on the whole ....
f aim; intention   ....
g modernising   ....
h concerning   ....

8 Are the expressions more suitable in a formal report (R) or a lively article (A)?

1 Details of the research are to be found ...   .
2 It seems to me that ...   .
3 The most immediate priority would be to ...   .
4 You must take action now.   ....
5 It is believed that this would benefit ...   .
6 Personally, I think ...   .
7 Is there any way to fix this problem?   ....
8 ... is highly recommended.   ....

Learner tip

Reports generally require formal language. Use neutral, non-emotive verbs and avoid personal pronouns. Passive structures can make your writing sound more objective, but only use these where appropriate.

9 You see the following advertisement in your local newspaper. Write a report (180–220 words) in answer to the advertisement.

We want to encourage more young people in your area to study science. We would like you, our readers, to send us reports about your experience of learning science at school or university. In your report you should

- highlight any positive parts of your experience of studying science
- describe any negative aspects
- make recommendations on how more young people could be encouraged to study science.

READING

1 Quickly read the article opposite. What is the main topic of each of the paragraphs 1–5? Choose five of the ideas in the box.

an idea for the future	an outline of the issue
an unsolvable problem	media relations
online coverage	visual media
worldwide publicity	

2 Complete the summary of the article with one or two words in each gap. You may need to use different forms of words or phrases that appear in the text.

According to the writer, effective ¹.................. is essential if scientists want to gain support for their research. There are several ways in which this goal is being pursued.

PR experts ².................. by numerous scientific organisations to promote and disseminate research. Some scientists write ³.................. , often distinguished by their ⁴.................. and accessibility. Science programmes on TV have also boosted the subject's image. Presenters such as Brian Cox, formerly a ⁵.................. , now a ⁶.................. , have also helped make science seem ⁷.................. geeky. Thanks to companies such as *SciVee*, scientists can also present their research online in ⁸.................. .

Some scientists still need to work on improving their media image. The writer suggests that young scientists should be ⁹.................. in effective communication skills while they are still ¹⁰.................. .

3 Choose the correct words.
1 Press officers help scientists *present / show* their research to the public.
2 Scientific documentaries can *create / inspire* young people to become scientists.
3 Using the latest technology, scientists *estimate / guess* the age of the skeleton to be approximately 10,000 years old.
4 Colourful visual images *sense / stimulate* interest and make the topic more appealing.
5 Scientists usually *give / release* information to the public after extensive research.
6 An official visited the research institute to *assess / check* its funding requirements.

Professor Brian Cox

Communicating science

1 One of the major problems for scientists lies in communicating the value of research to the people that matter: policymakers and the general public. In recent years, scientific organisations have come a long way in developing ways to make science more accessible to non-specialist groups.

2 Universities and research institutes now employ press officers to create user-friendly press releases which are intended to communicate new developments effectively, without hype or exaggerated claims. These professionals are able to target specific audiences, and estimate the best time for releasing information to them. They are careful to avoid over-selling a product and make sure that the press release includes information about risk as well as the limitations of a particular study. Occasionally, scientists may address an audience directly to lend weight to a campaign or initiative, but the press officer will assess whether the product will benefit from this or not.

3 The development of blogs has helped substantially in bringing science closer to the public. According to Wikipedia, the *ScienceBlogs* network is now ranked 37th among the most authoritative blogs worldwide, with two of its sections having won weblog awards. In 2008 the network launched a German-language edition, and the following year saw the introduction of *ScienceBlogs Brazil*. Released from editorial restrictions, science bloggers generally focus on areas of science that they are both passionate and knowledgeable about. They often write about science in an accessible, lively manner, and it is this that perhaps most attracts members of the public. Ed Yong's *Not Exactly Rocket Science*, for instance, is imbued with the writer's enthusiasm and down-to-earth attitude towards the subject. His chatty, youthful style appeals to a wide range of readers, whereas a formal, two-page article in a science journal might be neglected.

4 Television has also boosted the image of science. Early pioneers such as Jacques Cousteau, whose beautifully filmed documentaries opened up the oceans to millions, quickly realised the potential of TV to make science come alive for viewers. Other science disciplines have eagerly followed suit. Entertaining presenters carry out daring experiments or explore amazing scientific phenomena in order to attract attention. High-profile personalities such as Brian Cox, once famous for playing music in D:Ream, have also been instrumental in bringing science into the realm of popular culture. Now working in the field of physics, Brian is presenter of the BBC TV series *Wonders of the Solar System*. His background means that his face is not only well known to younger viewers but is also deemed cool. Other organisations have been utilising the power of visual media via the internet. For example, *SciVee* offers scientists video services to create online presentations of their research.

5 Nevertheless, despite this progress, communication remains one of science's biggest stumbling blocks. A tendency towards a more old-fashioned academic approach means that scientists often underestimate the importance of becoming media-savvy, leaving them vulnerable to missing out on public and financial support for their research. Perhaps it is time that universities addressed this problem, and thought about adding communications training to the curriculum.

Glossary

press officer: someone employed to give advice on how to deal with the media; a PR official
media-savvy: aware of how to deal with the media

VOCABULARY Forming nouns and adjectives

4 Complete the table with the verb and noun forms. Put a cross (✗) if there is no verb form.

adjective	verb	noun
1 exploratory		
2 manipulative		
3 diverse		
4 implied		
5 preventative		
6 abundant		
7 varied		
8 probable		

5 Complete the sentences with the correct form of *one* of the words in brackets.
1 I feel he is too .... in his view of evolution. (cynicism / capability)
2 Her .... approach to her research has made her a number of enemies. (fatality / aggression)
3 We do not yet know the full .... of this technology. (capable / exploratory)
4 A number of .... in the data have rendered the study inconclusive. (vary / probable)
5 There were several .... in the explosion at the laboratory last night. (manipulative / fatal)
6 The director's .... handling of the media was widely criticised. (imply / manipulate)

6 Complete the words with the prefixes in the box. Use one prefix twice.

in	non-	un	im	ir	il

1 Luckily, the poisoning was ....fatal, and she recovered.
2 This theory is quite ....probable.
3 The physicist's reasoning was ....logical and far-fetched.
4 She's quite ....capable of passing her chemistry exam.
5 ....fortunately, the operation is .... reversible.
6 This avenue of research has been hitherto ....explored.

VOCABULARY Statistics

1 Match the sentence halves.

1 The company has a vested
2 The figures showed a negative
3 Since the subject group was female only, the research is
4 Unhappy with the test results, the researcher twisted the
5 Close examination shows that the data doesn't stand
6 There's so much conflicting

a seriously flawed as it is not representative.
b up to scrutiny.
c evidence that it's difficult to draw a conclusion.
d correlation between addiction to video games and poor reading.
e interest in the test results being positive.
f figures to suit his own ends.

2 Complete the sentences with suitable words.

1 .... to popular belief, the human body does not burst in space. That is a myth.
2 The idea that a coin dropped from a high building can kill someone below doesn't stand .... to scrutiny.
3 The research assistant wanted to gain favour with the head of research, and so twisted the figures to .... her own ends.
4 In order to gain financial support, scientists have a vested .... in communicating with policymakers.
5 This sudden drop in numbers may simply be a statistical .... , i.e. an exception to the general trend.
6 Researchers have been successful in establishing a causal .... between chemical waste from the cement factory and the rise in the incidence of skin cancer in the area.

> **Learner tip**
>
> Language to discuss statistics is frequently used in news stories or scientific articles. It can be very useful for writing reports, academic essays or other types of formal texts, so keep a record of any useful examples you notice.

LISTENING

3 ⬤ 7.2 Listen to the first part of a speech about a hearing loss charity. Who is the main speaker?

a a university professor
b an entrepreneur
c an inventor

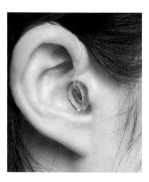

4 ⬤ 7.3 Listen to the second part and choose the correct answers.

1 How many people in Europe suffered from hearing loss in 1995?
   a 25 million
   b 70 million
   c 95 million
2 What does Dr Vermeulen say is a particular problem for younger people with hearing loss?
   a They're worried about the appearance of hearing aids.
   b They don't know what treatments and advice are available.
   c They don't realise how serious their problem is.
3 What *can't* people do on the *Hear-It* website?
   a read about hearing aids
   b review hearing aids
   c buy hearing aids
4 Dr Vermeulen cites the case of Ashkan Tehrani as an example of someone who
   a proves that life with a hearing impairment need not be any different.
   b has had his life transformed by technology.
   c has always had a positive attitude towards his problem.
5 Dr Vermeulen mentions a scientific development which suggests that
   a sounds can also affect our perception of sensations, tastes and smells.
   b our skin is of equal importance to our ear as a hearing organ.
   c when we listen, we use three senses.
6 The main purpose of Dr Vermeulen's talk is
   a to raise awareness of the scale of the issue.
   b to describe recent technological developments in the field.
   c to promote the charity's website.

GRAMMAR Passives

5 Rewrite the sentences using the words provided.

1 Government agencies twist statistics to suit their own ends.
Statistics ....

2 They regularly check the animals' health for signs of deterioration.
The animals ....

3 A Cardiff scientist has invented virtual ears to test acoustics.
Acoustics can ....
which ....

4 According to a report, rangers have illegally killed 30,000 elephants.
It ....
30,000 elephants ....

5 They gave the scientists the award in recognition of their work.
The award ....

6 People think that online translation services will bridge the language barrier.
It ....
the language barrier ....

Language note passive state verbs

Some verbs describing states, such as *know*, *think*, *believe* and *own*, can have a passive form.
He's believed to be studying science.
Other state verbs, such as *have*, *become*, *belong* and *wish*, cannot be used passively.
Other scientists have a similar approach
not *A similar approach is had …*

---

6 Complete the sentences with the active or passive form of the phrases in the box.

bees / resemble	~~it / discover~~
doubts / raise	findings / present
flower / once / belong	previously / think

1 *It has been discovered* .... that dinosaurs were larger than ....

2 Since 2005, ... about the validity of the test results, which may have been flawed.

3 Notice that the .... wasps in appearance.

4 The .... to the conference next month.

5 This extinct .... to the poppy family.

Vocabulary Builder Quiz 7

Download the Vocabulary Builder for Unit 7 and try the quiz below. Write your answers in your notebook. Then check them and record your score.

1 Are the definitions of the <u>underlined</u> words correct (C) or incorrect (I)?

1 <u>Anomalies</u> are unusual or unexpected.   ....
2 If you <u>extract</u> something, you add to it.   ....
3 A <u>breakthrough</u> is the act of stealing someone's invention or design.   ....
4 A <u>fragrant</u> flower smells nice.   ....
5 If you <u>duplicate</u> something, you repeat it.   ....
6 <u>Variables</u> are different kinds of things.   ....
7 <u>Random</u> actions are well planned.   ....

2 Complete the sentences with suitable prepositions.

1 The scientist was unable to come up .... a solution to the problem.
2 The pharmaceutical company has a vested interest .... the new drug trials.
3 It is hoped this development will pave the way .... further research.
4 The cuts are the thin end .... the wedge. Worse is to follow.
5 Forensic scientists need to ensure that evidence will stand .... in court.
6 Contrary .... expectations, the test flight was unsuccessful.

3 Complete the sentences with a suitable word.

1 Einstein's theory of relativity has stood the .... of time.
2 The atomic bomb .... devastation on the whole area.
3 This concept represents a potentially slippery ....
4 Research suggests that a genetic .... is the cause of the disease.
5 Your argument is full of ....
6 The evidence supporting the theory is .... , so we can publish our findings.

4 Complete the sentences with the correct form of the word in brackets.

1 The .... (accelerate) of my new car is impressive.
2 I didn't say that. That journalist .... (twist) my words.
3 The test involves the .... (insert) of a probe into the brain.
4 Recent .... (reveal) about research into chemical warfare have caused an outcry.
5 Visual .... (stimulus) are important in the primary classroom.
6 Management have given us an .... (undertake) that there will be no redundancies.

Score ___/25

Wait a couple of weeks and try the quiz again.
Compare your scores.

08 NATURE AND NURTURE

VOCABULARY Describing scenery

1 Match the definitions with the nouns in the box.

cliff	crater	dune	glacier	gorge	plain

1 a hole at the top of a volcano ....
2 a small hill of sand found in the desert
   or by the beach ....
3 a wide, flat area of land ....
4 a very deep valley, usually with a river
   running though it ....
5 a high, steep rock face, often next to the
   sea or part of a mountain ....
6 a slowly moving mass of ice ....

2 Complete the sentences with the correct words from exercise 1.

1 A variety of sea birds have built their nests on rocky
  ledges on the ....
2 The .... are constantly changing shape as the
  wind blows.
3 The .... was formed at the peak when Mount
  Etna first erupted.
4 In the summer, many visitors like to kayak down the
  river in the ....
5 You can see for miles and miles across the wide
  ...., where bison used to graze hundreds of
  years ago.
6 Many .... are melting rapidly because of climate
  change.

3 Match the sentence halves.

1 I saw below me a landscape of soft, rolling
2 This was once an area of dense
3 As a child I would follow the dirt
4 There were several rocky
5 We were impressed by the breathtaking
6 I couldn't wait to jump into the crystal clear

a scenery that we saw all over the island.
b beaches which we used to explore.
c hills which reminded me of home.
d sea that we had seen from the coastal road.
e woodland before it was all cut down.
f track through the woods to the village.

Language note *landscape* versus *scenery*

- -

Landscape refers to the general appearance of a place,
as in *a mountainous / flat / barren landscape*.
Scenery refers to things a landscape might contain, such
as trees or waterfalls. We don't usually use *scenery* with
negative adjectives: *beautiful scenery*, not ~~ugly scenery~~.

LISTENING

**4 ♫ 8.1 Listen to a woman called Monique talking about
rock-climbing. Who is she?**

a an amateur rock climber
b a rock-climbing instructor
c a professional rock climber

5 Listen again. Tick (✓) the statements Monique agrees with.

1 I took up rock-climbing because friends encouraged
  me to do so. ....
2 I found climbing difficult at first. ....
3 Rock-climbing is always a competitive sport. ....
4 I train just as much on indoor climbing walls as I do
  on real rock faces. ....
5 Female rock climbers have certain physical
  advantages over men. ....
6 I have encountered little prejudice from male rock
  climbers. ....
7 I believe that rock climbers probably reach their
  peak by 40. ....
8 My immediate plan is to improve my time on a
  climb I've done before. ....

DEVELOPING CONVERSATIONS
Emphatic tags

6 Find and correct *five* mistakes in the emphatic tags in the sentences.

a If I were you, I'd move back a bit, I really wouldn't.

b Mmm. The scenery can be incredibly varied, they really can.

c Yes. Amazing. I love the sea, I really love.

d We'll never make it, we really won't.

e Incredible. I've never seen wildlife like this so close before, I really have never.

f That sounds terrifying, it really is!

7 Complete the dialogues with the responses (a–f) in exercise 6.

1 A: I think we can get across the river if we go down a bit farther.
   B: ....

2 A: Wow! Can you see those wolves by the rocks?
   B: ....

3 A: Standing here on the edge of the cliff, I can see for miles and miles.
   B: ....

4 A: Our helicopter flew over the crater just as the volcano started erupting.
   B: ....

5 A: The bay looks so calm.
   B: ....

6 A: We've seen so much so far. Waterfalls, gorges, mountains ...
   B: ....

PRONUNCIATION Strong and weak forms

> **Language note** strong and weak forms
>
> Many function words (which include auxiliary verbs, pronouns, articles and some modal verbs) have strong and weak pronunciations.
> We use a strong form when the word
> • is emphasised
> • appears at the end of a sentence
> • is said on its own.
> *You can see for miles and miles from there, you really can.*
> /cən/   /cæn/

8 (Circle) the underlined words that have a strong form of pronunciation.

1 <u>The</u> mountains <u>are</u> awesome, they really <u>are</u>.

2 It <u>is</u> normally safe but sometimes problems <u>do</u> occur.

3 'Did <u>you</u> see James? Was <u>he</u> on the tour?'
   '<u>He</u> was, but <u>she</u> wasn't.'

4 <u>The</u> scenery <u>can</u> be stunning, it really <u>can</u>.

5 <u>You're</u> not well, <u>are</u> <u>you</u>?

9 ◐ 8.2 Listen and check. Practise saying the sentences.

GRAMMAR Auxiliaries

10 Quickly read the conversation, ignoring the gaps. Which adjective best describes the landscape?

a forested

b arid

c mountainous

d coastal

A: It looks like it's going to be a pretty good day for a hike, ¹.................... it? What with all the rain we've had recently, you probably didn't imagine we'd be setting out today. Neither ².................... I, in fact. But here we are. Well, anyway, as you know, we'll be heading up the gorge this afternoon and staying in a cabin at the foot of the slopes. It actually has proper beds.

B: ³.................... it? Great! I thought we'd be sleeping on the floor.

A: No, it'll be a comfortable first night at least. Now, one thing I ⁴.................... have to make clear is that when crossing the river, you must stay within reach of one another while ⁵.................... so. The water can be treacherous and I wouldn't want to lose anyone!

B: Neither ⁶.................... we!

A: Now, if you've been here before, you'll know that weather near the peak can be incredibly changeable, ⁷.................... it? So the one thing that I can't emphasise enough is to be careful. While most hikers return without incident, occasional problems ⁸.................... occur. Most of you will have arrived with the right equipment, but I suspect not all of you ⁹....................! Luckily, there's a shop just near here which sells everything you'll need.

B: ¹⁰.................... there? Can we go there first?

11 Complete the conversation in exercise 10 with the correct auxiliary verbs.

VOCABULARY Communicating

1 Choose the correct words.

1 He's always *pushing / butting* into other people's conversations.

2 Joe's always putting words *onto your tongue / into your mouth*.

3 You know exactly what Aisha thinks; she never *minces / chops* her words.

4 At times I find it quite a *battle / struggle* to express myself.

5 I wish you'd stop beating about the *trees / bush* and tell me what the matter is.

6 If you ever need a shoulder to *cry / rest* on, I'm a pretty good listener.

7 Marta hardly lets you get a word in *edgeways / longways*!

8 In my culture, it's quite rude to get to the *point / aim* too quickly.

2 What would you say in the following situations? Complete the responses with the correct form of the phrases in exercise 1.

1 Your friend looks very upset.
Do you want a .... ?'

2 A colleague is taking ages to explain something.
'Could you ...., please?'

3 In an argument, the other person has accused you of saying something you didn't.
'Don't .... !'

4 You're annoyed because someone keeps talking and won't let you speak.
'You're not letting .... !'

5 You think someone was much too direct with you.
'Well, you certainly didn't ....'

6 You think a friend of yours needs to be clearer about what he wants.
'Can you .... and tell me!'

7 You admit to a tutor that you can't always explain things clearly.
'I do find .... myself.'

8 You're annoyed with someone who interrupts when you're already talking.
'Do you mind not ....?'

READING

3 Quickly read the extract from a book of nature essays. Which two adjectives best describe the writer's attitude towards the Venus Fly Trap?

a concerned

b impartial

c frightened

d indifferent

e obsessed

f uncritical

g fascinated

4 Seven parts of the essay have been removed. Write the correct letter (a–h) in the gaps in the essay. There is one extra sentence that you don't need to use.

a Then there are the serious enthusiasts who delight in every tiny variation in the subspecies grown in their own greenhouses.

b We now know that the Venus Fly Trap is not unique.

c The plants are dug out of the soil and illegally sold on to traders.

d They therefore depend on insects to provide the nitrogen for protein formation that enables their growth.

e It's attacked by enzymes and slowly liquefied and absorbed.

f It's a member of this very small group of plants which are capable of movement.

g This allows the plant to distinguish between food and raindrops, and obviously, children's probing digits.

h It's also more accurate to refer to the 'mouth' as a leaf.

Learner tip

You will often encounter unfamiliar words in English texts. If you don't have a dictionary, don't panic! First, try to work out the part of speech (Does the word have a suffix or a prefix? How is it used?) Then look carefully at the context. This will often give you useful clues to understanding the meaning.

5 Match the definitions (a–f) with the underlined words in the essay.

a contradicted ....

b stealing plant (or animal) species ....

c attractive in an exciting way ....

d provide space ....

e open to harm or danger ....

f inaccurate description ....

87: The Venus Fly Trap

Dr Lars Bohr, Department of Botany, Aalborg University, Denmark

A great green jaw, red-rimmed, lies wide open and perfectly still on the forest floor. The sweet smell it gives off is <u>alluring</u>. It is not long before an inquisitive creature arrives and unwittingly steps inside. In an instant, the mouth has closed and the victim is sealed within. [1]....... Sound horrifying? It's just nature. Be grateful that the Venus Fly Trap is a mere six centimetres high.

Even people who otherwise have little interest in plants are familiar with Venus Fly Traps. For small children, the temptation of poking the open 'mouths' is irresistible. [2]....... When I'm lecturing on botany, I find that the name of the plant draws more attention than many other of my special interests. So what is it about the Venus Fly Trap that arouses such fascination?

Well, firstly, the idea of a carnivorous plant is intriguingly gruesome. When specimens first arrived in Europe in the 18th century, many scientists could not conceive of a plant with an insect diet, as it <u>confounded</u> their beliefs about natural order. This species seemed a hideous anomaly. [3]....... Actually, more than 630 species of 'meat-eating' plants exist.

The name, 'Venus Fly Trap', is a <u>misnomer</u>, as it's more likely to consume ground-level insects such as beetles and millipedes than actual flies. [4]....... This is lined with a number of tiny hairs. When an insect crawls onto one of the trigger hairs, the leaf snaps shut. This incredible mechanism will only operate if the same hair is rapidly touched twice, or a second nearby hair is touched within 20 seconds. [5].......

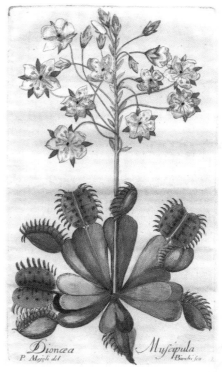

Dionæa *Muscipula*
P. Majoli del *Bianchi fec*

Here's another fact. The Venus Fly Trap is actually rather rare, so much so that local conservationists want it officially classified as '<u>vulnerable</u>', one step away from 'endangered'. The plant's habitat is a mere 100 miles across northern South Carolina and southern North Carolina in the USA, where they live in sandy, acidic soil that offers little in the way of minerals. [6]....... Constant sunlight is also a necessity as their modified leaves are poor at photosynthesis. And to gain sufficient access to sunlight, they rely on regular forest fires to reduce other vegetation.

Herein lies one of the threats to their survival. Their habitat has been encroached on by development, and residents are understandably keen to put out any fires which might start. Then, many of the wetlands have been drained to <u>make way</u> for golf courses, parking lots and hotels. On top of this, there is relentless <u>poaching</u>. [7]....... There are fines in place to deter their theft but local authorities do not have the manpower to set up regular patrols. If serious action isn't taken soon, the legendary plant may soon only exist in folklore.

> ### Glossary
>
> **carnivorous:** that eats meat
> **photosynthesis:** (in plants) the process of creating energy from light, air and water.
> **folklore:** the body of traditional beliefs and legends

133

VOCABULARY Animals

1 Complete the sentences with the words in the box. There are two extra words.

claws	feelers	beaks	fur
horns	humps	wings	scales

1 Be careful! That cat has sharp ....
2 Both lizards and fish are covered in ....
3 Beneath their white .... , polar bears actually have black skin.
4 Rhinos have curved, pointed .... above their noses which they may use in attack.
5 Insects use their .... , also called antennae, to help them forage for food.
6 Camels use the .... on their back to store fat.

2 Complete the sentences with suitable verbs. Then match the descriptions with the animals in the box.

penguin	beaver	mole
shark	spider	chameleon

1 It .... out of the water and snatches its prey in the air. ....
2 Its densely packed feathers help it to .... freezing temperatures. ....
3 It .... into the background by changing colour. ....
4 Its feelers help it to .... the slightest movement on the web. ....
5 It .... down into the earth using spade-like feet. ....
6 It spends its day .... through the bark with its teeth. ....

VOCABULARY Compound adjectives

3 Match the compound adjectives (1–10) with the nouns (a–j).

1 water-resistant   a suit
2 life-threatening   b guide
3 five-mile   c effort
4 long-term   d watch
5 child-friendly   e charity
6 self-help   f run
7 award-winning   g environment
8 high-powered   h disease
9 tailor-made   i unemployment
10 praise-worthy   j vehicle

4 Complete the sentences with a suitable phrase from exercise 3.

1 Jake wore this stylish .... to his wedding, and almost outshone the bride!
2 I've bought this .... to get some tips on how to improve my job prospects.
3 The .... charity Euan's Guide has received recognition for its innovative website offering support and guidance to children entering hospital.
4 We've bought Tim a .... to time himself during swimming practice.
5 Chronic arthritis is not a .... but it can be extremely debilitating for the sufferer.
6 In designing the house, we wanted to create a .... , as the clients have four-year-old twin boys.
7 The local council has set up a job-sharing scheme to tackle ....
8 I go for a .... every morning before work to try and keep fit.

DEVELOPING WRITING

A competition entry – describing a place

5 Read the description of Kaikoura. What are the two main activities which the writer recommends for visitors?

....
....

If you're planning a trip to New Zealand's South Island, make sure you include Kaikoura on the north-east coast on your itinerary. Originally a small fishing town, Kaikoura is now a popular destination for nature lovers. Its stunning alpine scenery and fascinating wildlife are truly unmissable.

In my opinion, there are two main activities which every visitor must try. Firstly, sign up for a boat trip on the harbour and go dolphin-spotting. It's an unforgettable experience to see these playful creatures swimming alongside you, so don't forget your camera.

An excursion to the seal colony is also highly recommended. Head to the top of the cliff behind the Kaikoura Peninsula. Walk away from the car park and wander along a track that takes you past rolling hills on your left. On your right, gaze at the breathtaking views of the crystal clear bay. Make your way down a wooden staircase to the base of the cliff. Here you can see dozens of seals sunning themselves on the rocks. It's an incredible sight! Beware of getting too close though, as they'll attack if they feel threatened.

Kaikoura is a fantastic place for seeing nature up close. It's a must-see destination for anyone who loves the wild.

Learner tip

Use imperatives to give instructions and make recommendations in a concise, direct style. This can add impact to your writing, but take care: imperatives can sound quite forceful so are generally best avoided in very formal or academic writing.

6 Complete the imperative sentences with the verbs and phrasal verbs in the box.

Avoid	Beware	Don't forget	Gaze	Make
Sign up	Take	Wander		

1 .... along a dirt track to the coast.
2 .... upward at the mountain peaks.
3 .... some time to admire the view.
4 .... for a tour at the Information Office.
5 .... to bring binoculars.
6 .... the forest as this is private property.
7 .... of the tide, and .... sure you don't get caught.

7 Match the sentence halves. Use the underlined words to help you.
You can see
1 hundreds of butterflies
2 tiny green lizards
3 groups of shivering monkeys
4 shoals of tropical fish
5 solitary eagles
6 thousands of tiny glow worms

a bathing in the hot springs to warm up.
b darting through the shallow water.
c soaring majestically over the gorge.
d flitting from flower to flower.
e sparkling on the roof of the cave.
f scaling swiftly up the cliffs.

8 You see this advertisement on your favourite travel website. Enter the competition and write your description (180–220 words).

COMPETITION – calling all nature lovers!

Write a description of your favourite wild place and recommend things for visitors to see and do there.
The descriptions will appear on our website. The writer of the best one will win a holiday.

Vocabulary Builder Quiz 8

Download the Vocabulary Builder for Unit 8 and try the quiz below. Write your answers in your notebook. Then check them and record your score.

1 Which adjective can't describe the noun?
1 sheer / jagged / narrow   cliffs
2 barren / murky / rugged   landscape
3 narrow / winding / lush   ridge
4 sweeping / articulate / blunt   person
5 thick / dense / barren   woodland

2 Write the missing prepositions in the correct place.
1 I hate the way he butts when we're talking.
2 The beaver gnawed the wooden fence.
3 Authorities are cracking on illegal poaching.
4 Stop beating the bush and just say it!
5 The insect can blend with its surroundings.
6 He saw the snake and let a scream.
7 The blow fish will puff when it is alarmed.
8 Researchers draw their knowledge of the species' nocturnal habits to locate it.

3 Choose the correct words.
1 They strayed / scrambled up the hill to escape from the angry bear.
2 She says what she thinks and doesn't mince / nurture her words.
3 The researcher cited / dismissed Jane Goodall's book My Life with Chimpanzees as uninteresting.
4 His TV show is designed to popularise / polarise science.
5 These days language skills are vital / valid.
6 Young people here defy / conform to the rules. They're very rebellious.
7 Prey / Predators catch prey / predators.

4 Complete the sentences with the correct form of the words in brackets.
1 Claire is very .... and never walks under ladders. (superstition)
2 My new watch is water- .... , so I can wear it when I go diving. (resist)
3 Dolphins .... sense when a human is in danger in the water. (intuition)
4 As an underwater photographer, she explores the world's oceans .... (extend)
5 He was devastated when he had to sell his .... home. (ancestor)

Score ___/25

Wait a couple of weeks and try the quiz again. Compare your scores.

09 WORK

VOCABULARY Roles and tasks

1 Match the people and departments in the box with the definitions (1–7).

Admin	CEO	HR	IT	PA	R&D	rep

1 the person responsible for a company's operations ....
2 someone who travels and sells a company's products ....
3 someone who assists another person who has a senior position ....
4 the department for organising and managing the business ....
5 the department for training and managing employees ....
6 the department responsible for computers and communications equipment ....
7 the department for researching and developing new products ....

2 Replace the underlined words and expressions with the words in the box.

come up with	draw up	input	liaise
oversee	process	schedule	troubleshoot

1 I facilitate communication with managers to agree on best working practice in the office. ....
2 Could you supervise this new research project? ....
3 We need to find a solution to the problem on the website immediately. ....
4 Janet's working hard to enter all the dates into the group's calendar. ....
5 We'd like you to create exciting new products. ....
6 I'll arrange for someone to write out the full-time contract and send it to you tomorrow. ....
7 I deal with any job applications in the usual way. ....
8 Could we arrange a meeting of all the executives for Monday morning, Raoul? ....

3 Which people or departments in exercise 1 do you think are responsible for the tasks and activities in exercise 2?

LISTENING

4 9.1 Listen to three people talking about their work. Tick (✓) the two things they have in common.
All of them
a studied the same course at university. ....
b set up their own businesses. ....
c have worked in business for many years. ....
d have changed careers. ....
e are interested in environmentally friendly products. ....

5 Listen again. Are these statements true (T) or false (F)?
1 Olivia started her business while she was at university.
2 Olivia's design uses energy produced from human activity.
3 She doesn't have any regrets about her business.
4 David's business started during the economic recession.
5 He has invented more than one product.
6 He thinks that employing someone to help him in the early stages was unnecessary.
7 Rafaela turned her hobby into a business.
8 Rafaela's professional experience helped her to draw up a business plan.

6 Choose the correct words to complete the sentences. Listen again and check.
1 What if we could *harness* / *create* at least some of that energy and use it?
2 It's still early *times* / *days* yet, but I've been receiving a lot of interest.
3 I *patented* / *experimented* my product so that no one would be able to copy my idea.
4 I had to employ someone to organise files and *deal* / *process* orders.
5 She's helped to *generate* / *grow* business and keep us going.
6 The thing was to think of a *catchy* / *sticky* brand name so it would stand out.

Learner tip

Read the audioscripts at the back of the book after you listen and make a note of any new vocabulary. Don't forget to learn and revise it!

DEVELOPING CONVERSATIONS
Making deductions

7 Write suitable responses using the correct form of the verbs and *then*.

1 Mike's got to finish that project by tomorrow.
he / not able / come / to the party
He won't be able to come to the party, then.

2 She does a lot of shift work.
she / not have / a lot of free time

3 I'm a journalist based in Stockholm.
you / must / be able / speak / Swedish

4 She's at a conference all next week.
she / not able / finish / that report

5 I'm starting a new job in Dubai next week.
you / must / hand in / your notice

6 Gys is working in R&D at the moment.
he / be / a good person / talk to about this new product

GRAMMAR Continuous forms

8 Find and correct *five* mistakes.

1 I'm now developing other products along similar lines.

2 A number of new colleagues will be join us over the next couple of weeks.

3 I work for the same pharmaceutical company for 15 years.

4 The machine was being developed for the international market at that time.

5 We'll have been finishing the project by next week.

6 It's still early days yet, but I've been receiving a lot of interest from various business sectors.

7 This time next week we're supposed to celebrate the book launch, but I'm not sure it'll be ready in time.

8 I've been having a lot of trouble with that photocopier before it broke down.

9 Choose the best verb forms.

A: Someone's ¹*broken / been breaking* into the workshop!

B: Oh no! I ²*'ve been / was* telling Mark to get that lock fixed for weeks!

A: They must have ³*looked / been looking* for the cash box.

B: Probably ... Luckily, I ⁴*'d left / been leaving* it in Admin last night.

A: Yeah. It ⁵*contained / was containing* all this week's takings, and it ⁶*'s been / was being* a good week, too!

B: I ⁷*was / 'd been* thinking of leaving it here, but at the last minute decided I'd better not.

A: Just as well. You know what, I think I may have seen the thief! I ⁸*was / 've been* waiting for the bus outside when I saw someone running down the road with what looked like a tool box.

B: Oh, that! They won't ⁹*have felt / be feeling* very pleased with themselves when they opened it, because there was nothing in it but old equipment. I ¹⁰*'d go / was going* to take it to the tip ...

Language note future passives

Future continuous passives (*will be being* + past participle) and perfect continuous passives (*has / have / had been being* + past participle), although correct, are unusual in English. We are more likely to use alternative constructions.
At 3 p.m. today we're having the office cleaned.
not *At 3 p.m. today the office will be being cleaned.*

VOCABULARY
Adverb–adjective collocations

1 Add *one* of the adverbs in brackets in the correct place.

1 Advertising is competitive and can be quite stressful. (fiercely / entirely)
2 I'm not interested in working with children because I have no patience with them! (highly / remotely)
3 Caring for people with Alzheimer's can be draining, so I try to remain detached. (emotionally / mind-numbingly)
4 Factory workers should take frequent breaks to stay alert. (mildly / reasonably)
5 Accountancy was rewarding but I hated it. (utterly / financially)
6 I'm content with my present job and have no plans to retire. (inherently / blissfully)
7 Working as a receptionist is straightforward, although problems occasionally arise. (not terribly / technically)
8 I'm exhausted by the work and really need a break. (highly / utterly)

PRONUNCIATION *quite*

> **Language note** meanings of *quite*
>
> *Quite* has several different meanings. In British English, *quite* can be used as a modifying adverb to mean *fairly / rather* with gradable words and *completely* with non-gradable words.
> *I'm quite tired but I'll do a bit more work.*
> *I'm quite exhausted; I can't work any longer.*
> In American English, *quite* almost always means *completely* when used as a modifying adverb.
> *Quite* can also be used to express agreement.
> *'I wish they didn't always argue in public.' 'Quite.'*

2 Does *quite* mean *fairly* (F) or *completely* (C), or is it being used to express agreement (A)?

1 It was quite nice there. ....
2 'His behaviour was out of order!' 'Quite.' ....
3 Have you quite finished? I've had enough of your attitude! ....
4 This new product's quite amazing! ....
5 'It was an inspiring performance.' 'Quite.' ....
6 The presentation was quite interesting, if you like that sort of thing. ....

3 ❧9.2 Listen. Practise saying the sentences, imitating the intonation.

READING

4 Quickly read the web page opposite. Complete the subheadings (1–3) with the options (a–e). There are two extra options that you don't need to use.

a Show a willingness to correct your mistake
b Learn from your mistake
c Help colleagues deal with their mistakes
d Admit your mistake
e Don't make any more mistakes

5 Read the web page again. Tick (✓) the opinions the writers would generally agree with.

1 Making a mistake is the worst thing that can happen at work. ....
2 Making a mistake needn't be a disaster. ....
3 Focus on the solution more than the problem. ....
4 Most mistakes sort themselves out by themselves. ....
5 Employers are generally too critical of employees who make mistakes. ....
6 Don't try to deal with your mistakes alone. ....

6 Complete the notes with ideas from the web page. Write one or two words in each gap.

SEVEN TOP TIPS: DEALING WITH MISTAKES

1 Don't panic. Everyone .... sometimes. It's normal!

2 .... about your mistake, then go and .... your boss.

3 Don't .... your colleagues as this won't gain you any favours.

4 Show a desire to .... for your mistake by working overtime.

5 .... committing future mistakes through effective organisation.

6 Don't make unrealistic promises, or your boss won't .... you in future.

7 Never stop .... new skills to help you .... your performance.

Hear it from the experts: what to do when you've made a mistake

| HOME | WHAT TO DO WHEN YOU'VE MADE A MISTAKE | ABOUT US | CONTACT US |

▼ What to do when you've made a mistake?

▶ Mistakes: FAQs

▼ Experts' Tips

Three leading career experts offer some tips on how to deal with mistakes in the workplace.

STEP ONE – [1] Carina Blake, management consultant

It's inevitable that at some point, you will make a mistake at work. This is only human. Even bosses make mistakes, so they won't necessarily be as angry or hostile as you might expect. A lot depends on what you do to ameliorate the situation. Firstly, face up to the problem. Acknowledge to yourself what has happened and take a few moments to think about how you can handle any problems which may arise as a consequence. Then go and inform your boss of the situation and tell her your plans for dealing with it. Being honest and accepting responsibility will reduce the amount of anger aimed at you. Don't pass the buck and place blame on others even if they are partly responsible. Getting colleagues into trouble will not make you a popular member of the team. If colleagues feel they can trust you, they will be more likely to support you.

STEP TWO – [2] Paulo Berusa, careers officer

Most managers accept that staff will make mistakes at some point, but what concerns them more is that any mistakes should be rectified quickly and effectively. The golden rule is to talk it over with your boss and show a willingness to make amends. Make sure that correcting a mistake doesn't interrupt the overall flow of work you are doing, however, by doing it in your own time. Work through your lunch hour and stay late if necessary. If people notice the extra effort you put in, then they'll respect you for it. Organise your time carefully to avoid further problems. If you're very busy, keep a prioritised list of things to do and delete items as you complete them. It is also prudent to keep a note of any corrective procedures you follow in case you need to explain your actions later on.

STEP THREE – [3] Bernhard Bouwman, CEO

Mistakes needn't be the end of the world – they can be opportunities for development. Don't waste time feeling guilty, but try to take a more constructive approach. Think: what has this experience taught me? Where can I go from here? But be realistic and don't make promises you can't keep. Failed promises will not curry favour with anyone and could result in your boss losing faith in your ability to do the job. Don't be afraid to ask for assistance if necessary – many people are flattered to be asked! In particular, listen carefully to any advice your boss may give you on how to avoid making the same mistake again. That way you'll be sure to impress in future. Finally, don't become complacent. No one's perfect, and it's easy to make mistakes when you take your eye off the ball. It's vital to keep abreast of the latest developments and skills at work, so make sure you keep learning and keep making progress.

Glossary

management consultant: someone employed to give advice on improving managerial practice
curry favour with: make you popular with

---

7 Are the definitions of the <u>underlined</u> words and phrases true (T) or false (F)?

1 If something is <u>inevitable</u>, you cannot prevent it from happening.

2 When you <u>ameliorate</u> a situation, you make it easier.

3 If you <u>pass the buck</u>, you accept responsibility for something.

4 If you <u>take your eye off the ball</u>, you lose your focus.

5 If you <u>keep abreast of</u> news, you ensure you are aware of developments.

VOCABULARY The world of work

1 Choose the best options to make collocations.

1 *industrial / collective* tribunal
2 *voluntary / compassionate* redundancy
3 *biased / unfair* dismissal
4 *subsidised / statutory* travel
5 *compassionate / compensation* leave
6 *crackdown / minimum* wage
7 *swingeing / early* retirement
8 *state / absentee* pension

2 Complete the sentences with the collocations in exercise 1. There are two extra collocations that you don't need to use.

1 As he had a substantial pension, Henry decided to take .... in his 50s, to the disappointment of the CEO.
2 An .... ruled that the company had acted fairly with regard to the employee's dismissal for repeated absenteeism.
3 Elderly people are finding it increasingly difficult to get by on the .... It doesn't provide for a high standard of living.
4 We need to raise the .... so that everyone, from cleaners to factory workers, can earn enough to live on.
5 Her company needed to make cuts, so she agreed to take .... and is now looking for a job elsewhere.
6 Alan's boss let him take two weeks' .... when his sister died.

3 Complete the paragraph with suitable words.

One of the ¹p.................... of my job is that I get a company car with ²s.................... travel – the company pays for some of my petrol. The union also managed to negotiate the introduction of a ³c.................... at head office, where I can leave my two-year-old daughter during work hours. This saves me a lot of money on ⁴c.................... , such as nurseries or nannies, and also means I get to check on her from time to time. There was some ⁵o.................... from the management at first, who wanted to avoid the extra expense. Then Howard Kendall suggested that launching a ⁶c.................... on the problem of ⁷a.................... would reduce money lost in that area, and so offset any costs incurred. Management finally agreed, for which I'm eternally ⁸g.................... . It's made a real difference.

DEVELOPING WRITING

A job application – making a positive impression

4 Choose the most important *four* points from options a–g which, in your opinion, should be included in a job application.

a relevant experience
b your skills and qualifications
c your interests and hobbies
d explanations of why you would be suitable
e queries about salary and working conditions
f expressions of enthusiasm about the role
g personal details (age, marital status, etc.)

5 Quickly read the email. Which of the options a–g in exercise 4 are included?

To	
From	jy-klein@interweb.home.com
Subject	Application for position ref KLT/33

Dear Ms Fields,

I'm writing to apply for the post of Customer Services Manager advertised on your company's website.

I graduated with a degree in Marketing in 2010 and since then I have been working in the Customer Services department of a large corporation. During this time I have ¹.................... a range of effective management skills in liaising with customers and company sales representatives. I have personally ².................... and overseen a number of improved customer service initiatives, including the development of new staff training programmes. In recognition of these achievements I was ³.................... early promotion to the role of Department Manager last year.

For some time now I have been following your company's activities in the business press and I am highly ⁴.................... by your company's commitment to offering excellent customer support. I feel that I could use my knowledge and experience to help your Customer Services department to ⁵.................... its maximum potential in the future.

I attach my curriculum vitae and would ⁶.................... the opportunity to discuss some of my ideas with you in person. I look forward to hearing from you.

Yours sincerely,
Jannette Klein

6 Complete the email with the correct form of the verbs in the box.

award	demonstrate	develop	impress
realise	relish		

Learner tip

Remember that a letter or email of application acts as an advertisement for you!
- Only include relevant information.
- Use the appropriate register.
- Use persuasive language.

To strengthen your application, career advisors recommend using a variety of positive verbs, or 'power verbs', such as *develop*, *promote* and *advance* instead of *have*, *do* and *make*.

7 You see the advertisement below in a local newspaper. Write your letter of application (180–220 words).

WANTED:
International Student Officers

This autumn, we are looking for part-time Student Officers to help us welcome new international students to our university.

Interested applicants must have a good level of spoken English. Please write to Marco Wilde, answering the following questions:

- What do you think international students need to know when they first arrive at the university?

- Do you have any useful skills or experience?

- Why would you like the position of International Student Officer?

Vocabulary Builder Quiz 9

Download the Vocabulary Builder for Unit 9 and try the quiz below. Write your answers in your notebook. Then check them and record your score.

1 Match 1–5 with a–e.
1	draw up	a	a biscuit tin
2	dip into	b	a clever idea
3	settle in	c	to a new job
4	pick up	d	a plan of action
5	come up with	e	a language easily

2 Choose the correct words.
1 The *tribunal* / *trial* decision was unanimous. Everyone agreed with the verdict.
2 We strongly *condemn* / *commit* this attempt by big companies to rig the market.
3 It's vital to *liaise* / *conspire* closely with other departments.
4 The work is *inherently* / *remotely* dangerous.
5 The spectators cheered *enthusiastically* / *blissfully* as the runners crossed the line.
6 My boss tried to *neglect* / *screw* me out of a pay rise. He's so mean.

3 Complete the sentences with the correct form of the words in brackets.
1 We have to accept the .... of cutbacks being made to the workforce. (inevitable)
2 She's .... (bliss) happy in her new office.
3 He's .... (fierce) competitive.
4 His job is .... (numb) boring and repetitive.
5 He went to court for unfair .... (dismiss).
6 He took voluntary .... (redundant) after cuts were announced.
7 We want someone with .... (technically) skills.

4 Complete the sentences with suitable words.
1 Let's .... the wheels in motion.
2 We need to .... this software bug.
3 .... your weight and do some work!
4 This job is .... boring.

5 Choose the odd one out.
1 lean   nod   slump   back
2 oversee   perk   delegate   schedule
3 subsidise   compensate   screw   sponsor

Score ____/25

Wait a couple of weeks and try the quiz again. Compare your scores.

VOCABULARY Operations

1 Match the sentence halves.

1 I suffered severe burns because
2 The hospital doctors recommended a steady supply of liquids and painkillers, so
3 I'm fine now. Once the wound had healed,
4 I was put on a waiting list after the doctors confirmed that
5 They couldn't operate on my leg again after the injury, so to repair the muscle damage
6 As I hadn't been able to clean the cut properly,
7 When the ambulance arrived,
8 It wasn't serious. After the doctor took my temperature and listened to my cough,

a I underwent extensive physiotherapy.
b I was diagnosed with the flu.
c I was put on a drip.
d I would need an operation.
e I actually got an infection.
f I'd had to fight my way out through the fire.
g I had my stitches removed and that was that.
h I was rushed to hospital.

Language note vocabulary

Be careful of commonly confused words in English. A *wound* is a type of *injury* in which the skin is torn, cut or pierced. A medical professional can *cure* someone of a disease, but some injuries can *heal (up)* by themselves.

---

2 Choose the correct verbs or phrasal verbs.

1 She had to *undergo* / *suffer* surgery to remove the lump in her leg.
2 I have to *starve* / *fast* for at least 12 hours before the operation, with no food at all.
3 She had to have an operation to *insert* / *graft* metal rods to hold the bones together.
4 The bite *swelled* / *expanded* up horribly until it was the size of a grape!
5 The headaches became worse, so he had to have a *transplant* / *scan* to see what was wrong.
6 After the car accident, Stephen had to *take part* / *take place* in a long rehabilitation programme.
7 The cut was so deep I had to have *stitches* / *a skin graft* to close the wound.
8 When I crashed into the tree, I *broke* / *severed* my arm in two places, and it took months for it to heal.

DEVELOPING CONVERSATIONS
Vague language

3 Find and correct *five* mistakes.

1 It may take a few years so until they find a cure.
2 When Martin was in a coma, I knew he could hear somehow me.
3 He made a kind of bandage or somehow.
4 I knew I needed to do some sort exercise but I wasn't sure what type.
5 I suppose Shanti was acting as a kind of doctor when there was no one else to help us.
6 He managed to mix up somehow the children's medical records.
7 I find it sort of uncomfortable to look at someone bleeding.
8 There were about a hundred people or so involved in the train accident.

4 Complete the conversations with *(some) kind of*, *somehow*, or *so* or *something*. You can use these expressions more than once.

A: So, what can I do for you?
B: Well, I've ¹.................. got a strange rash on my arm. Here, I mean.
A: Oh, yes. When did it first appear?
B: Erm, about a week ².................. ago.
A: Have you ever had anything like this before?
B: I've had a rash or ³.................. there before but it wasn't this bad. I tried ⁴.................. natural antiseptic on it and it went away.

A: How can I help you?
B: Well, I managed to cut my foot open ⁵.................. . I think it's ⁶.................. infected, by the looks of it.
A: Yes, it looks that way. Well, with antibiotics, it'll only take a day ⁷.................. for the inflammation to go down.

DEVELOPING WRITING
A story – describing events

5 Quickly read the story. What was the holiday disaster?

....

It was in my last year of high school when the accident happened. The whole class had gone on a camping trip to the mountains, including myself and my best friend, Juri. We'd been looking forward to the trip for ages. Having just finished our exams, we saw it as a real chance to let off some steam.

So there we were: it was our second day in the camp and we'd been divided into five teams. We were having a competition. To win, each team had to build its own raft and be the first across the river.

We were madly chopping up bits of wood and tying them up with rope when Juri suddenly tripped over a log. Landing on the ground, he hit his head. At first it seemed funny. It wasn't until he stood up that we saw the blood pouring out of a gash on his head. So we abandoned the rafts and Juri and I made a rather unexpected journey to hospital.

After a three-hour wait, Juri ended up getting a whole row of stitches. Poor Juri. Poor me! A trip to the hospital was hardly the way we'd pictured spending our holiday!

6 Complete the table with the expressions in the box.

It was (back) in … when …	After all that, …
In the middle of all this, …	So there we were, …
It all started when …	I ended up …
One thing it's taught me is …	While all this was going on, …
Have I ever told you about the time …?	
But the … part of … was yet to come	

1 introducing the story; setting the scene	
2 moving from one event to the next; re-establishing the situation	
3 concluding the story; giving the outcome of an event	

Language note emphasising

To emphasise exactly when something happened, you can use the structure
It was + only when / only after / not until / at this point + that …
For even greater emphasis, you can use inversion:
Only when he got up did we see what had happened.

7 Rewrite the sentences correctly.

1 It was at this point that I did notice my foot was bleeding quite badly.

....

2 It was until we had been walking for a couple of hours that we remembered our flashlights.

....

3 It was only when Lois reached the village that felt she a sense of relief that the trip was over.

....

4 Not until midnight we could find our way back.

....

5 Only after standing up did I realise how much I have hurt myself.

....

8 Write a story (180–220 words) ending with the sentence *A trip to the hospital was hardly the way I'd pictured spending my holiday!* Use one of the ideas in the pictures or your own ideas.

VOCABULARY Mind and body

1 Complete the sentences with the pairs of words in the box.

clench / fist	flutter / eyelashes	mind / drift
raise / eyebrows	shrug / shoulders	stretch / legs

1 I was vaguely aware of the tutor's voice as my .... started to .... towards lunch.
2 I saw Grant .... his .... in anger at the news.
3 Anya just thinks she can .... her .... at the boss and get whatever she wants.
4 I saw my doctor .... her .... in disapproval when I confessed I never did any exercise.
5 Most people will just .... their .... and admit they don't know much about allergies.
6 After spending hours in the waiting room, I needed to go out and .... my ....

2 Choose the correct words.

1 In Thailand, it's taboo to *clutch / pat / crouch* children on the head.
2 People usually *raise / clench / shrug* their shoulders to show they don't know or care about something.
3 In my country, it's illegal to *spit / kick / scratch* your gum on the pavement.
4 In Japan, people tend not to *glare / grin / hug* one another in public.
5 It's not socially acceptable to *punch / blink / sniff* in public when you have a cold.
6 You may *wipe / flutter / click* your forehead when it's very hot.

3 Correct the errors in the sentences.

1 She stretched her eyelashes at the good-looking waiter.
2 Leaving the building, he glared as the strong sunlight hit his face.
3 She raised her chest desperately. Was she having a heart attack?
4 I've been on the computer all morning, so I'm going out to support my legs.
5 He fluttered down to stroke the small dog, and almost fell flat on his face.
6 When she saw what he was wearing, she blinked her eyebrows in surprise.
7 Use a cushion to crouch your back while you work at your desk, Mrs. Jones.
8 He clutched angrily at the woman who had taken his parking space.

READING

4 Look at the picture opposite, then quickly read the article. Why is the woman behaving like this?

....

5 Read the article again. Choose the best options.

1 The writer didn't immediately go to the doctor because
   a she'd had similar symptoms before.
   b she didn't believe the doctor would help her.
   c she didn't want to be prescribed antibiotics.
2 What is the main point made in paragraph 2?
   a GPs' surgeries should be more comfortable.
   b It isn't always possible to see a doctor at a convenient time.
   c It doesn't take long to do research online.
3 After completing the questionnaire, she
   a discovered things could be worse than she'd imagined.
   b found the results unconvincing.
   c was reassured by reading the diagnosis.
4 What was the result of her visit to the doctor?
   a The doctor confirmed what she'd suspected.
   b She doubted the doctor's assessment.
   c She had mixed feelings about the diagnosis.
5 What does she find particularly worrying about cyberchondria?
   a The amount of time people spend researching medical conditions.
   b The inaccuracy of some online information.
   c The failure to recognise that it's just as serious as hypochondria.
6 What final point does she make?
   a It's better to visit a doctor than search for symptoms online.
   b The internet is a completely unreliable source of diagnoses.
   c The more information we have, the better.

6 Replace the underlined words with the correct form of five of the phrases in the box.

clear up	come down with	come up with
head off to	take up	turn out

1 It was discovered that Andreas had a rare disease.
2 Marius started going towards the pharmacy.
3 As soon as summer is finished, my hay fever should get better and disappear.
4 We must think of a cure for this disease.
5 Researching my symptoms has occupied a lot of my time recently.

A CURE FOR
cyberchondria?

1 It started with a bit of casual itching and scratching on the scalp, but after a week it had spread to the back of my neck, enough to lead me to my laptop. Annoying as it was, I was reluctant to take up my doctor's time with such a silly complaint and then have a wasted journey only to be informed that it would clear up by itself and that, no, antibiotics would be of no use at all.

2 As soon as I'd tapped in 'online self-diagnosis', the search engine provided me with over 11.5 million results. And in the fraction of the time normally spent in my GP's waiting room absorbing the *Woman's Weekly* – and plenty of germs – I was able to find a site that would provide a free assessment in the comfort of my swivel chair, and with no need for an appointment.

3 I scrolled down the series of 'Yes / No / Go to' questions until I eventually reached a description exactly matching my symptoms. As I clicked on 'More Information', I was hit with a prognosis I'd never anticipated. The worst case scenario was complete hair loss. At best, it would be bare patches. I couldn't have been more alarmed.

4 I headed off to the doctor for what I thought would be a blood test but which turned out to be a valuable lesson in not believing everything you read on the internet. It took him less than a minute to guess at and locate head lice. I was simultaneously relieved to know that I would be keeping my hair, and horrified to know that it was being occupied. I guess it's not just homework that kids bring home from school these days.

5 I learnt my lesson, but for some the preoccupation with looking up every twitch, ache and spasm has led to a new form of hypochondria. Dubbed 'cyberchondria' by the print media back in 2000, this particular affliction has increased exponentially. Although most people's main port of call is still the doctor's surgery, it's estimated that health worries are now the second most researched topic on the web. This is truly a serious concern when approximately 25% of the medical information online is thought to be misleading.

6 Once upon a time, hypochondria required time and effort: you had to go to the library to research your ailments and painstakingly go through the glossary. Now it's just a matter of a few clicks of a mouse. But whereas your doctor will make a diagnosis taking into consideration your age, appearance and medical history, a search engine will rely simply on algorithms. These come up with results graded according to popularity or numbers of key words. So the most highly ranked hits might actually be for very genuine diseases, which are nonetheless extremely rare. One minute you think you've come down with the flu, the next you're under attack from sub-tropical, flesh-eating bacteria. Time spent going to the doctor's for peace of mind suddenly seems fair enough.

> **Glossary**
>
> **GP:** a British term for a non-hospital doctor
> **head lice:** small insects that live in human hair
> **hypochondria:** the belief that you are seriously ill when you are actually fairly healthy
> **algorithm:** a mathematical process

LISTENING

1 🔊 **10.1 Listen to part of a radio phone-in show about health.**

Why have Iris and Brett phoned the show?
a to discuss ways in which hospital services could be improved
b to comment on new government policies relating to health care
c to complain about the medical staff in hospitals

> **Learner tip**
>
> Always read the questions carefully *before* you listen and think about the kind of language you might expect to hear. For example, words relating to *money* in question 1 in exercise 2 might be *income, funding, earn, pay* or *spend*.

2 Listen again and match the opinions with Iris (I) or Brett (B).
1 Hospitals don't have enough money. ....
2 Hospital food needs to be improved. ....
3 It's worth getting an additional diagnosis from another doctor. ....
4 People who smoke should not receive free treatment. ....
5 More private health care would be a good idea. ....
6 The number of visitors a patient receives should be restricted. ....
7 Young doctors are less effective. ....
8 Nurses receive adequate salaries. ....

3 Does Steve, the radio host, agree (A) or disagree (D) with Iris and Brett about the opinions in exercise 2?
1 ....   3 ....   5 ....   7 ....
2 ....   4 ....   6 ....   8 ....

VOCABULARY
Nouns based on phrasal verbs

4 Match the nouns (1–7) with their definitions (a–g).

1	outbreak	a	act of making major improvements
2	breakthrough	b	exercising in a gym
3	upbringing	c	sudden widespread occurrence of a disease
4	workout	d	period leading to an event
5	dropout	e	way in which someone is raised as a child
6	shakeup	f	act of leaving university before finishing
7	runup	g	major new discovery in science

5 Complete the sentences with a noun from exercise 4.
1 This new drug represents a .... in the quest for a cure to Parkinson's disease.
2 Mary's .... on the slopes of Mount Pelion provided her with a knowledge of wild herbs, and fostered her later interest in herbalism.
3 The acupuncture course is so well-organised that there are hardly ever any ....
4 In the .... to Christmas, there is invariably an increase in the number of road accidents.
5 The sudden .... of measles in the school caused widespread concern among the parents.
6 The recent .... in hospital management is already having a positive impact on staff efficiency.
7 Shelley's doctor recommended she go for a .... session at her local gym three times a week.

GRAMMAR   Modal auxiliaries

6 Match the sentence halves (1–4 with a–d, and 5–8 with e–h).
1 John shouldn't have taken the medicine
2 He couldn't have taken the medicine
3 He would have taken the medicine
4 He could have taken the medicine

a because it's still here.
b because it's out-of-date.
c if you'd told him it was necessary.
d but I'm not sure because the bottle isn't here.

5 The antibiotics should have worked
6 They must have worked
7 They can't have worked
8 They might have worked

e by now. That's what we were told.
f because the infection is still bad.
g if they'd been prescribed earlier on.
h because the infection has cleared up.

7 Rewrite the sentences using the words provided. Use modal verbs and the words in brackets.

1 I'm certain you are better.
You .... better. (feeling)
2 Dr Hollis has been on holiday. You certainly didn't see her.
You .... Dr Hollis because she's been on holiday. (possibly)
3 Without his glasses, it was a really bad idea for Ernesto to drive.
Ernesto .... without his glasses. (been)
4 It was possible to have a vaccination but I didn't want one.
I .... I'd wanted one. (if)
5 Perhaps I got food poisoning from that hamburger!
It .... food poisoning! (gave)
6 It was a mistake not to tell your parents that you don't want to become a doctor.
You .... wanting to become a doctor. (about)

PRONUNCIATION Linking sounds

Language note linking

When native speakers are talking at normal speed, they often link words together. A consonant sound at the end of one word is often linked to a vowel at the start of the next word.

8 Underline the places where a word which ends with a consonant sound is followed by a word which starts with a vowel sound.

1 He saw his old doctor.
2 I don't know why he felt unwell.
3 You shouldn't have ignored your injury.
4 I think it was some kind of natural medicine.
5 The doctor asked me to get dressed again.
6 He could have picked up the disease on holiday.
7 I was put on a waiting list for my heart operation.

9 🔊 10.2 Listen. Then practise saying the sentences.

Vocabulary Builder Quiz 10

Download the Vocabulary Builder for Unit 10 and try the quiz below. Write your answers in your notebook. Then check them and record your score.

1 Complete the sentences with the correct form of the word in brackets.
1 Looking down, he saw that his knee had .... (swell) like a balloon.
2 Clara takes .... (diet) supplements daily to combat her anaemia.
3 The WHO has declared that the .... (eradicate) of diseases like Ebola is now a priority.
4 They .... (anaesthesia) the injured rhino in order to be able to examine its wounds.
5 The reputation of this hospital is .... (pin) by a strict policy on patient welfare.
6 The findings of Dr. Mason's .... (extend) research on the MAOA gene have formed the basis for this report.

2 Complete the sentences with suitable nouns based on phrasal verbs.
1 Fortunately, he wasn't badly hurt, but his car's a complete ....
2 The hospital porters are staging a .... to protest against the new policy.
3 They had a .... over who owned the apple tree which stands in both gardens.
4 Plans to build a .... around the town have just been approved.
5 There was a .... at the Medical Centre, and apparently they stole medical supplies.
6 Following the .... in the hospital administration, things have been running much more smoothly.

3 Which three sentences describe a form of treatment?
1 He had a lump.
2 He is undergoing rehabilitation.
3 He relapsed last week.
4 He's going through remission.
5 He had a skin graft.
6 He was prescribed morphine.

4 Choose the word or phrase which *can't* complete the collocations.
1 mounting *tension / pressure / mortality / evidence*
2 a bout of *illness / nausea / cure / anxiety*
3 breach *aftercare / a contract / safety rules / confidentiality*
4 undergo *disease / physiotherapy / treatment / an operation*
5 clutch *your chest / at your heart / at straws / your fingers*
6 extensive *remission / scarring / research / experience*
7 clench your *teeth / head / fist / muscles*

Score ___/25

Wait a couple of weeks and try the quiz again.
Compare your scores.

VOCABULARY Sports and events

1 Complete the sentences with the verbs in the box.

blowing	challenging	doping	fading
sending	substituting	sponsoring	thrashing

1 Rumour has it that Lufthansa are thinking of .... the Olympic team

2 That was a clear foul and the referee is .... him off.

3 After yesterday's injury, hopes of his winning the gold medal are ....

4 Federer looks unhappy and seems to be .... the umpire's decision.

5 It looks as though the coach is .... the injured player with Mealamu.

6 The team's been accused of .... before, but the allegations of drug-taking have never been proved.

7 The young Korean is absolutely .... his opponent and surely he knows he's going to win!

8 The Russians know that with even the slightest mistake they'll be .... their chances of a medal.

2 Choose the correct words.

1 We were knocked *down* / *out* of the World Cup by Brazil.

2 Personally, I always like the *underdog* / *bottomdog* to win. It's nice to see outsiders striking it lucky.

3 I think the referee's decision needs to be *overtaken* / *overturned*. It's a joke!

4 By the end of the race, I was definitely *fading* / *vanishing*. I was exhausted.

5 We managed to *scratch* / *scrape* through in the last round, qualifying by just one point.

6 For the entire match, it was a very *closed* / *close* game. We didn't know who would win.

7 His verbal abuse towards the referee resulted in Rooney being *dropped* / *suspended* from playing in the next match.

8 There have been allegations that the fight was *fixed* / *set* in advance, but nothing has been proven as yet.

LISTENING

3 ◆ 11.1 Listen to five people talking about sport. Who are the speakers (1–5)? Choose from the ideas in the box.

a current sportsperson
a doctor
a fitness instructor
a referee
a retired sportsperson
a sports commentator
a team supporter

1 ....
2 ....
3 ....
4 ....
5 ....

4 Listen again and match the speakers (1–5) with their opinions on sport (a–f). There is one extra opinion that you don't need to use.

a It's too focused on image. ....

b It forces people to take too many risks. ....

c It's not as exciting as it used to be. ....

d It offers amazing opportunities. ....

e It costs too much money for supporters. ....

f It's become appealing to wider audiences. ....

5 Choose the best definitions for the underlined phrases.

1 ... you have to <u>give it everything you've got</u>
   a try as hard as you possibly can
   b spend lots of money on something

2 ... to <u>get the edge</u>
   a be brave   b be better than the rest

3 ... keeps the fans <u>on the edge of their seats</u>
   a angry and likely to get violent
   b thrilled, waiting to see what happens next

4 ... the players <u>have a go at</u> you
   a attack or criticise   b try to compete with

5 that's where I <u>come in</u>
   a can help   b work

6 ... to <u>get a bit of a lucky break</u>
   a have time to get better
   b have an unexpected chance

DEVELOPING CONVERSATIONS Irony and humour

Language note irony versus sarcasm

Sarcasm is a special use of irony when a speaker is trying to tease or upset someone. You can refer to a *sarcastic person* or *sarcastic comment*, but **not** a ~~*sarcastic situation*~~. However, a *situation* can be *ironic*, when something is not as you expected.

6 Which replies are ironic? Look at the pictures and read the opening questions or comments. Choose one reply (a or b), both replies (a+b) or neither reply (–).

1 'Are you worried about the conditions?'
   a 'Not personally, but the less experienced drivers might have problems.'
   b 'No. It looks like we've got perfect weather.'

2 'Finally! I beat her!'
   a 'Yeah, and you managed to do it in only eight hours!'
   b 'Of course you did. She's a child.'

3 'The match is due to start soon!'
   a 'Where are all the fans?'
   b 'Great support!'

4 'Did you see that jump?'
   a 'Yeah, she can't fail to win the championship now!'
   b 'Yeah, that was fantastic timing!'

5 'Ouch! That must have hurt!'
   a 'Yeah. Are you guys all right?'
   b 'Yeah, a great display of teamwork!'

6 'Keep up, will you!'
   a 'Why? I'm not exactly training for the Olympics!'
   b 'I'm trying!'

VOCABULARY
Talking about gaming

7 **Match the sentence halves.**
1 Violent role play games are a great way
2 The group and guild quests enable players
3 The well-developed chat system fosters
4 As your character grows stronger, you can
5 The incredible skills displayed by some
6 Some parents worry that their children are

a modify it by adding extra abilities to it.
b interaction and relationships between players.
c exposed to too much violence in online games.
d to collaborate, and are a great way of meeting people.
e players defy belief.
f to let off steam at the end of a long day at work.

8 **Complete the sentences with words from the box.**

engrossed	attached	informed
confronted	grasped	

1 He was so .... in the game that he didn't hear me come into the room.
2 At the next level, you'll be .... by a number of more challenging monsters.
3 It was a while before I .... the point of all the different champions, quests and that, but once I did, I was hooked.
4 Ask Jane, as she's well-.................... about all the latest developments in the gaming industry.
5 You get a month's free trial with no strings ...., so you don't have to purchase the game afterwards.

9 **Correct the mistakes.**
1 I'm not against you playing online games as long as it's done with moderation.
2 It seems to be a universal fact that online games provide a thrilling alternative to watching TV.
3 Online games are more thrilling, true and simple.
4 I like cooperative games where you play in teams.
5 Multi-tasking online role-play games can be useful tools for staff training sessions.

11

GRAMMAR Linking words and phrases

1 Choose the correct options. Choose both options when both are possible.

1 I went along to the tennis match *even though* / *even if* I found the game really boring!

2 You should stretch first, *provided* / *otherwise* your muscles are really going to hurt!

3 *Although* / *Even though* he's a really keen reader, he's quite useless at word games.

4 The judges will have to decide *whether* / *if* or not to disqualify him.

5 She's having some physiotherapy *in order to* / *so as to* be ready for the match.

6 *Provided* / *So long as* we win this match, we might still have a chance in the final.

2 Match 1–9 with a–i to complete the sentences.

I'll never be fit enough for the race,

1	even if	a	I'm going to quit.
2	although	b	I'm training really hard.
3	so	c	I train very hard.

I'll be fit enough for the race,

4	provided	d	my injury gets worse.
5	unless	e	I train very hard.
6	even though	f	I suffered an injury last year.

You need to start training harder,

7	otherwise	g	you like it or not.
8	until	h	you're fit enough for the race.
9	whether	i	you won't be fit for the race.

3 Rewrite the sentences using the words in brackets.

1 Johnson's resting to recover from his injury.
Johnson's taking ....
.... (so)

2 The only way you'll improve is by training more.
You ....
.... (unless)

3 Despite his protests, Marc was still disqualified.
Marc ....
.... protested. (though)

4 I'm sure you only won because you cheated!
You must ....
.... won. (otherwise)

5 I can't give up my job, so professional training isn't possible.
I'm unable ....
.... professionally. (order)

READING

4 Quickly read the letter opposite, which is to a magazine editor. Who is the writer?

a a concerned parent

b a researcher

c a fanatical gamer

5 Read the letter again. Are the statements true (T) or false (F), or doesn't the writer say (DS)?

1 The author of *An end to play* helped to make people with children feel better.

2 The view that only lonely men play video games is untrue.

3 There is no link between video games and aggressive behaviour.

4 Fewer women enjoy playing games than men.

5 Video games are unsuitable for very young children.

6 Games can help people to preserve their mental faculties for longer.

7 Video games should replace outdoor sports.

8 The enjoyment of video games is entirely beneficial.

6 Complete the sentences with the missing prepositions. Look again at the letter if you need to.

1 I think they've made a good job .... creating the main characters.

2 There's no place .... competitive gaming for genuine friendship.

3 There appears to be a correlation .... the number of hours spent on gaming and the loss of clear vision.

4 I feel that the time spent on gaming should be limited .... a few hours per week.

5 He was accused .... uploading the game illegally.

6 We'd like to present you .... the latest in gaming consoles.

7 Contrary .... popular belief, women do buy video games to play themselves.

8 Please enjoy fast food .... moderation.

Learner tip

When you make a note of new vocabulary, make sure you include any dependent prepositions, by writing an example sentence:

They engaged in a long discussion.

In the case of video games, I tend to agree with you.

THIS MONTH'S LETTERS

To the Editor

The article *An end to play* in the June edition of your magazine lacked balance and perspective in the way it presented the role of video gaming in young people's lives. If it was your writer's intention to overwhelm already guilt-laden parents, he certainly did a good job of it.

The popular media has long portrayed the players of video games as socially inadequate, under-achieving young males who are doomed to remain glued to a screen for much of their waking lives, without the prospect of any kind of career or normal human relationship. Such tired stereotypes should have no place in serious writing. Moreover, journalists such as your writer are all too keen to assume a strong correlation between violent or criminal tendencies and familiarity with shooting games. Research by the well-regarded sociologists Ian Macquarie and Karina Rylands (published 2009), amongst others, has proved that societal and even genetic factors have much more of an influence.

The truth is that the appeal of gaming is not limited to those of a particular gender or age. Even I enjoy it now and again! It's a popular form of entertainment and is a far more mentally stimulating way of spending your time than watching television, which, funnily enough, was also accused of being 'the downfall of culture' when it first began appearing in homes. Indeed, to deny even infants

access to video games is to hold them back. It has always been the case that game play engages developing minds in the learning process, and modern technology offers exciting new opportunities in this regard.

I would like to present you with some areas of published research your writer chose to neglect, but which is nevertheless widely available to those of us who take a genuine interest in our children's social and intellectual development. First of all, scientists from the University of Wisconsin have established in a key study that traditional video games actually sharpen the mind, and not only in the case of young people. It has been shown that, by regularly engaging in this type of activity, the elderly are more likely to retain cognitive skills such as the ability to reason and multi-task into later life. Surely this is a highly desirable benefit, which could even lead to savings in health care?

It may also surprise you to know that, contrary to your claims that video gaming automatically leads to childhood obesity, games are now increasingly being used for fitness training in the USA. In fact West Virginia has provided such a game to all the middle schools under its authority. People run, walk, jump, squat and dance on special mats, following instructions on a screen. When the weather impedes an outdoor physical education programme, children can still take indoor exercise using these 'active' games, increasing their range of options.

I am not saying that – taken to excess – gaming does not have some serious side effects, but enjoyed in moderation, the advantages are numerous. The one-sided view of video gaming that your magazine seems to favour is simply frustrating.

Yours sincerely,
Fiona Robson (54!)

Glossary

be glued to: look at something intently
sociologist: someone who studies human social behaviour
multi-task: perform more than one task at the same time

An END to play?
Or NOT the end of the world?

11

DEVELOPING WRITING
An essay – expressing personal opinion

1 Read the task in the box and then the essay, ignoring the gaps. Which is the best summary of the writer's opinion?

a Participation in school sport should be a matter of personal choice.

b Sport is an essential part of a student's education.

c If a wider range of sports were available, more students would participate.

> 'It should be compulsory for all students to have a daily sports lesson.' What do you think?

Sport is usually part of the school curriculum in most countries. [1].................... whether young people should still be forced to practise physical exercise as part of the school week or whether their participation in sports should be optional.

My belief is that physical education is vital [2].................... . First of all, there is an increasing tendency nowadays for students to lead a sedentary lifestyle. [3].................... , fewer young people are engaging in physical activity. [4].................... , sport creates a strong sense of team spirit. The members of winning teams can take pride in themselves and their institution, which is good for their personal and social development.

[5].................... , students who have an acute dislike of sports or have little natural ability will find little benefit in compulsory lessons. If they are forced to attend, they might grow resentful and unhappy. It would be far better for them to focus on the development of skills and knowledge in subject areas they are passionate about.

[6].................... , I would say that making sports lessons compulsory is beneficial for some students but not all. In my opinion, schools should take a flexible approach, providing regular sports lessons but making them optional.

2 Complete the essay with the phrases in the box.

| in other words | in summary | in two respects |
| moreover | on the other hand | the question is |

> **Language note** abstract nouns
>
> Using abstract nouns rather than adjectives can sometimes help to reinforce your opinion in a more formal essay. For example, *they take pride in ...* sounds stronger and more authoritative than *they are proud of ...*

3 Complete the sentences with nouns formed from the adjectives in the box.

| able | believable | comparative | determined |
| developing | free | participating | resentful |

1 Contrary to this view, there is a common .... that these types of hobbies are only for children.

2 There is a growing tendency amongst athletes to boast about their own .... and achievements.

3 Our .... in and enjoyment of board games is what counts, not whether we win them or not.

4 In .... to the previous generation, the sportsmen of today earn much higher salaries.

5 Athletes need great .... to succeed and will need to stay highly committed.

6 .... may arise if people feel that life is all about work and not play.

7 Playing sport can improve a child's .... , mentally as well as physically.

8 Allowing people the .... to have fun can make them more productive at school and work.

4 Match the opinions (1–8) in exercise 3 with statements a and b.

a Winning is everything in sport.

b Playing games is a waste of time.

5 Choose one of the statements in exercise 4. Write an essay (180–220 words) saying whether you agree or not with the statement.

VOCABULARY Alliteration

6 Complete the extract from an alliterative poem with words from the box. There are more words than you need.

kith	thin	gloom	marriage
nothing	family	right	disappointed
lost	heels	test	bred
care	preach	meet	

Love's Lesson Learned

Rob and Rose were lovers,
Theirs a true ¹................... of minds.
They had no need of others,
Sharing a love one rarely finds.
It was beautiful.

Yet little love was ²...................
Between Rob and Rose's mum,
And friends and ³................... alike
Declared that Rob was far from
Being suitable.

For Rob was not wealthy,
But working class born and ⁴...................,
And worse still he had next to ⁵...................
To offer Rose. They said,
'He's just not eligible.'

Faced with such opposition
From Rose's ⁶................... and kin,
Rob said he felt deeply ⁷...................
That they couldn't even begin
To be more reasonable.

7 Find three more examples of alliteration in the poem.
8 What 'lesson' do you think Rose's family learned? Complete the poem. Use alliteration where possible. Here are some suggestions.

head over heels	test of time	thick and thin
bite the bullet	words of wisdom	

PRONUNCIATION

Different spelling, same sound

9 Find six pairs of words in the box that have the same vowel sound.

bluff	coach	court	cushion
down	football	ground	hurdle
pawn	show	tough	world

....
....
....

10 🔊 11.2 Listen and check your answers. Practise saying the words.

Vocabulary Builder Quiz 11

Download the Vocabulary Builder for Unit 11 and try the quiz below. Write your answers in your notebook. Then check them and record your score.

1 Complete the pairs of sentences with words that are both nouns and verbs.
1 The demonstrators .... slogans as they marched.
2 The deafening .... of their fans inspired the team.
3 They're bringing on two .... for the injured players.
4 It's a real shame they had to .... Ronaldo.

2 Complete the sentences with suitable verbs.
1 We'd better .... the bullet and find a solution.
2 I get so caught up in the game that time just .... by.
3 The paintballing day allowed staff to .... off steam.
4 It also .... effective collaboration, as you play in teams.
5 The chess game .... on for three hours. I got tired of watching.
6 Don't .... the gun. You'll need to train harder before you're ready for the tournament.
7 After playing WoW all night, he .... off in class, and started snoring.
8 We're losing, guys! What can we do to .... the rot?

3 Complete the sentences with the correct form of the words in brackets.
1 Gaming is not a bad thing, in .... (moderate)
2 The player was give a three game .... (suspend)
3 Posts with .... language will be deleted by the forum moderators. (abuse)
4 Sims 4 is my favourite .... game. (simulate)
5 This huge guy just hurled himself at me. It was quite .... , actually! (trauma)
6 Would the introduction of educational gaming make children more .... in class? (attend)

4 Are the definitions of the <u>underlined</u> words correct (C) or incorrect (I)?
1 If an online game <u>comes with no strings attached</u>, it is easy to play.
2 A <u>pun</u> may make someone laugh.
3 You <u>cement</u> a friendship if you let someone down.
4 <u>Textures</u> in video games are the surface appearances in the game's environment.
5 If a room is <u>ship-shape</u> it needs tidying.
6 Some endangered languages have a strong <u>oral</u> tradition, with little information actually recorded.
7 A <u>hybrid</u> sheep is one that has been cross-bred.

Score ___/25

**Wait a couple of weeks and try the quiz again.
Compare your scores.**

VOCABULARY Personal histories

1 Replace the words and phrases in brackets with the words and phrases in the box.

broken home	coup	deprived	flee
orphaned	radical	saw active service	

1 I was forced to .... (leave) the country after the .... (takeover of the government).
2 She was involved in .... (fundamentally extreme) politics, committed to change.
3 He came from a .... (very poor) background, his overriding childhood memory being of constant hunger.
4 She was .... (left without any living parents) when her parents died in a fire.
5 My grandfather .... (was on military duty) during the Second World War.
6 They grew up in a .... (family in which the parents were separated), their mother having left when the twins were six years old.

2 Complete the story with the correct form of the words in the box. You may need to expand some of the words.

deprive	evacuate	flee	knit
privilege	scholar	scratch	shelter

Some people might say that I've had a
¹................... childhood because my family is
quite poor, but it never felt that way to me.
I've enjoyed a loving, ²................... upbringing,
protected and cared for by my wonderful
parents. My village, Calderas in Guatemala, is
a close-³................... community, where everyone
knows each other.
   My only sister, Anna-Maria, won a ⁴...................
to an elite school in the area. She was ⁵...................
to go there as there are very few places. I miss
her, because we only see her in the holidays.
   Not much has ever happened in Calderas
– until last May, when the Pacaya volcano
suddenly erupted. Buildings were quickly
⁶................... and many people ⁷................... from
the area as fast as they could. Luckily, my
family was safe although the damage to our
home was terrible. We've had to rebuild it from
⁸..................., but we're so grateful to all be
alive that this seems a small price to pay.

LISTENING

3 🔊 12.1 Listen to an interview with a woman called Penelope Fowles. What is Penelope's job?

a history professor
b historical biographer
c researcher for history programmes

4 Listen again and complete the sentences. Write *exactly* what you hear in the recording, using *one to three* words in each gap.

1 Penelope recommends choosing a .... subject to write about.
2 Writers who focus on shocking and .... details will attract more readers.
3 If the subject is famous, you should try to say something original about them so that your book appeals to .... and booksellers.
4 The greatest difficulty for writers is ....
5 When planning, first of all you should create a ....
6 The most useful items for your hard copy collection are ....
7 Interviewees are often .... at first.
8 Penelope compares her work to that of a ....

> **Learner tip**
>
> Before you listen, read the sentences you have to complete and try to predict the kind of information you need to listen for. Will the answer be a noun or an adjective, for example?

VOCABULARY Similes

5 Correct the mistakes in the similies.

1 I felt like a fish in a sieve at the party, as I was the only one under 40!
2 Don't annoy him. He's as hard as a dodo.
3 Ha! That joke is as old as the plague.
4 She smokes like mud. I wish she'd quit!
5 That's as clear as a chimney. What do you mean, exactly?
6 They're like chalk and nails. You'd never know they were brothers.
7 She's unbearable! I avoid her like mud.
8 Oh, I've got a memory like a sheet! What's his name again?

DEVELOPING WRITING

Contribution to a longer piece – a profile

6 Read the task in the box. Tick (✓) what your profile should do.

a describe several people   ....
b engage the reader's interest   ....
c describe everything that happened ....
d include a timeline   ....
e include a personal response   ....

> A new website is being produced in your area for people who are interested in local history. The website will include profiles of interesting local people. You have decided to contribute a profile to the website. Your profile should
> • describe one person who lived / lives in your area (it can be a relative or neighbour, or any local figure from the past or present)
> • describe some key life events
> • suggest why he or she is interesting or important.

7 Read the profile on the right. Match the events (a–f) with the paragraphs (1–3).

a an act of friendship ....   d a memoir   ....
b outbreak of war   ....   e upbringing   ....
c moving on   ....   f tragedy   ....

8 Rewrite the sentences using the correct form of the underlined phrases in the profile.

a Life was difficult during the recession.
  The recession ....

b They accused her of theft and arrested her.
  She ....

c We felt guilty for a long time.
  For many years, ...

d She tried to understand what had happened.
  She ....

e She wrote very emotionally about the events.
  Her book is ....

f It appreciates how brave some people were.
  It ....

Apostolos Dountis

1 My grandfather, Apostolos, was born to a very loving and close-knit family near the village of Haraki, on Rhodes, in 1931. The island was occupied by German soldiers in the 1940s, which ªbrought a time of great hardship for the family. His father joined the resistance and went away to fight, never to return. This meant that Apostolos, his sister and mother often had to go and hunt for food to survive.

2 Then he and his sister ᵇwere arrested on suspicion of spying. Aged fourteen, he was sent to prison, where he eventually befriended one of his guards, a boy not much older than himself. One night, he helped Apostolos escape but he wouldn't talk to him or look at him. It wasn't until the next day that my grandfather discovered that his sister had been shot. He was devastated and for many years, ᶜhe was consumed by grief.

3 Eventually, ᵈstruggling to make sense of it all, he wrote a book about what had happened on the island. ᵉIt is a moving account of the Occupation, which ᶠpays tribute to the courage and compassion shown by a few on both sides, like his sister and the guard. Apostolos passed away in 2005 but he will always be remembered by me and many others from my neighbourhood as a hero.

> **Learner tip**
> To make your account more interesting, vary your language as much as possible. Include a range of grammatical structures and vocabulary.

9 Read the task in exercise 6 again. Write your contribution to the website (220–280 words). Follow *all* the instructions in the task and include a range of language.

12

READING

1 Quickly read the web page opposite. What is the main point we learn?

a Our view of history is influenced by prevailing social attitudes.

b It is impossible to learn the truth about historical events.

c Few historical figures are as heroic as has been claimed.

2 Read the web page again. Are the statements true (T) or false (F)?

1 Shakespeare's portrayal of Cleopatra represented an original viewpoint.

2 Many people now believe that Cleopatra cared deeply about her country.

3 The writer cites Hector to show how social ideas of heroism have changed.

4 Modern historians are still divided in their views of Alexander.

5 Drake's illegal activities were frowned on by the English ruling powers.

6 We know that Francis Drake had a good relationship with some freed slaves.

7 It's been established that Marie Antoinette had an affair during her reign.

8 Modern portraits of Marie Antoinette are all much more flattering.

3 According to the writer, who

1 has been assessed in different ways depending on their gender? ....

2 brought prosperity to their country? ....

3 was inspired by a legendary historical figure? ....

4 brought new ways of life to different countries? ....

5 was pitied by someone after being accused of a crime? ....

6 has different reputations in different countries? ....,...................

4 Choose the correct verbs. All the verbs appear in the web page text.

1 Historians sometimes *manipulate / favour* the facts to support their political views.

2 He is often *portrayed / modelled* as the world's greatest military leader.

3 Historians often *condemn / promote* Drake for being a ruthless pirate.

4 She was unfairly *maligned / plagued* by journalists, who wanted to discredit her.

5 One history book *contended / hailed* that she was the greatest queen of all time.

History module 2.1>Historical perspectives

Students should prepare for the seminar by reading the introductory article below and consulting the reading list.

A matter of perspective?
by Professor Xavier Broudel

Cleopatra

Views of Cleopatra have largely depended on changes in the perception of women in power. The earliest historians, influenced by a general mistrust of women rulers, portrayed Cleopatra as an evil seductress who manipulated men for political gain. In *Antony and Cleopatra*, Shakespeare depicts her as a helpless victim, promoting the patriarchal views of women's fragility common to his time. Films and TV programmes present us with an ambitious, resourceful politician who was by-and-large devoted to her people, thus reflecting the prevailing expectations of women in contemporary society.

Alexander the Great, b.356, d.323 BC

Alexander the Great is generally hailed by Europeans as having 'civilised the barbaric east', by enlightening that part of the world with the more sophisticated Greek culture. However, the territories in Asia that he conquered view him as an evil usurper of power, a murderer and pillager on a par with Genghis Khan. Alexander admired Achilles and modelled himself on the warrior hero, whose reckless display of courage inspired soldiers in battle.

Such values were admired until the Second World War, but today history books are more likely to favour the peace-loving Hector who tried his best to avoid war. The new wave of commentators either condemn Alexander for committing innumerable atrocities or contend that he was comparatively fair and reasonable for a soldier of his era.

Sir Francis Drake,
b.1540, England, d.1596

A controversial figure even in his day, Francis Drake is viewed in the UK as a heroic rogue, while to the Spanish he is El Draque, a ruthless pirate. His methods were unlawful, but Queen Elizabeth I, who made enough money from his exploits to pay off the national debt, was prepared to turn a blind eye, and indeed he became a national hero in the eyes of many. Several modern historians claim he was ruthless, and criticise him for his involvement in the slave trade. However, conflicting accounts suggest that Drake in fact made friends in the Caribbean with many escaped African slaves, who then helped him attack the Spanish bases there. The truth of this is still open to speculation.

Marie Antoinette,
b.1755, France, d.1793

Marie Antoinette was plagued by scandal throughout her short life. An Austrian princess, her marriage was one of political convenience. French people viewed her with suspicion from the start, and she was much maligned. Early historians claimed she was unfaithful, though modern scholars agree there is no solid evidence to support this. She was also falsely accused of fraud, a libel which aroused the sympathy of a leading historian of the day, Edmund Burke, who portrayed Marie Antoinette as a helpless victim. Modern historians have uncovered accounts of her showing kindness to the poor, yet Coppola's recent film features a frivolous woman who took little seriously. Surrounded as it was by rumour and gossip, the truth about her life is unlikely ever to be fully unravelled.

Glossary

seductress: a woman who sexually entices
pillager: historical term for someone who steals goods by force
marriage of political convenience: marriage made for political reasons rather than for love

DEVELOPING CONVERSATIONS
Contextualised questions

5 Complete the students' comments to Professor Broudel with the correct form of the verbs. Make any other changes that are necessary.

1 *You mentioned* Drake's connection to the slave trade. (mention) ....

2 .... Shakespeare's portrayal of Cleopatra as weak and helpless. (cite) ....

3 .... modern history books favour peace-loving leaders. (suggest) ....

4 You seemed to .... Drake was a controversial figure in his day. (argue) ....

5 .... early historians viewed Cleopatra as evil. (make the point) ....

6 .... Edmund Burke's view that Marie Antoinette was a victim. (refer) ....

7 .... all historical study is a 'work in progress'. (claim) ....

6 Match the comments (1–6) in exercise 5 with the follow-up questions (a–f).

a Could you back that up with an example from the play?

b Do you think this is because our sense of morality has changed?

c Could you explain what you mean by that expression?

d What evidence is there that he was involved?

e Do you have the full reference for that?

f Could you elaborate on that with examples of people who disapproved of him?

g Isn't that a bit of an overstatement?

Language note referring

Note the different verbs for referring to information.
You *mention* something when you refer to it briefly.
You mentioned a book you'd written. (but you didn't say much about it)
You *cite* something when you refer to it or quote it as an authority or example.
I'd like to cite your book in my essay.

VOCABULARY Historical events

1 Match the causes (1–10) with their consequences (a–j).

1 Following the declaration of war,
2 Revelations that he had been embezzling funds
3 The recent massacre at a Scottish primary school
4 The success of the petition to save the Arctic
5 The reforms implemented by the last government
6 The rebels finally overthrew the dictatorship
7 As a result of the break-up of the committee
8 Winning the by-election by such a large margin
9 Their historic victory in 1928 pointed
10 The introduction of surveillance cameras in urban areas

a strengthened the resolve of environmental activists.
b marked a turning point in the young politician's career.
c and established a new socialist government.
d the way forward for British women's struggle for equal rights.
e thousands of people fled the region.
f the organisation entered a period of uncertainty.
g undermined people's faith in the Ambassador.
h saw a reduction in the overall number of muggings recorded.
i led to calls to restrict public access to all schools and colleges.
j sowed the seeds of the current economic crisis.

PRONUNCIATION
Stressed and unstressed suffixes

2 ✪ 12.2 Listen to the words. Practise saying them, paying attention to the main stress.

1	●○○	uprising
2	○●○	employer
3	○○●	employee
4	○●○○	reliable
5	○○○●	evacuee

3 Add the words in the box to the table in exercise 2.

assassinate	editor	engineer	industry
portrayal	reflection	refugee	scholarship
validity	Vietnamese		

4 ✪ 12.3 Listen and check. Practise saying the words.

VOCABULARY
Discussing arguments and theories

5 Complete the quiz with the correct form of the verbs in the box.

cast	challenge	claim	establish	give
play	put	stem		

Women in history

Who

1 became the world's first woman prime minister in 1960 and was instrumental in .... Sri Lanka as a new Republic in the 1970s?
2 was a physicist who .... forward the theory that radioactivity was an atomic phenomenon?
3 .... a significant role in the development of modern medical procedures during childbirth in the 1950s?
4 was perhaps the greatest Russian woman poet, whose appeal .... from her ability to describe romance?
5 was the politician who successfully .... the dictatorship of Ferdinand Marcos in the Philippines and restored democratic rule?
6 won four gold medals at the 1948 Olympics, even though experts .... this Dutch athlete was too old at 30?
7 created innovative designs that .... rise to the trend towards simple, chic clothes for women?
8 .... doubt on the necessity for the war when she was elected to the US Congress as the first African American woman?

6 Now answer the quiz with the names in the box.

Anna Akhmatova	Corazon Aquino
Fanny Blankers-Koen	Gabrielle Chanel
Marie Curie	Shirley Chisholm
Sirimavo R. D. Bandaranaike	Virginia Apgar

GRAMMAR Dramatic inversion

7 Choose the correct adverbial phrases.

1 *At no time / Not only* during the 22-hour rescue mission did the firemen complain of being tired.
2 *No sooner / Not until* had they declared war than the bombing started.
3 *Only after / Not only* did she win the 100 metre sprint, but the relay race as well.
4 *At no time / Nowhere else* in the world could you find such a diverse multicultural society right now.
5 *No sooner / Not until* 1956 were Greek women permitted to vote in parliamentary elections.
6 *Only after / Never before* all possibilities were exhausted did the government call off the search for survivors.

8 Rewrite the sentences using the words provided.

1 It was the first time I'd ever seen such a huge crowd of people gathered in one place.
Never before ....
....

2 The crowd didn't disperse until the police fired tear gas at them.
Only when ....
....

3 The tsunami killed eleven villagers and also destroyed nearly all of the fishing boats in the area.
Not only ....
....

4 Only two people signed the Declaration of Independence on 4 July, and the last signature was added five years later.
Two people signed the Declaration of Independence on 4 July, but not until ....
....

5 Thirty-eight minutes after war had been declared between Britain and Zanzibar in 1896 the latter surrendered.
No sooner ....
....

6 Although he was frightened, the little boy didn't cry during the earthquake.
Despite being afraid, at no time ....
....

Vocabulary Builder Quiz 12

Download the Vocabulary Builder for Unit 12 and try the quiz below. Write your answers in your notebook. Then check them and record your score.

1 Complete the sentences with the correct form of the word in brackets.

1 The .... of civilians began as war seemed inevitable. (evacuate)
2 Self-employed workers have to submit a tax .... every year. (declare)
3 Foreign .... undoubtedly prolonged the civil war. (intervene)
4 Soon after that, they .... the railway network. (nation)
5 It's a bit of an .... to say that all labourers are lazy! How many do you know? (state)
6 Nowadays, students often leave university with .... debt due to high fees. (cripple)

2 Complete the similes.

1 The twins may look identical, but they're like chalk and ....
2 When she saw the results she went as white as a ....
3 She won't remember your name. She's got a memory like a ....
4 I find him creepy, and generally avoid him like the ....
5 That was as clear as .... ! I haven't got a clue what he was on about!
6 I can't believe she gave up. She used to smoke like a .... !

3 Add the missing prepositions.

1 Due to his skill with horses, the young officer was assigned .... the cavalry.
2 I've dedicated my life to building .... this business.
3 Our son dropped .... of university as he didn't like the course.
4 She designed and built the machine .... scratch.
5 The police uncovered fraud .... a massive scale.
6 This evidence casts doubt .... our findings.
7 Could you go .... these figures again? They don't match up.
8 She couldn't get her head .... the fact that she wouldn't see him again.

4 Choose the correct words.

1 The rebels *massacred / assassinated* the entire village.
2 She had a very *deprived / privileged* background, having gone to one of the top private schools in the country
3 She was not happy with the outcome and *contended / challenged* the judge's verdict.
4 He's as hard as *nails / a dodo*; nothing seems to frighten him.
5 She had a sheltered *uprising / upbringing*, surrounded by a close-knit, protective family.

Score ___/25

**Wait a couple of weeks and try the quiz again.
Compare your scores.**

VOCABULARY Newspaper headlines

1 Match the <u>underlined</u> words in the headlines (1–8) with the definitions (a–h).

1

Earthquake <u>toll</u> reaches 2,000

2 President <u>hails</u> French investment in region

3

Government <u>crackdown</u> on credit card fraud

4 **Manos <u>cleared</u> of murder charge**

5

Scandal over <u>leak</u> of lab data

6 Amsterdam put in <u>bid</u> to host the Olympics

7

Rail workers and bosses <u>clash</u> over cuts

8 **Government <u>rules out</u> deal with strikers.**

a	number of deaths	e	offer
b	excludes the possibility of	f	find innocent
c	act of revealing secrets to the public	g	fight
d	strong action to repress something	h	welcome

2 Rewrite the sentences as headlines. Include the correct form of the verbs in brackets, and miss out grammar words where possible.

1 Scientists are on the point of a breakthrough in finding a cure for Alzheimers. (brink)
Scientists on the brink of breakthrough in finding cure for Alzheimers

2 Emile Cole is going to withdraw from the contract with Arsenal. (pull)
....

3 The chancellor states that there definitely won't be a tax increase. (rule)
....

4 President Carver is going to reduce arms spending. (slash)
....

5 Drugs have been captured in a warehouse raid. (seize)
....

6 Landlords promise to stop hooligans from visiting city centre pubs. (vow / bar)
....

DEVELOPING CONVERSATIONS
Rhetorical questions and common opinions

3 Read the mini-dialogues (1–6) and complete the responses with the opinions (a–h). There are two extra opinions that you don't need to use.

1 A: The boys showed no concern for the old lady's safety.
B: Why would they? ....

2 A: Anyway, they were convicted of robbery and given community service.
B: And that's meant to be a punishment? ....

3 A: They get their first pay check, then they're off!
B: Well, what do you expect? ....

4 A: I reckon Southampton might just beat Man United tomorrow.
B: You're kidding me, right? ....

5 A: Even though she'd been bitchy to colleagues to get promoted, she was amazed when Karina did the same to her.
B: What did she expect? ....

6 A: The new tax law will hit lower-income families the hardest.
B: So, what's new? ....

a They're just in it for the money.
b It's one rule for the rich and another for the poor.
c If you live by the sword, you die by the sword.
d It's all about oil.
e They should lock them up and throw away the key.
f They haven't got a hope in hell.
g Young people today! They have no respect.
h It's about time they did something about it.

DEVELOPING WRITING
A proposal – being persuasive

4 Complete the headings in the proposal below with suitable words.

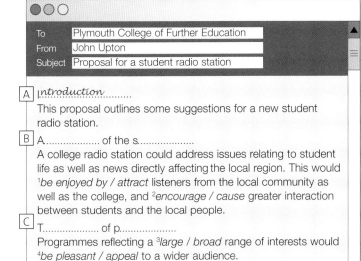

⚫⚪⚪

To	Plymouth College of Further Education
From	John Upton
Subject	Proposal for a student radio station

A *Introduction* ....
This proposal outlines some suggestions for a new student radio station.

B A................... of the s...................
A college radio station could address issues relating to student life as well as news directly affecting the local region. This would ¹*be enjoyed by / attract* listeners from the local community as well as the college, and ²*encourage / cause* greater interaction between students and the local people.

C T................... of p...................
Programmes reflecting a ³*large / broad* range of interests would ⁴*be pleasant / appeal* to a wider audience.

1 Music
Music would form the greater part of the radio programming. An emphasis on world music would ⁵*generate / encourage* interest among the college's large international student community.

2 News
News programmes would also play a major role, with a special focus on such themes as further education, scientific developments and environmental issues. These could be supported by a radio phone-in slot to ⁶*make / allow* listeners to express their views.

3 Others
A regular feature on arts news would also be of interest to the target audience. This could include reviews of both college and local events, plus interviews with people in the public eye.

D C...................
The creation of a student radio station would be ⁷*a benefit / an asset* to the local community as well as students. It would help to ⁸*improve / increase* relations between students and the rest of the community, and inform listeners as well as entertain.

Learner tip

Use persuasive language in your proposal to convince the target reader of your ideas. Emphasise your ideas by using positive language, including strong nouns and verbs as well as adjectives.

5 Choose the most effective words to complete the proposal.

Learner tip

Get rid of unnecessary words and details to make your writing clearer and more powerful.

6 Rewrite the sentences more concisely and include the words in brackets.

1 In order to encourage more people to read the paper, it would be a good idea to include a review supplement. (appeal / wider)
A review supplement ....
....

2 If we use clear headings, this would make the web page easier for people who use the page to understand. (more accessible / users)
Clear headings ....
....

3 We could make the page more appealing to lots of different kinds of readers by including colourful images. (attract / broad / readership)
Colourful images ....
....

4 More businesses might want to put advertisements in our paper if we created a careers supplement. (encourage / advertise)
A careers supplement ....
....

7 Read the task in the box. Write a proposal (220–260 words) for the website suggesting what it should include and how it could be made appealing to as many students as possible.

You are a student at an international college in your area. The Principal of your college has asked you to write a proposal for a new student website.

VOCABULARY Common sayings

1 Complete the responses to the comments with a suitable saying from the box. There are more than you need.

When the going gets tough, the tough get going.	Too many cooks spoil the broth.
The grass is always greener on the other side.	The early bird catches the worm
If it ain't broke, don't fix it.	When in Rome, do as the Romans do.
If you can't beat them, join them.	It takes all sorts to make a world.
Don't count your chickens before they hatch.	Every cloud has a silver lining.

1 A promotion means more money, so we can have that holiday in Hawaii!
Steady on! ....

2 They've got a lovely house, and they never seem to argue. Why aren't we like that?
You know what they say. ....

3 After me complaining about having to work the last three weekends, the boss invited me to join the team going to the conference in Paris!
You see! ....

4 She's nice but weird. I mean, she wears funny clothes, and listens to all that strange music.
So what? ....

5 So Jill and Zeta came, and then Mum started interfering, and no-one could agree. It was a nightmare.
That's a real case of ....

6 Fran's leaving at the end of the month. Is it too early to ask Mark for her job?
Certainly not. Remember, ...

7 They take their shoes off whenever they go into a house. Should we do the same?
Well, ...

8 Right! This project's got to be finished in two weeks. We're going to have to work long hours and weekends to meet that deadline.
No problem! ....

READING

2 Quickly read the handout from a media studies seminar opposite. Complete the handout (A–D) with the subheadings (1–5). There is one extra subheading that you don't need to use.

1 Use of images
2 Corporate influence
3 Article selection
4 Bias through statistics
5 Style and tone

3 Read the handout again and choose the best options.

1 Newspapers today are subject to
a fewer restrictions.
b rising overheads.
c fierce competition.
d falling advertising revenue.

2 Editors don't put some stories on the front page because
a they are too sensationalist.
b important stories require more room.
c political news doesn't sell papers.
d they aren't exciting enough.

3 In paragraph B, the writer explains that some papers try to affect readers' opinions by
a selecting words to achieve a particular effect.
b using highly sensationalist language.
c explicitly criticising people or actions.
d exclusively using exciting language.

4 In the writer's view, effective headlines
a do not need to exaggerate the facts.
b reflect the editor's political views.
c can boost newspaper sales.
d are less important than good quality articles.

5 According to the writer, a photograph which focuses on a particular scene of aggression
a is misleading and unethical.
b highlights the event's significance.
c glorifies violence.
d ought to include more context.

6 The writer's attitude towards the printed press is best described as
a critical.   b positive.
c dismissive.   d cautious.

4 Complete the sentences with suitable words from the handout.

1 Colour supplements can attract more readers and increase .... figures.
2 The .... reader knows how to separate fact from fiction.
3 She .... precedence over other celebrities in the magazine because readers loved her.
4 The .... angle in the photograph focused on a small section of the scene.
5 Police hope that the outbreak of violence was simply an .... incident and not the beginning of widespread hooliganism.
6 They focused on the scandal to the .... of other news stories, which were ignored.

EXAMINING **BIAS** IN THE NEWS

The top priority of any newspaper is to sell. Never before has this been as important as it is today. The sudden growth of online news reporting means that printed newspapers have to struggle to maintain circulation figures. As a result, they are heavily dependent on commercial concerns and marketing. While many journalists and editors try to be as objective in their approach as possible, a certain amount of bias is inevitable. Be aware of this and keep a lookout for certain characteristics and you will become a more discerning reader.

A ....

Editors know that eye-catching 'shock stories' shift more copies. For this reason, you are more likely to see news of a bombing or the latest victim of a serial killer on the front page than an account of firemen saving someone's life. Similarly, coverage of national parliamentary elections will take precedence over everything else, including major world news. Positioning other stories further back subconsciously affects the reader's view of their significance. What's more, restrictions on the number of stories in any one issue may mean that some stories will simply be omitted.

B ....

Some newspapers may try to avoid seeming overtly sensationalist, but they still influence the reader indirectly by using language to convey excitement, to show approval or to criticise. For example, a public demonstration attended by 560 protesters can be described in positive terms with 'Over 500 people took to the streets to protest against the proposal' or, conversely, in a negative way with 'The protest march was marked by a poor turnout of fewer than 600 people'. It all depends on the journalist's point of view. Headlines are often particularly revealing in this respect and are often the deciding factor for a reader when considering whether or not to buy the newspaper. Editors will aim to make stories sound more dramatic, knowing that the headline 'Six die in train crash' will probably attract more attention than 'Two trains collide outside station'.

C ....

Newspapers make choices about the kind of pictures they show in order to influence public opinion. A photograph of a presidential candidate, for instance, could be taken from a flattering or unflattering perspective. At a football match, the camera angle can be narrowed onto a scene of hooliganism, suggesting that violence was widespread, or widened to play it down as one isolated incident.

D ....

Newspapers rely heavily on advertising for revenue. Those that receive a large part of their income from a particular company are therefore unlikely to publish information to the detriment of that company's products. They may even include press releases promoting the firm's latest creation, while ignoring that of its chief competitor.

To obtain a broader view of what's happening in the world, it is best to read widely. Luckily, major newspapers now have their own websites, so it is easier than ever to access information on a news item from a range of sources.

Glossary

serial killer: murderer who kills three or more people over a period of time
shift: (of media publications) sell
the deciding factor: the factor which determines someone's choice

13

LISTENING

1 🔊 **13.1** Listen to part of a radio show in which guests discuss the week's news. What are the three main stories on the show and in what order do they appear? Write 1–3 next to pictures a–d. There is one extra picture that you don't need to use.

a

b

c

d

2 Listen again and write the speaker, Marie (M), Araminta (A) or Roy (R), next to the opinions.

Story 1
1 The arrest represents a major success in the fight against crime. ....
2 The arrest is merely part of a political strategy. ....
3 The suspect is too important to be merely part of a political ploy. ....

Story 2
4 Children in cities have virtually no contact with nature. ....
5 Most children's knowledge of nature is gained passively. ....
6 We are too concerned about children's safety. ....
7 People are already concerned about keeping fit. ....

PRONUNCIATION
Short and long vowel sounds

> **Language note** vowel sounds
> --
> Vowel sounds can be different in different forms of a word. For instance, a long vowel in a noun may become a short vowel in an adjective.
> p*a*rent /eə/ → p*a*rental /ə/
> Similarly, the vowel sound in a present tense verb may change in the past form.
> dr*i*ve /aɪ/ → dr*i*ven /ɪ/

3 (Circle) the word in each pair with the *short* vowel sound.
1 (d**ea**lt) / d**ea**l
2 n**a**tural / n**a**ture
3 s**o**ciety / s**o**cial
4 r**i**sen / r**i**se
5 legisl**a**tion / legisl**a**ture
6 adv**e**rtising / adv**e**rtisement
7 st**a**tion / st**a**tute

4 🔊 **13.2** Listen, check your answers and repeat.

GRAMMAR Patterns after reporting verbs

5 Complete the table with verbs in the box. Some verbs match more than one pattern.

acknowledge	assure	blame	claim	confirm
deny	express	praise	refuse	reject
urge	vow			

reporting verb pattern	verbs
1 verb + (*that*) clause	
2 verb + object + (*that*) clause	
3 verb + *to*-infinitive	
4 verb + object + *to*-infinitive	
5 verb + noun phrase	
6 verb (+ object) + preposition	

6 Choose the correct verbs.

Solar plane breakthrough

The aviation pioneer Bertrand Piccard ¹*expressed / assured* relief as well as excitement over the success of the test flight of the first solar-powered plane yesterday. He ²*acknowledged / declared* his initial fears that something might go wrong. However, he ³*assured / urged* reporters that the plane had exceeded all expectations, ⁴*praising / vowing* his team for all their hard work. Piccard ⁵*claimed / assured* that the plane will be able to operate without using a drop of fuel. He also ⁶*confirmed / admitted* rumours of a planned transatlantic flight in the near future.

7 Rewrite the sentences in reported speech using the words in brackets.

1 'Taxes will be cut in the next six months,' declared the Prime Minister. (vowed)

....

....

2 'So sign the petition and let's make the outcry too loud to be ignored!' cried the speaker to the crowd. (urged)

....

....

3 'I've decided not to accept your offer,' said Gerard to the committee. (rejected)

....

....

4 'I now realise that I was misguided in my calculations,' said the physicist. (acknowledged)

....

....

5 'We did not try to play down the importance of the problem,' replied the company spokesperson. (denied)

....

....

6 'Children have lost contact with nature due to the nanny state,' says Marie. (blames)

....

....

7 'Yes, Parliament is going to pass the new education bill this year,' said the minister. (confirmed)

....

....

8 'No, I won't discuss the issue with the press until tomorrow,' said the MP. (refused)

....

....

Vocabulary Builder Quiz 13

Download the Vocabulary Builder for Unit 13 and try the quiz below. Write your answers in your notebook. Then check them and record your score.

1 Complete the headlines with the correct form of the words in the box.

slash	hail	raid
clash	pull	

1 B&Q .... out of deal to merge with Habitat after redundancy row.
2 Prime Minister .... police crackdown on inner city crime as violence falls.
3 Nine injured as Man Utd fans .... with Liverpool fans after 0–2 defeat.
4 Government plans to .... jobs in the public sector.
5 Daring bank .... gang escapes with $20 million.

2 Choose the correct verbs.

1 The PM *denied / refused* the allegations.
2 The reporter was *punched / tipped* off that the meeting would take place that night.
3 If you can't beat them, *spoil / join* them.
4 The case was *thrown / pulled* out when the witness admitted lying.
5 Police have managed to *clash / slash* imports of heroin in recent years.

3 Choose the best synonyms.

1 proceeds   *profits / trial*
2 suppress   *cover up / counter*
3 hail   *praise / criticise*
4 hike   *tack / rise*

4 Add the missing prepositions.

1 He was convicted .... murder.
2 They sentenced him .... life imprisonment.
3 She was .... the brink of signing the contract.
4 She suddenly pulled out .... the deal.
5 The scandal was just a storm .... a teacup.
6 She's touring the country in a bid .... become the next President.
7 They sued him .... breach of contract.

5 Tick (✓) the sentences which make sense.

1 You get on well with people you clash with.   ....
2 An intrusion is usually unwelcome.   ....
3 Libel is usually complimentary.   ....
4 Going bust means the end of a business.   ....

Score ___/25

Wait a couple of weeks and try the quiz again. Compare your scores.

VOCABULARY How's business?

1 Complete the conversations. There is an extra phrase in each box that you don't need to use.

flooded	made	picked up	taken on

A: Over the last quarter, we've been so [1]................... with orders that we can hardly keep up with demand.

B: Are you saying we should have [2].................... more staff to help with the workload?

A: Well, not yet, but it's great to see that sales have [3].................... since last year's difficulties.

consolidating	hanging in	making	relocating

A: How's it going? I heard your company was [4]................... to Conway Street.

B: That's right. The rents are cheaper there. I think they're [5].................... redundancies too as part of the whole cost-cutting strategy.

A: Well, at least the company's [6].................... there. A lot more have gone under this year.

client base	downturn	overheads	upturn

A: This year has seen a sharp [7].................... in profit.

B: I thought we had a solid [8].................... . Our customers seem pretty loyal to me.

A: They are, but the fact is that our [9].................... have increased. The rent has almost doubled!

DEVELOPING CONVERSATIONS
Small talk

2 Match the questions (1–7) with the answers (a–g).

1 So, how's the family?
2 What are you up to this weekend?
3 Disgusting weather, eh?
4 Did you watch the match?
5 Did you hear about those burglars?
6 How's the house coming along?
7 You heading out for lunch?

a Slowly. We should have hired professionals!
b Yeah. Terrible. They're going to get relegated.
c Good! Ali joined the football team this term.
d Yes. I'll probably just grab a quick bite.
e Not a lot. Just having the in-laws over, probably.
f Yeah. They should lock them up.
g Yes, but it's supposed to clear up tomorrow.

DEVELOPING WRITING
An information sheet – making suggestions

3 Complete the gaps (1–3) in the information sheet with the subheadings (a–e). There are two extra subheadings that you don't need to use.

a Physical activity and rest
b Effective communication
c Healthy eating habits
d Prioritising commitments
e Recognising the symptoms of stress

Avoiding stress in the workplace

We place great importance on staff health and job satisfaction. While some degree of stress is normal in working life, we know that excessive stress can be highly damaging. For this reason, we have produced this information sheet to help you stay on top.

1 ....

It is essential to recognise which projects need to come first and which can be tackled later. Try making yourself a to-do list and cross off each task as it is achieved. This will give you a sense of moving forward. Perhaps you should also stop taking responsibility for every last detail yourself and try delegating some projects instead.

2 ....

To be at your best, it is vital you maintain your body's blood sugar levels. Make sure you eat frequently throughout the day, which may mean bringing in light snacks to consume whenever you feel tired.

3 ....

Exercising is often something people mean to do but never quite manage. Even 30 minutes of aerobic exercise a day will provide considerable stress relief. Try to include some kind of physical activity in your daily routine – by walking or cycling to work, for example. Take regular rest breaks and avoid doing too much overtime in the evenings. Aim for at least seven hours' sleep per night.

4 Match 1–6 with a–f to make work collocations.

1	work-life	a	management
2	time	b	break
3	action	c	balance
4	job	d	satisfaction
5	to-do	e	plan
6	rest	f	list

5 Complete the sentences with the collocations in exercise 4.

1 Practical ....s might include lists of aims, schedule overviews and summaries of the key outcomes required.

2 If your work does not provide you with any ...., it may be time to find a new one.

3 Take a regular .... to relax.

4 When there is so much pressure to work long hours, it becomes difficult to maintain a good .... and then your personal life suffers.

5 Prioritising the most urgent projects is an example of effective ...., enabling you to meet your deadlines faster and more effectively.

6 I ticked off three items on my .... this morning.

Language note verb + -ing or verb + infinitive

Some verbs, such as *stop, try, remember, forget, regret* and *come,* have a different meaning depending on whether they are followed by an *-ing* form or an infinitive.

---

6 Choose the correct forms in the pairs of sentences.

1 a Stop constantly *to check / checking* your emails.
  b When you're tired, stop *to have / having* a break.

2 a Reduce interruptions. This may mean *to put / putting* a 'Do not disturb' sign on your desk.
  b Decide what you mean *to do / doing* in the morning and stick to the plan.

3 a Whatever you do, try not *to leave / leaving* important tasks until the last minute.
  b If you suffer from insomnia, try *to read / reading* a book instead of watching TV.

4 a We regret *to inform / informing* staff that some redundancies will be necessary.
  b Many people regret not *to spend / spending* enough time with their families.

5 a Remember *to eat / eating* healthily.
  b I remember once *to get / getting* extremely anxious about getting all my work done.

7 Write an information sheet (220–260 words) with the title Managing Your Time Effectively. Include information and advice either for colleagues at your workplace or for students at your school or college.

LISTENING

8 🔊 14.1 Listen to the first part of a speech. Who is speaking?

a a company director
b a university lecturer
c a business advisor

9 Listen again. Tick (✓) the good reasons for going into business and put a cross (✗) by the bad reasons, according to the speaker.

1	making more money	....
2	pursuing a passion	....
3	being your own boss	....
4	supplementing a less fulfilling job	....
5	fulfilling a need in the market place	....
6	showing you can start again after failure	....
7	spending more time with your family	....

10 🔊 14.2 Listen to the second part of the speech and complete the list. Write *exactly* what you hear, using *one* word in each gap.

Reasons why businesses fail

- not having enough management knowledge, especially about finance and how to deal with difficult [1]....................

- having unrealistic expectations of the amount of [2].................. which is required

- not recognising problems to do with location such as accessibility and nearness to [3]....................

- not providing an online [4].................. and not promoting [5].................. strongly enough

- not focusing on [6].................. rather than short-term business

---

VOCABULARY Loanwords

1 Choose the correct word or phrase to complete the sentences.

1 Entering the room, she had an overwhelming feeling of .... She was sure she had been there before.
a zeitgeist   b plus ça change   c déjà vu

2 The rest of the family presented him with a .... and so he had no choice but to agree to the plan.
a fait accompli   b faux pas   c au fait

3 Frankly, he's rather a .... , and keeps reminding us that we're lucky to have him.
a guerilla   b chef   c prima donna

4 The .... , boasting an impressive 14th century church on its north side, forms the centrepiece of the town.
a fiasco   b plaza   c angst

5 These brassy, ... accessories are particularly popular among teenagers.
a kitsch   b prima donna   c macho

6 There have been reports of fighting between .... and government troops in the area.
a chefs   b zeitgeists   c guerillas

7 I'm afraid I'm not really .... with the way the security system operates yet, so I'll need to see the manual.
a au fait   b faux pas   c déjà vu

8 The wedding was a bit of a .... as the organisers got the seating wrong, and the band failed to turn up.
a trek   b fiasco   c fait accompli

PRONUNCIATION Intonation in questions

Language note question intonation

We use a falling tone at the end of questions when we want to find something out, and a rising or fall-rising tone when we want to make sure about something.

2 ⏺ 14.3 Listen to the questions. Is the speaker finding something out (FSO) or making sure (MS)?

1 So, how's the family? Tell me all!   ....
2 What are you up to this weekend? I thought you were going camping.   ....
3 So, did you go out? Only I didn't see you.   ....
4 Did you catch the news this morning? I couldn't believe it.   ....
5 Where are you going for your holiday? I can't remember if Clare said Greece or Italy.   ....
6 What are you doing this evening? I fancy going out.   ....
7 How's the house coming along? I'd love to see it!   ....

3 Practise asking the questions in exercise 2, copying the intonation.

READING

4 Quickly read the four texts opposite. Who has the most negative view of corporate responsibility?

....

5 Read the texts again. For questions 1–9, choose from the people (A–D). Sometimes more than one answer is required.

Who

1 admits to changing their view on the topic?   ....
2 thinks that large corporations act responsibly because they are concerned about their image?   ...., ...
3 believes they may personally become responsible for harming some other businesses?   ....
4 expects to change career path in the future?   ....
5 supports the idea that a company ought to prioritise making money?   ....
6 implies that companies are deliberately unclear about their policies and practices?   ....
7 is not impressed when large corporations give away money?   ....
8 is concerned about the impact of business on the environment?   ....
9 feels that some corporations believe their customers can be easily fooled?   ....

6 Complete the sentences with the words and phrases in the box. All these phrases appear in the texts.

agenda	buzz word	do-gooder	give it a go
grey area	Plan A	spin	undercut

1 I don't see how the company could put a positive .... on this disaster.
2 The difference between truth and lies is a .... in this company – the boundaries aren't clear.
3 'Best practice' is an irritating .... that managers use all the time.
4 Let's go for .... If it doesn't work out, we'll come back to the alternatives.
5 Michelle's only being nice because she has a hidden .... I think she wants to get promoted.
6 Bill Gates has been criticised for being a .... , but I think his charity work should be praised.
7 Let's see if we can .... our competitors by offering bigger discounts.
8 You'll never find out if you're good at business unless you ....

Corporations:
in what sense responsible?

We asked four alumni from the Williams Business and Accountancy School what corporate responsibility means to them.

A Jason

Corporate responsibility? I think it's just a buzz word. Maybe I shouldn't be saying this, given that I've recently changed direction and decided to enter the corporate world myself. I know that some corporations profess to be bringing huge benefits to local people, and maybe some are. However, in other cases, they're paying low wages or undercutting small, family-run firms who can't compete. It may not be a pretty image, but that's the nature of capitalism. I'd like to hope I won't end up as part of this process, but I suspect it's inevitable. Essentially, your biggest responsibility is ultimately to return value to your stakeholders. Positive employee relations are desirable, but not actually a legal requirement in many countries.

B Anya

Thanks to my sister, I've recently had a shift in thinking. As far as corporate responsibility is concerned, I'm no longer a complete sceptic! Christina recently transferred to an overseas branch. She was surprised and delighted to discover the branch was running local programmes to improve basic literacy skills amongst employees as well as to conserve the environment. She's now currently retraining as a teacher and moving over to that side of things. The branch isn't a bunch of do-gooders and this isn't just for show. They genuinely seem to be making a difference. Now that I've seen this side of corporate responsibility, I've been persuaded to give it a go myself in later life, although I'll stick to Plan A and pursue a solid career in finance for a few years first.

C Andre

For me, what it comes down to is sustainability. Whatever your product, it shouldn't have a detrimental effect on the planet. Many companies make a big noise about how much cash they give away to charity, but they should implement changes in the way they make their profits in the first place. Quite aside from the ethical arguments, there's also a sound commercial incentive here. These days the consumer has access to far more information than ever before thanks to the internet, so if a scandal goes viral, it'll tarnish a reputation forever. Companies are well aware of that. For that reason, more are starting to face up to their responsibilities – or so they claim.

D Lisa

In the USA, corporations often support community development projects by donating books or equipment to schools. However, this apparent altruism is not all it professes to be. There's a large grey area between corporate giving and company branding. Nowadays every corporate website includes a summary of so-called 'core values'; vague descriptions of how they're 'giving back' to society. I can't help thinking they're obscure for a reason and that it's all just spin for good PR. I'm particularly irritated by the claims of fast food companies, and if I thought it would do any good, I'd join a protest march. But what can you do against these giants? They pretend to be concerned with obesity levels while promoting special offers on larger portions. The hidden agenda is clearly to boost margins. It's an insult to consumer intelligence.

Glossary

go viral: spread as or like an online virus
PR (public relations): the activity of promoting a good reputation with the public
altruism: caring more about other people and their needs than your own

14

GRAMMAR Relative clauses

1 Add the correct relative pronoun where necessary. Omit the relative pronoun whenever possible. You may also need to add a preposition.

Poor customer service can cause terrible harm to a company's image, depending on the extent [1] *to which* reports of customer dissatisfaction are taken up by the media. A case in point was the hardware chain Homemakers, [2] .... was established as a small family-run business in the 1970s and [3] .... had grown into a chain of eleven nationwide stores by the late 1990s. During this time, it was known as the place [4] .... you went for friendly, expert advice and quality products. However, it got to the point [5] .... Andrew Tyson, the original owner, was ready to retire and in 1999 the store was bought out by Reed & Shaw. Almost immediately, there were a number of ways [6] .... the new company policy failed to meet customer expectations. To begin with, local delivery, [7] .... had long been provided free of charge, was now a service that came at a cost. Items [8] .... customers returned as faulty were not refunded. Furthermore, numerous stories soon spread about customers [9] .... the wrong information or even change had been given. The reason [10] .... these problems were occurring was an ill-advised cost-cutting measure. The new company had replaced the staff [11] .... Tyson originally hired with a cheaper workforce, [12] .... basic training was limited. Ultimately, this concern with short-term profits was [13] .... cost the company its long-term survival.

2 Complete the sentences with a relative clause. Use the information provided (a–f) and make any other necessary changes.

1 The company was originally set up by Andrew Tyson , *who took out a loan to finance it*

2 Some customers were full of praise for Tyson
....
....

3 Reed & Shaw took over Homemakers in 1999
....
....

4 Several cheaper brands were introduced into the stores
....
....

5 In 2007 the directors published a report for the company's shareholders ....
....

6 In 2008 Reed & Shaw began to reverse some of its policies
....
....

a A number of changes to company policy were made.
b It was too late to win back a solid customer base by then.
c The report described how profits had plummeted.
d His policy of employing experienced staff was very successful.
e ~~He took out a loan to finance it.~~
f None of these were of good quality.

VOCABULARY Business situations

3 Complete the collocations with the words in the box.

deal	concessions	gap	line	meeting	stakes

1 a .... in the market
2 to raise the ....
3 to negotiate a ....
4 to chair a ....
5 to affect our bottom ....
6 to win ....

> **Language note** *rise* versus *raise*
>
> *Rise* is an intransitive verb.
> *The share price is likely to rise again.*
> *Raise* is a transitive verb.
> *The company is going to raise salaries this year.*

4 Choose the correct words.

1 We have *upped / exceeded* our targets, thereby increasing our profits by nearly 150%.
2 Thankfully, we finally managed to *seal / scale* the deal with the Canadians and our joint venture will be going ahead in the near future.
3 XR Electronics Ltd was acquired by Taylor-Rees Inc. in a hostile takeover *threat / bid*.
4 OK, I'll *outsource / recommend* your proposal to the shareholders and see if they agree.
5 In order to cut costs the company will *make / undertake* a certain amount of restructuring.
6 No decision has been reached and negotiations are likely to be *competitive / ongoing* for several weeks.
7 Before launching the project, we really need to *conduct / drop* a focus group to see what kind of advertising campaign will work best.
8 I don't think we should give in to the union's *demands / lobby* for a pay rise.

5 Complete the sentences with the words that you *didn't choose* in exercise 4.

1 Because they carry such a high tax, our goods are a lot less .... than the cheaper Australian products.
2 The .... to persuade the Government to reduce business tax has been gaining ground lately.
3 For a start, we'll need to .... back the number of staff and make some redundancies.
4 If delivery is late again, we'll need to .... our suppliers and find someone more reliable.
5 If we .... marketing to a specialist firm, we'll be able to optimise our own manpower.
6 In the end, Smith & Davis .... their offer, increasing it by 15%.
7 We have to take seriously the union's .... to go on strike unless we agree to their terms.
8 Well, if we want to avoid a strike, we'll need to .... a few concessions and agree to some of their demands.

Vocabulary Builder Quiz 14

Download the Vocabulary Builder for Unit 14 and try the quiz below. Write your answers in your notebook. Then check them and record your score.

1 Which *four* sentences relate to money?

1 The layoffs failed to restore profits.
2 The share price began to recover in the first quarter.
3 The company recognised the need to consolidate its position in the market.
4 The cutbacks in the budget will mean downsizing.
5 We need to scale up now the downturn is over.
6 We'll take a look at overheads in the meeting.

2 Replace the underlined words and phrases with idioms from the Vocabulary Builder for Unit 14.

1 He <u>went to prison</u> for fraud.
2 Times are hard but so far we're <u>managing to survive</u>.
3 We've just <u>gained permission to mine</u> in the area.
4 What really <u>got him to sign the contract</u> was when I told him about the bonuses.
5 Remember, the <u>most important thing</u> in this business is trust.

3 Complete the sentences with the correct form of the word in brackets.

1 There'll be a .... (float) on the stock market.
2 The company is thinking of .... (locate) its head office away from the city.
3 We're thinking of .... (diverse) into other areas of the industry.
4 I don't know whether they'll sign but negotiations are still .... (go)
5 A .... (terminate) of the contract seems likely.
6 There was a sharp .... (turn) in profit and the business rapidly picked up.

4 Add the missing prepositions.

1 We buy all our supplies .... bulk.
2 She's really taken .... the new job.
3 We're expanding and will need to take .... more staff.
4 The bank was bailed .... by the government.
5 Can you talk me .... your proposal?
6 There's a rumour the company's in danger of going ....
7 We've been inundated .... queries about the new product.
8 Justice was brought .... bear on the CEO for embezzling company funds.

Score ___ /25

Wait a couple of weeks and try the quiz again.
Compare your scores.

VOCABULARY Style and fashion

1 Choose the correct options.

1 Those jeans are too *scruffy* / *stripy* for school, Jimmy! Put on a smarter pair.
2 OK, I'll wear *flares* / *high heels*, but my feet'll be killing me all night.
3 She wore this backless number, and it was very *conventional* / *revealing*, I can tell you!
4 As soon as I bent down, they *spotted* / *split* at the seam. It was so embarrassing!
5 What a lovely necklace! Those *beads* / *laces* really set off your top!
6 I tried on this *ripped* / *linen* shirt, and it felt lovely and cool.
7 I'm not sure about the fur *collar* / *flats* on this jacket. Have you got anything plainer?
8 When it's hot, I pull my hair back in *wedges* / *a ponytail*.

2 Match 1–6 with a–f to make collocations.

1	smart	a	jacket
2	woollen	b	collar
3	zipped	c	sweater
4	sturdy	d	dress
5	summery	e	clothes
6	frayed	f	shoes

3 Complete the sentences with a word from box A and a word from box B.

A	bob	checked	lining
	conventional	silk	worn out

B	shades	formal	ripped
	trainers	knee-length	spotted

1 She decided on a cream-coloured .... shirt and a .... skirt in olive-green for the meeting with the board.
2 He's very .... in the way he dresses, wearing quite .... clothes to work, and this belies his rather wild, bohemian lifestyle.
3 Those .... old .... of yours need throwing out. Go and buy some new ones before football practice tomorrow.
4 He's wearing a .... shirt with a .... tie. They really clash!
5 She has her hair in a .... , and hides her face behind huge dark ....
6 The .... in my jacket is .... , Mum. Can you repair it for me?

LISTENING

4 🔊 15.1 Listen to five short extracts in which people talk about fashion. Match the professions / people (a–g) with the speakers. There are two extra professions that you don't need to use.

Speaker 1 ....   Speaker 4 ....
Speaker 2 ....   Speaker 5 ....
Speaker 3 ....

a online shopping consultant
b clothes shop manager
c manufacturer of beauty products
d consumer
e fashion editor
f male model
g fashion designer

5 Identify the places and say which speaker mentions them.

1 .... Speaker ....   2 .... Speaker ....

6 Listen again and match the statements about fashion (a–h) with the speakers (1–5).

a Items sold to men need to be presented differently. ....
b Striking accessories are very effective. ....
c Men are no longer restricted in what they wear. ....
d There is a huge discrepancy in the treatment of the sexes. ....
e The industry can be intimidating. ....
f Both men and women can enjoy exactly the same products. ....
g Really original items can rarely be found in mainstream shops. ....
h The industry is ageist. ....

7 Choose the correct adjectives.

1 She wore a very *skimpy / curvaceous* skirt to show off her long legs.
2 He wears very *flamboyant / subtle* clothes to get attention.
3 That bracelet is really *eye-catching / off-putting*. Where can I get one?
4 That dress is very *feminine / female* and pretty.
5 His usual style is very *bland / bold* – he doesn't like to draw attention to himself.

DEVELOPING CONVERSATIONS
Backtracking and correcting

8 Choose the correct words to complete the questions.

1 Don't you like my hair permed, *then / right*?
2 So, you think I should *lose / quit* the beard?
3 What's *bad / wrong* with my jacket?
4 So you think these colours *clash / suit*?
5 *Are you saying / Do you say* I look silly in these boots?
6 You're not keen *with / on* this dress?

Language note confirming opinions

When someone thinks you don't like something about them and asks for confirmation of your opinion with a negative question, we usually give a negative reply.
A: *Don't you like my hair, then?* (I'm worried / angry because you've given me the impression you don't like my hair.)
B: *No, no, I think it suits you!* (No, I didn't say I don't like it. I actually like it.)

9 Match the questions in exercise 8 (1–6) with the replies (a–f).

a .... No, not at all! They're just rather bright, that's all.
b .... I like the design. I'm just not sure about that collar.
c .... I do! All I meant was I'm not used to you with it like that.
d .... It's not that it doesn't suit you. It's just more low-cut than you normally wear.
e .... No, I didn't say that. I'm just used to you being clean-shaven.
f .... No, that's not what I meant. I just think you should have worn something smarter for the wedding.

DEVELOPING CONVERSATIONS Defining yourself

10 Match the sentence halves.

1 As both a teacher and a parent,
2 As a male model,
3 As a creator of beauty products,
4 As a teenager who's interested in fashion,
5 As an image consultant,
6 As a psychologist and a mother,

a obviously I'm concerned about getting a fair deal for my work.
b I try to encourage young people to maintain a positive self-image.
c I'm concerned about the extent to which even young children are influenced by fashion.
d I believe grooming for men is just as important as it is for women.
e I worry about how I look.
f I feel appearance is vital if you want to create a good impression.

PRONUNCIATION
Stress in corrections and contradictions

Language note corrections and contradictions

When we correct or contradict someone, we stress the word or words which make clear what we want to correct or contradict. We sometimes stress syllables which are not normally stressed to show a contrast.
A: *You thought he was pleasant?*
B: *No, I thought he was unpleasant!*

11 🔊 15.2 Listen and underline the stress in B's replies.

1 A: You didn't like him, then?
  B: But I did, actually.
2 A: So, you liked the show?
  B: No, I said I disliked the show.
3 A: You must have overslept!
  B: No, you're early!
4 A: So it's true. You were laughing at me!
  B: No, I wasn't laughing. That's not true!
5 A: It's your turn to do the shopping.
  B: No, it's not my turn. I did it yesterday.
6 A: You must have seen her!
  B: No, I can't have seen her. I wasn't there!

12 Practise saying the mini-dialogues in exercise 11, copying the intonation.

READING

1 Quickly read the web page opposite, ignoring the gaps. What sort of website would you expect to find this page on?

a the website of an online fashion store for men

b the website of an image consultant agency

c the website of a business magazine for people in the fashion industry

2 Read the web page again. Choose the sentence (a–h) that best fits each gap (1–7). There is one extra sentence that you don't need to use.

a But they also like confidence, so remember to stay true to who you are.

b An image consultant will help you to achieve this.

c Find out which image consultants are members of a recognised association.

d Then, to save you precious time, our experts can do the leg work, gathering samples and bringing them to you.

e You will be amazed how paying attention to such small details can make a huge difference to the message you convey to the world.

f Personal shoppers earn commission so will encourage you to buy expensive brands.

g In contrast, image consultants have no such restrictions placed on them.

h In our view, this makes them a bargain!

3 Replace the underlined phrases with the correct form of the phrases in the box.

build a rapport with	do the leg work
drag around	go about
rip off	speak volumes

1 The way you dress <u>tells other people a lot</u> about who you are.

2 I got <u>taken unwillingly around</u> the shops yesterday – for three long, terrible hours!

3 Let me <u>do the physical work</u> around the shops while you stay here and relax.

4 To be honest, I'm a bit concerned about being <u>cheated out of a lot of money</u>.

5 So, let's sit down and think about how we're going to <u>do</u> this.

6 The important thing to do is to <u>create a good relationship with</u> a potential client.

Style matters

The need to dress with style is no longer reserved exclusively for women. In today's society, your image speaks volumes.

Consider the following questions:

Do you feel confident in what you wear?

Are you making the impression you want?

Here are some FAQs and answers.

Why should I spend money on an image consultant when many department stores offer their own personal shoppers for free?

Remember that the personal shopper is employed to promote the store's products. [1]....... This means that they won't put pressure on you to buy something you don't really like. In fact, they may actually save you money by helping you to avoid making expensive mistakes. [2]....... What's more, they won't just assess your clothes but will take into account your whole image – something you won't get from a store shopper.

I hate shopping. Will I get dragged round lots of shops?

Hiring an image consultant makes shopping fast and easy. An initial interview will give the consultant an idea of your personal tastes, needs and budget. [3]....... All you have to do is try them on.

Glossary

FAQs: frequently asked questions

personal shopper: someone employed to help you shop

venture: (business) project

Q I'm looking for investors for my new venture. How can I look like I'm worth it?

A In business, presentation is everything. Your appearance acts as an advertisement, so you need to sell yourself well! [4]....... He or she will help you make the right fashion choices to impress colleagues and clients, and may also give you advice on such things as the right haircut or watch. [5].......

Q How can I make myself more attractive to women?

A This is quite simple. Either get a woman's perspective or ask a consultant for help! Women prefer a man who dresses with style. [6]....... A good image consultant will help you to create a style which will not only suit you, but will also reflect your individual personality. Then you're ready for that date!

Q How do I know I'm not getting ripped off?

A With so many style consultants available, you should be careful choosing one to work with. First, do your research. [7]....... You can use our website to help you with this. Then interview at least three people before making your choice. If they are unwilling to meet you before they get paid, cross them off your list. During the interview, pay attention to the kind of questions they ask you, and decide whether they really understand what you're looking for.

GRAMMAR Prepositions

4 Choose the correct prepositions.

● ○ ○

The sari

Entry Links

The Indian sari is reputedly the most enduring fashion item [1]*in / of* the world. Its origins are obscure, but it is at least 5,000 years old, dating back [2]*to / in* the beginnings of the Indus Valley civilisation. [3]*On / At* one point [4]*in / of* time, both men and women wore the dhoti or lungi, [5]*from / with* which the sari is said to have evolved. Originally, it was worn only around the lower part of the body, but [6]*by / with* the arrival of the British, women began wearing a petticoat or 'ghagra' and a blouse known as a 'choli' underneath the sari. Technically, it is a long piece of cloth made [7]*from / by* silk or cotton. Now the material is manufactured in factories, but formerly it was woven [8]*from / by* hand, each piece with its own unique pattern or theme. Hindus believed that cloth pierced by a needle was impure, which is why no seams, buttons or zips are sewn [9]*in / into* the sari.

VOCABULARY Snowclones

5 Complete the sentences with a suitable phrase in the box.

my middle name	the flatmate from hell
life's too short	the new 'speak'
of whom you speak	it was the mother of all
the word 'mutt' in the dictionary	not as we know it

1 'Is that Nagu playing the violin?' 'Yes. It's music, but ....'
2 Oh no! Gareth's left all his dirty dishes again! He's ....!
3 'You go base jumping? Awesome!' 'Don't you know, 'Danger' is ....'
4 Did you hear that thunder last night? .... storms.
5 Who is this guild master .... ?
6 If you look up ...., you'll find a picture of our dog, Scampy.
7 'Everyone tweets these days!' 'I know. 'Tweet' is ....
8 'Pink hair, brightly patterned tights ... What's that all about?' 'Well, ... for dull colours.'

VOCABULARY Verb forms and word families

1 Complete the word family table.

verb	noun	adjective
		simple / simplified
	mystery	
		commercial / commercialised
lighten		
	authority	
		(un)justified / (un)justifiable
idealise		
	width	

2 Complete the sentences with the correct form of the word in brackets. You may need to add a suffix, prefix or both.

1 I think the manager was .... in dismissing Tom for being late. It hadn't happened before. (justify)
2 She was .... by his disappearance. He'd had no reason to leave. (mystery)
3 .... is when you view yourself not as a person but as a physical object. (objectify)
4 Attributing all teenage violence to the prevalence of online gaming is a vast .... of the issues surrounding this problem. (simple)
5 I worry about the consequences of using skin-.................... products on a daily basis. (light)
6 She felt .... by the fact that after dieting continuously for two months she had only lost two kilograms. (heart)

DEVELOPING WRITING
An informal letter – using input material

3 Last summer Henny had a job at a fashion show. She has received a letter from her friend Isadora asking her about her job. Read an extract from the letter and an extract from Henny's diary for last year. On balance, do you think Henny will recommend the job?

....

Would you recommend the job? I really want to meet some designers and make contacts for my fashion career. If I could use my English and get useful work experience too, that would be great! Would I make enough money for a holiday at the end? Thanks!
Isadora

10 July

Been here a week but haven't spoken to any designers yet - too busy! Translating for the English and American models is fun, but lots of boring admin work! Luckily, money's not bad and I get to see the show for free.

4 Read Henny's reply and check your answer to exercise 3.

Dear Isadora,

Great to hear from you! How's it going? It's been quite full-on here, but I'm looking forward to the summer break! About the job I had last summer, there are a couple of things you should think about.

Making useful business contacts may be tricky. You won't have a lot of free time. The only contact I had with a designer was when I took one a coffee one morning.

The work's quite repetitive. Most of the time you'd be backstage, doing dull admin jobs like answering the phone and stuff like that. I did get to act as an interpreter for the English and American models, though, which was a fantastic experience.

You'll be glad to know, however, that the pay was pretty good and I managed to save. Don't forget that I travelled round Peru for two weeks after I'd finished. I also saw the fashion show for free, which would otherwise have been beyond my reach!

So, would I recommend it? Definitely, if you're hoping to practise your English and make a bit of money. It probably isn't the best place for making contacts or varied work experience, but it's a start, and it isn't a bad way to begin. Let me know what you decide.

Best wishes,
Henny

5 For 1–8, find words and phrases in Henny's letter that are more informal.

1 difficult ....
2 How are you? ....
3 other, similar activities ....
4 the job was well remunerated ....
5 please inform me ....
6 busy ....
7 unaffordable ....
8 with regards to ....

6 Read the task in the box and the extracts that follow. Then write a letter to your friend (200–240 words) saying whether or not you would recommend the job and giving reasons.

> Last summer you had a job with a large department store in a city that is popular with international tourists. Your friend Enrique has written to ask you about it. Read an extract from Enrique's letter and an extract from your diary below, then write your letter.

> Would the job suit me? I'd particularly like to work in the fashion department because I think it'd be more interesting. It would be great if I could get some useful work experience and practise my languages. I'd like to make enough money for a holiday too.
> All the best,
> Enrique

> **11 August**
>
> End of first week! Hard work. Head of Fashion's a bit strict but music department's really friendly. Lots of variety. Good for meeting people – customers and staff from all over the world. Money's not great but might pay for a camping trip to the beach.

Vocabulary Builder Quiz 15

Download the Vocabulary Builder for Unit 15 and try the quiz below. Write your answers in your notebook. Then check them and record your score.

1 Replace the <u>underlined</u> words and phrases with phrasal verbs from the Vocabulary Builder for Unit 15.
1 At the formal dinner, he <u>was really conspicuous</u> in his electric blue suit.
2 She <u>chose</u> a strapless satin dress for the party.
3 It was a hard game but they <u>managed to win</u>.
4 The bob <u>is likely to</u> make a comeback next season, according to fashion experts.
5 Clever marketing persuades teenage consumers to <u>accept new fashion items</u>.
6 The craze for asymetric hairstyles is <u>dying down now</u>.

2 Choose the correct words.
1 The *incidence / implication* of credit card fraud in the area is on the rise.
2 Many of our personality *markings / traits* are genetically inherited.
3 In most cultures, facial and body hair is seen as a sign of *masculinity / obscurity*.
4 We are investigating every angle to try and *shield / pinpoint* the cause of the accident.
5 For many people, their height and weight can have a *valid / profound* impact on their self-esteem.
6 Sports shoe manufacturers tend to rely on *endorsements / epidemics* from celebrity athletes to promote their products.
7 I often feel *worn out / disorientated* by the rate at which technology develops.

3 Choose the odd one out in each set.
1 bob gelled seam ponytail
2 lining laces lapel sleeve
3 loud revealing scruffy flares
4 flats high heels shades wedges
5 bangle zip beads belt
6 bushy paisley stripy tartan

4 Add the missing words.
1 Her new book is set top the best seller list a week after its release.
2 We need to take board feedback from our customers, even if it's negative.
3 60% of the men in the group opted keep their beard.
4 I think this trend is on wane now.
5 Many parents want to shield their children the negative influence of the media.
6 She likes to wear her hair a ponytail.

Score ____/25

Wait a couple of weeks and try the quiz again.
Compare your scores.

LISTENING

1 🔊 16.1 Listen to three extracts of people talking. Identify the main speakers in each extract. Choose from the list a–h.
a police officer
b writer
c office worker
d member of a rescue team
e mother
f manager
g soldier
h competitive climber

Speaker 1 ....
Speaker 2 ....
Speaker 3 ....

2 Read the situations and the questions. Then listen again and choose the correct answers.

Extract 1
You hear part of an interview with a man called Jacek Grzes, who's talking about his job.

1 Jacek says that most people who visit the mountain
   a are aware of the possible danger.
   b are ill equipped to deal with the weather.
   c intend only to stay for a short time.
2 How did the English tourist react to being rescued?
   a He appeared to be embarrassed.
   b He seemed to be annoyed.
   c He was relieved to be safe at last.

Extract 2
You hear part of an interview with a woman called Geraldine Grey, who's talking about her family history.

3 Geraldine's grandfather did not marry her grandmother because
   a he was unaware she was having his child.
   b he was forced to rejoin the war.
   c she had told him their relationship was over.
4 What does Geraldine say about risks?
   a It's better to take a risk than to regret letting an opportunity pass by.
   b People often don't think about the consequences of taking a risk.
   c Men and women tend to have a different attitude towards risks.

Extract 3
You hear a man telling a friend about something that happened at work.

5 Why did he decide to take a risk?
   a He wanted to impress his work colleagues.
   b He needed an increase in salary.
   c He believed it was what his employer wanted.
6 After having taken the risk, he felt
   a justified.   b humiliated.   c confused.

PRONUNCIATION Final /t/

Language note /t/

In normal, fluent speech, the /t/ sound is often omitted at the end of a word. However, the /t/ is pronounced if
• the word stands alone
• the next word begins with a vowel sound or /h/.

3 **Underline** the words in which the final /t/ sound can be omitted.
1 They've come with the right gear.
2 Wait. I'll just catch my breath.
3 'The next step could have been fatal.' 'Quite.'
4 We're leaving on the first of March.
5 He was sent home to get over a leg wound.
6 I remember quite clearly. I left it there.

4 🔊 16.2 Listen, check and repeat.

DEVELOPING CONVERSATIONS Interjections

5 Choose the best responses.
1 And after two nights stuck on the mountain, the fog finally lifted and we were safe!
   a Oi!   b Phew!   c Mmm …
2 And I said, well, what with the weather and one thing and another, you know what it's like …
   a Mmm …   b Wow!   c Ahem!
3 I dropped the big dictionary on my foot.
   a Oi!   b Sshhh!   c Ouch!
4 What's happening in the meeting? Can you hear anything through the door?
   a Gosh!   b Woah!   c Sshhh!
5 You've got time to hear all about my trip to the train museum, haven't you? Well, …
   a Oops!   b Phew!   c Umm …

6 Read the situations and complete the responses with suitable interjections. Use some of the words that you *didn't* choose in exercise 5.

1 A friend is talking about eating some roasted snake on holiday. It was a local delicacy.
You: .... That sounds disgusting!
2 You're talking to someone who drops their phone on the floor.
You: .... That was kind of clumsy.
3 Your good friend surprises you with the news that he's about to get married.
You: .... You've been keeping that one quiet!
4 Your aunt is going on holiday and she is giving you a very long list of all the tasks she wants you to do while she's away.
You: .... Find another slave!
5 You're trying to study, but your neighbours are having a loud party.
You: .... Would you mind turning it down a little?

VOCABULARY Accidents and injuries

7 Choose the option which is not correct.
1 I could see blood *streaming / tearing / pouring* from the wound.
2 With the heat and lack of air, I *came to / passed out / fainted* and lay unconscious on the ground.
3 All around us people were *panicking / freaking out / banging* in the rush to escape.
4 After the accident, I was in *consciousness / agony / terrible pain*.
5 The cyclist had a *gash / cut / burn* across his forehead from hitting his head on the kerb.
6 His leg was bleeding *deeply / profusely / heavily* and we knew it was serious.
7 The faulty hairdressing equipment actually *ripped / tore / sliced* some of her hair out.
8 The bone *whacked / broke / snapped* loudly.

VOCABULARY Laws and regulations

8 Complete the mini-dialogues. Use a verb from box A and a noun from box B. You may need to use them the other way round.

A			
	awarded	set	dismissed
	opposed	overturned	sued

B			
	conviction	damages	legislation
	precedent	libel	grounds

1 A: What's the news on Dan's lawsuit?
   B: Oh, the judge .... the case on the .... of reasonable doubt. It seems the evidence wasn't conclusive.
2 A: Look at this. I hate it when the newspapers write such obvious lies about celebrities.
   B: Yeah, but then the celebrities go to court and get .... loads of money in .... if they can prove it was all untrue.
3 A: You heard about that millionaire accused of murder? Well, he was found guilty this morning.
   B: Yeah, but his lawyers will probably invent some new evidence and his .... will be .... on appeal. There's no way he's actually going to go to prison!
4 A: I notice that the documentary didn't mention the company's name, even though everyone knows they've been selling fake goods.
   B: Yeah, but at the time that hadn't been proved in court. If anyone mentioned their name, the company could have .... them for ....
5 A: Have you heard? They've agreed to the union's terms after all.
   B: I know, but the management's decision to agree to all their demands will .... a dangerous .... for future industrial disputes.
6 A: Why did it take so long for the new law about safety regulations to come in?
   B: A lot of people really .... the .... , and there were big campaigns against it. Some companies felt it would affect their profit margins.

READING

1 Quickly read the first paragraph of the web page opposite. What is the writer's main intention?

a to promote adventure holidays for a travel company

b to give useful warnings to travellers planning an adventure holiday

c to give information about the best adventure holidays available

2 Now read the whole web page. For questions 1–11, choose from the descriptions (A–D).
Which holiday or activity

1 might you want to remember with a particular kind of souvenir? ....

2 will still affect you after you've returned? ....

3 is no longer dangerous? ....

4 may result in your getting lost if you don't take care? ....

5 should you research first to make the most of it? ....

6 does the writer not recommend to people with a fear of heights? ....

7 may include some historical sight-seeing? ....

8 would be too intimidating for the writer to undertake? ....

9 may require certain documentation in advance? ....

10 do you have to use the equipment supplied? ....

11 is best avoided at a certain time of year? ....

3 Choose the correct words.

1 Check out the online video of El Caminito. Just watching it makes my stomach *churn / jut*!

2 I like adventure, but I *draw / cross* the line when it comes to free climbing. No way!

3 After seeing *Jaws*, even going into shallow water will *conjure / post* up feelings of terror!

4 The skydiving sounds more like me, but I guess I've got a reasonable *head / heart* for heights.

5 Feel the adrenalin *rush / plunge* as you sky-dive over the Grand Canyon. It's electrifying!

6 They pushed me out of the plane without a *word / caution* of warning.

○○○

Holidays for ... **thrill-seekers**

For most people, the thought of leaping out of a plane or getting up close to a shark conjures up feelings of terror. But if you're a **thrill-seeker**, these may sound like ideal vacation options. Having posted up some of my own adventures a few months ago, I've been inundated with your adrenalin-rushing recommendations. Here are some that particularly stood out.

A Swakopmund, Namibia

This seaside town has reinvented itself as a year-round adventure playground thanks to its wild surf and rough desert terrain. Quad-biking is the main attraction, but go out into the wilderness by yourself and you're likely to become utterly disoriented in the endless shifting sand. No need to get a map – simply hire one of the local guides, who are very good value and can also point out the disconcerting Horses Graveyard, a site where the sun-bleached remains of hundreds of horses from the Second World War still lie. It's an eerie sight which I've been told will haunt your dreams for a long time.

B El Caminito del Rey, Spain

Nerves of steel are required to take the pathway, three kilometres long and three metres wide, that runs along the steep walls of a narrow gorge in El Chorro, Malaga. Getting lost in the view is not an option – you'll be too busy concentrating. Closed for many years after several walkers fell to their deaths from its decaying paths, it re-opened in 2015 after extensive renovation. The new secure walkway and compulsory safety equipment mean visitors are no longer dicing with death, but the path is just as narrow, and still clings precariously to the sheer cliffs over 100 metres above the river below, so vertigo sufferers should give this one a miss!

Holidays for ... | Home
by Location

C Queenstown, New Zealand

Queenstown is an unbeatable destination for those wishing to sky-dive out of a plane at an insane altitude of 15,000 feet. Obviously, a professional will do all the necessary tugging of cords, but it's still a terrifying experience! Luckily, you'll quickly recover from the shock. Be aware, though, that elderly would-be divers might be required to show a certificate of fitness – heart attacks have been known! Most tourists opt for being filmed on the way down, and while I can't help feeling this is a bit of a vacation cliché, you'll definitely want to show off the footage back home. Going off-peak is a better bet to avoid the long waiting-list.

D Gansbaii, South Africa

Offering yourself up as shark bait? This is probably where even I would draw the line. If you've seen the classic film *Jaws*, you'll have already heard the line 'DON'T GO IN THE WATER'! But if you're made of sterner stuff than me, then head for Gansbaii and the local shark-infested sea. Come summer or winter, you can simply pop yourself into a cage and be plunged into the depths. The cage is attached to a boat, so you won't vanish completely. But check out the local operators carefully before signing up because they all have different deals – not to mention safety records!

Glossary

thrill-seeker: person who enjoys doing dangerous activities for fun
cord: rope
bait: food used to persuade an animal to come nearer

VOCABULARY Synonyms

4 Complete the pairs of sentences with the words in the boxes.

peril	threat

1 Many small business now under ....

2 Ignore your fatty diet at your .... !

hazards	menace

3 Clear up all the health .... on our beaches!

4 'We need help combating drugs .... ' admits Government

danger	risk

5 Strict parents run the .... of alienating teenagers says expert

6 Skipper survives journey fraught with ....

risk	threat

7 Protestors pose grave .... to peace talks says minister

8 Binge-drinking teens putting themselves at ....

5 For 1–4, use *one* word from exercise 4 to complete all three sentences in the set.

1 The accused was described as a .... to society.
We must tackle the .... of under-age drinking.
He was a man with .... – everyone avoided him.

2 A dirty kitchen is a serious health ....
These piles of cardboard are a potential fire .... , so clear them up.
Icy conditions are causing a major road ....

3 He told police he'd received a death .... in the post.
The villagers saw the new law as a .... to their way of life.
The .... of attack is now becoming all too real.

4 There's no .... of Andrew applying for the manager's job, is there?
We believe the patient is now out of ....
Children at school need to learn about .... so they know how to avoid it.

DEVELOPING WRITING

An online comment – linking ideas

> **Learner tip**
>
> Effective writers avoid repetition by using pronouns or other reference words to talk about points, things or people mentioned previously.

1 Read the online comment. What do the underlined words refer to?

1 it   ....
2 this   ....
3 these   ....
4 What   ....
5 so   ....

Blog spot ● YOUR SAY *This week's topic:*
the proposal to raise the legal driving age

● Does anyone else find it extraordinary that the government is considering raising the driving age to 18? We knew that ¹it always intended getting tough on crime, and I accept ²this also included stricter penalties for drunk and speeding drivers. ᵃ................. , punishing a whole age group is wrong, particularly when the vast majority have committed no crime.

● It's clear that the government is under pressure to act. A growing number of adolescents are involved in road accidents, drink- or drug-driving, illegal drag racing – all of ³these make sensational headlines in the media. The public is ᵇ................. convinced the roads are no longer safe. Obviously, something needs to be done. But how is raising the driving age going to remove all the risks? Dangerous driving isn't a habit that ends when you turn 18. ᶜ................. , countless middle-aged and elderly people cause havoc on the roads.

● ᵈ................. the best way to tackle this, there are a number of options. ⁴What's clear is that driving is hazardous, no matter who's behind the wheel. If we truly want to bring the accident toll down, we need to get tough with repeat offenders, whatever their age. ᵉ................. , all motorists should be obliged to take regular courses ᶠ................. keep their driving skills current. By doing ⁵so, everyone's potential to cause accidents will be reduced and we won't just be punishing young people.

2 Complete the gaps (a–f) in the online comment with the words and phrases in box A.

A	as for	as well as this	but still	in order to
	indeed	therefore		

3 Which words and phrases in box B could also complete gaps a–f?

B	consequently	in fact	on top of this
	nevertheless	so as to	with respect to

4 Complete the sentences with phrases from exercises 2 and 3.

1 Thrill-seekers put their own lives at risk. .... , they often endanger the lives of their rescuers.
2 Anyone who smokes is bound to be aware of the risks. .... , you cannot escape the constant health warnings in the media.
3 I can't help feeling that many people take up dangerous activities .... impress their friends.
4 Some activities, such as surfing and paragliding, need more regulation. .... climbing without ropes, it should be completely outlawed.
5 Most smokers know that they should quit. .... , the fact that nicotine is addictive makes this hard.
6 Smokers pay a particularly high tax on a packet of cigarettes. They should .... be entitled to full health care provision.

5 Write a comment (220–260 words) expressing your views about *one* of the new government proposals, a or b. Include ideas from exercise 4 or some of your own.

a People undertaking dangerous sports or activities should pay if they have to be rescued.
b Smokers should pay an extra tax for medical treatment.

GRAMMAR Talking about the future

6 Choose the correct words.

1 The story of the climbers' survival is due *to / for* release in cinemas this month.
2 With my luck, it's *bound / set* to rain for the entire weekend!
3 *With / In* all probability, there'll be at least a couple of accidents in this kind of weather.
4 There's a distinct *odds / possibility* that Patu will be injured in this game.
5 I'm due *to / for* start my new course on Monday.
6 The *possibilities / chances* of that kind of disaster happening are pretty slim.

7 Rewrite the sentences using the words in brackets. Use no more than *five* words in each gap.

1 The President's meeting with the Prime Minister is probably going to take place in December.
   The President ....
   the Prime Minister in December. (set)
2 We're supposed to renew your contract next month.
   Your contract ....
   next month. (due)
3 An accident is fairly likely for Logan.
   Logan ....
   an accident. (bound)
4 There's a strong chance we'll reach the summit within a couple of days.
   The ....
   reach the summit within a couple of days. (odds)
5 The researchers believe that they have almost found a cure.
   The researchers believe that they are ....
   .... a cure. (verge)
6 It's just possible that Nathan's plan will work.
   I think ....
   that Nathan's plan will work. (slim)
7 I doubt that Prash will survive the operation.
   In ....
   survive the operation. (likelihood)
8 The search party has just announced that they will probably stop looking soon.
   The search party has just announced that they ....
   .... quitting. (point)

Vocabulary Builder Quiz 16

Download the Vocabulary Builder for Unit 16 and try the quiz below. Write your answers in your notebook. Then check them and record your score.

1 Add the missing prepositions.

1 When I came ...., I was lying in a hospital bed.
2 The party was boring so we sneaked .... to a bar for a quiet drink.
3 This stretch of the river is fraught .... hidden obstacles like submerged rocks.
4 Then, to top the whole thing ...., she went base jumping.
5 Counsel for the Defence, kindly confine yourself .... the facts of the case.
6 We installed an alarm system to guard .... theft.

2 Match 1–7 with a–g to make collocations.

1	finalise	a	a case
2	set	b	a lawsuit
3	stumble	c	a law
4	repeal	d	a deal
5	file	e	a precedent
6	dismiss	f	the opportunity
7	welcome	g	over something

3 Choose the correct words.

1 I almost lost control of the car and was on the *verge / view* of crashing.
2 He had his skateboard *confined / confiscated* after he broke his leg.
3 Ignore this storm warning at your *peril / hazard*.
4 She knocked over the pan of hot soup and *scalded / sliced* her arm badly.
5 He made some *distinct / absurd* claim that I'd hit him on purpose. As if I'd do that!

4 Complete the sentences with the correct form of the words in brackets.

1 The student was found guilty of .... (plagiarise).
2 A case like this is .... (precedent); we've never seen anything like it before.
3 .... (Menace) clouds threatened rain.
4 We'll carry out an .... (appraise) of the risk.
5 The roadworks caused severe .... (disrupt).
6 The company was cleared of .... (negligent).
7 Hotel guests have legal .... (liable) for any damage they cause.

Score ___ /25

Wait a couple of weeks and try the quiz again. Compare your scores.

AUDIOSCRIPT

UNIT 01

🔊 **1.1**

P = Presenter; A = Aytak; E = Eileen

P: OK, so next up we're looking at student life in the city. First, I'd like to welcome two international students to the studio – Aytak from Turkey and Eileen from Canada.

A/E: Hello.

P: So, Aytak, how do you like the city? A bit chilly, eh?

A: More than a bit! I can't believe how many people go around in T-shirts. I've been piling on the layers.

P: So, you don't think much of the place, then?

A: Oh, no! Quite the opposite, in fact. The centre's so compact, for a start ... and there are no cars, so you can walk everywhere.

P: I agree, yeah, that's a real plus point ... And how are you liking it here, Eileen?

E: Well, personally, I can't get enough of this weather – I'm from Canada, so to me this is mild! But I agree with Aytak about the pedestrian zone. I really enjoy shopping on the high street. But ...

P: Go on, we can take a bit of criticism!

E: Hmm, yes, well, once you get out into the suburbs, it's not so nice. Some parts are filthy, actually – there's lots of litter.

A: Oh, you'd hardly notice it! My hometown's in a hot, dry part of the country, so there's a lot of dust and sand everywhere. To me, this place is practically spotless.

P: What about the locals? How're you getting on with them?

A: It was tough at first just to understand anyone. The thing is, I reckon my English is quite good ...

P: It's excellent.

A: Thanks, but when I first came here I felt like a beginner again! Everyone talks so fast!

E: Hmm, even I struggle to make out what people are saying sometimes. So you must have found it impossible, Aytak!

A: Yeah ... although I'm getting better now. Luckily, most people have been really helpful ...

P: Most people?

A: Well, a couple of times, I've had some hassle ... just teasing really, no big deal. In general, everyone's been really welcoming.

P: Good to hear it! What're your thoughts, Eileen? Are we a friendly bunch, or ...?

E: Oh, totally! And I've been amazed by the way people go out of their way to help you. In my first week, I asked this lady for directions ... She actually walked me all the way to where I wanted to go, because she said some places could be dangerous if you didn't know your way around.

A: Hmm, I've never felt in any danger.

E: Hmm, crime's a bit of a problem, I think, especially in some of the more deprived areas. You've got to take care.

P: Yes, just like in a lot of big cities, I think ... Oops, we're running out of time, so one last question: what about the nightlife, guys?

E: Yeah! Wild! I mean, some clubs are really buzzing.

A: Hmm, clubbing isn't really my thing, so I can't comment on that. I've been impressed by the restaurants, though.

P: All good stuff! Thanks, both of you! We're going to take a little break now, and ...

🔊 **1.2**

1   I swear, the shop was filthy inside!
2   The woman in the baker's was incredibly helpful.
3   Honestly, the stench was unbearable!
4   It was really, really great to see you again!
5   Seriously, he drove like crazy to get here!
6   Getting across town was a nightmare!

UNIT 02

🔊 **2.1**
Speaker 1

At work, the relationship has to remain professional. There's no room for domestic quarrels! I think, first off, establishing clearly defined roles is vital. Of the two of us, Tony's more of a 'people' person, so he's the one who tends to deal with clients. On the other hand, he's absent-minded about admin, so I run the organisational side of things. We meet in the office at the end of the day to address any problems there and then – we don't take anything home with us. Then, three times a week, we go to separate gyms after work – sometimes, you just need to get away from each other for a bit! We try hard to set boundaries and strike a balance. Going away together on vacation was a major problem in the beginning, because there were just the two of us and we couldn't leave the office unstaffed. This caused arguments and put a strain on our relationship, even though we'd been married for years ... I almost walked out, it was so bad. But now we close the office for ten days every August. You can overcome any challenge if you put your mind to it!

Speaker 2

Work out our differences? You must be joking! I'll never work with him again! You know, I thought I could trust him ... I mean, he's family, right? But I should have known. He was like that at school, always vying for attention, always had to be the best. Dad used to try and be fair to us both, but it didn't make any difference. Anyway, I thought we'd got over that, and when we first started working together, it was fine ... for a while. I think he's actually a pretty good salesman, and said so – but it turns out the feeling wasn't mutual. He was soon up to his old tricks again, always criticising my work, making bitchy remarks. To make things worse, it turned out he'd also been stealing my clients behind my back! I complained, of course, but nothing came of it. So, I quit ... Some problems just can't be fixed.

Speaker 3

Nan's getting on a bit now, but it still amazes me how fresh her art seems. You wouldn't know we were two generations apart. Her illustrations for each book have a youthfulness that I find inspiring and she always seems to capture the images I have in my mind ... But then, it was her pictures that inspired me to write in the first place, after all! She says my stories inspire her to paint, too, which is nice! The main hurdle we had to overcome was being able to accept each other's comments. It all felt too personal – after all, I could still remember sitting on her knee when I was a kid! But we got over it, eventually. We had to! And actually, having someone who can review your work constructively is incredibly useful, even if sometimes you end up agreeing to disagree. Luckily, we're both usually fairly easy-going, laid-back kind of people, so we haven't had too many major dramas!

✪ 2.2

1 I'd've thought you'd've been delighted!
2 He'll've finished it by tomorrow.
3 She said there'd be rain later, but I don't know if there will.
4 She couldn't've known who'd be there.
5 I would'nt've helped you, even if I could.
6 These're mine, but I don't know whose those are.

UNIT 03

✪ 3.1

Speaker 1

One of my favourite national celebrations is Martisor. It's celebrated in Romania and Moldova in early March, to welcome the end of winter. It's a very old tradition, possibly even pre-Christian, I think – largely without religious connotations now, anyway! Adults give each other inexpensive, often hand-made bows or bracelets made from interwoven red and white strings or ribbons. The two strands are supposed to symbolise winter and summer, and the relationship between men and women. If you wear one, it's supposed to bring you good fortune. These bows, called martisors, are worn for nine days. If someone gives you a martisor, you have to choose one of these nine days. If it's mild and warm on the day you picked, then you'll have a wonderful year ahead. Unfortunately I always seem to pick a day that pours!

Speaker 2

Chalandamarz is a Swiss festival – its name means the first of March. It's held in the Engadine valley region, near where I grew up. We used to celebrate it every year, although I don't know how authentic it is – apparently there aren't any records from before the last century, so I suspect it's a relatively recent custom. Anyway, it's certainly a very picturesque one and tourists love it! All the local boys dress up in blue shirts and red scarves and hang cowbells round their waists. You should see the size of some of them – I don't know how the younger boys manage to carry them! They march through the town, ringing the bells, and people give them sweets and cakes and sometimes a small amount of money. Last year we gave them hot chocolate too because it was freezing! The bells act as a blessing – according to folklore, any evil spirits are driven out by the sound. And believe me, by the end of the day, you'll be desperate for some peace and quiet, too!

Speaker 3

A couple of years ago I visited my friend Yoko in Japan and she took me to the Hinamatsuri festival at the Kada Shrine. It was amazing! This ornate temple was filled with thousands of dolls and figurines from all over Japan. It's a centuries-old tradition, from way back in the Heian period. The dolls are believed to bring happiness and prosperity to young girls. The dolls can cost families a small fortune – parents really go to town to get their daughters the best. People visit the temple in their finest, most colourful clothes and they give offerings to the gods. Many people bring peach blossom because the festival is held at the time the tree comes into bloom and the warmer weather begins. There's an elaborate ceremony, with priests and children praying and singing songs for the dolls – it's really quite beautiful, such a lovely sound. Then they load them all onto little boats and send them out to sea, taking all the girls' bad luck with them. It's a breathtaking sight.

✪ 3.2

A: It's important to respect religious beliefs.
B: Yes, I think that's essential.

A: We should teach religion in schools.
B: Oh, I don't know about that.

UNIT 04

✪ 4.1

1 charisma ... charming ... change ... charitable
2 compassion ... ruthlessness ... pressure ... obsession
3 wisdom ... pleasant ... hasty ... disaster
4 machine ... charming ... brochure ... chef
5 nature ... downturn ... statue ... fortunate
6 possessive ... issue ... dissolve ... scissors

✪ 4.2

Presenter

Hello and welcome to *World Watch*, our weekly look at issues shaping the world today. This week we're joining a debate which has risen to the top of the political agenda recently. The loss of plant and animal species around the globe is a growing concern, but what are governments really doing about the problems? And how will it affect us all, from the rich Western civilisations to the poorest countries in the Third World?

4.3

P = Presenter; S = Sara; L = Lyle

P: Now, I'm going to ask an obvious question. Several of the more right-wing ministers have suggested that the problem of loss of biodiversity is being over-exaggerated, while environmental scientists claim the issue's still being underestimated. Who's right?

S: Well, who do you think? Solving issues such as global warming and biodiversity loss will be expensive, but that's not what concerns me the most. We have to act now, not because what's happening is terribly sad – that's a given – but because it's irreversible. Once biodiversity has been lost, it's gone forever. This issue is about as serious as can be.

P: So, what should we do, Sara? Forgive me, I don't doubt your sincerity – it's your idealism that worries me. Are you suggesting we abandon our way of life and go back to living in huts?

S: No, of course not. However, drastic action is needed – yes, I agree with that.

L: I think I'll step in here, if I may ... Although I started out as a scientist, I'm now a politician, and I like to think I'm also a pragmatist, too. And I think we need to address this issue realistically.

S: *Slowly*, you mean, Lyle ...

L: Maybe, if necessary. I totally agree with you, Sara, that we need to develop environmentally friendly policies. The issue for me is whether we'd be sacrificing the economy in favour of wildlife.

S: But we can help both! In Brazil, for example, a group of farmers in the Amazon basin are currently planting an endangered species of wild cassava. As well as helping the plant, sales of the crop have also provided money for a hospital, new housing, and there's a school planned for next year. This in turn has given them a means to survive as they make money out of the crops. I'm totally in favour of initiatives like these.

L: Well, I don't know. That might work in the Amazon, but what could be done about farming in Europe? Despite being wealthy, these countries are also very heavily populated. The situation there is rather different.

S: That's why we've got to look at the issue globally. For me, the problem of biodiversity loss ranks alongside health care and defence in terms of seriousness, and way above local politics. We urgently need policymakers such as yourself to get together for some joined-up thinking, and ...

UNIT 05

5.1

1 You must be getting quite good at it.
2 It must've been amazing.
3 I bet that was awful.
4 I imagine she was quite relieved.
5 I bet she was mortified.
6 You must be getting pretty tired of it.

5.2

I = Ian; A = Amy

I: Hi, Amy! Goodness, you look awful! What have you been up to? Not another party again!

A: Umm? Oh, Ian! Hi. No, I haven't been to one for ages! Actually, I had a night in ... But I sat up till four playing *World of Warcraft*.

I: You? Playing *World of Warcraft*? Till four? I bet you're feeling a bit rough, then!

A: I am a bit, yeah.

I: I haven't played it yet, but I've heard it's really cool. But I didn't think you were into that kind of stuff?

A: Yeah. Well, I'd seen the adverts and they didn't really appeal – all those silly avatars, like something from *Harry Potter*. It was Mike who put me onto it, really. He'd been raving about it for months and eventually I just gave in.

I: So, uh, how did you rate it?

A: Oh, to be honest, I felt it didn't live up to the hype. I mean, I'd heard that the gameplay was pretty awesome, but the interface was really complicated and I was a bit overwhelmed by it all.

I: I wouldn't mind giving it a try ...

A: Well, I can lend it to you, if you like? Only not tonight. I was wondering about giving it another go, just to be fair. And then I'll quit, and it's all yours. I've done my last all-nighter ...

G = Gareth; J = John

G: So, John, don't you hit the town on Fridays any more, then?

J: Not as a rule. Now and again, but I've usually got other plans.

G: Such as ...?

J: Well, a group of us have set up this film club. We take it in turns to meet at each other's houses, someone sorts the food, someone brings the wine, and we're all set.

G: Huh, and you do that every Friday?

J: Pretty much.

G: You must get fed up of it sometimes, though. I mean, doesn't it get boring, doing the same thing all the time?

J: Not at all, it's great! Well, it's hard to beat the big screen at the cinema, but we more than make up for it with a great atmosphere – oh, and saving on cost!

G: Yeah, what got you started on that, then?

J: Well, we'd being talking about it for a while. Then Joanne got made redundant and we thought it would be a great way to cheer her up.

G: So what kind of films do you watch?

J: All sorts. The first time we did it, we chose a comedy with whatshername in it ... you know, the English actress with the posh name?

G: Er, oh, do you mean Helena Bonham Carter?

J: That's her! Can't remember the name of the film, but it was hilarious, and we were in stitches for most of the evening. Comedies aren't usually my sort of thing, but that's the great thing about this club, it broadens your mind. We've seen thrillers, horror flicks – I can't get enough of them. Even romances – although I'm not so keen on those.

G: Mmm, sounds interesting ... Well, perhaps I'll come and join you one Friday, then.

J: Sure, yeah. Why not?

UNIT 06

🔊 6.1
Speaker 1

That reminds me of the time when Carolyn, our old boss, had gone on maternity leave and they'd hired this new guy, Mark, to take over. He was pretty efficient, I guess, but well, it took about a week for office morale to go right down. He was just blatantly rude to people, even though he had a good team working for him. One day we had a meeting and I put an idea forward that I'd had ... something I'd been working on for a while ... and he just shot it down, like it was nothing. He said something sarcastic like, 'So how much money do you want the company to lose, Simon?' Hilarious. I couldn't believe he'd just spoken to me like that, in front of everyone. I didn't want to say something I'd regret, so I just sat there glaring for the rest of the meeting, refusing to participate. At the end, I spoke to him about it, but it didn't get me anywhere. It was a relief when Carolyn came back, I can tell you.

Speaker 2

A few years ago, I had a particularly unprofessional moment. You know, in my line of work, you're supposed to remain calm, no matter who your guest is or what they do. You can ask provocative questions, sure, but start a full-blown row – no. But when the Minister for Health came on, I just lost it. I started off fairly calm. I asked him to explain what had happened to the promises that had been made in the election campaign. He sort of made a joke and started evading the question, as they do. So I asked him again 'Why aren't you doing the things you committed to when you wanted our votes?' And he started talking about making efficiency savings, improving procedures, until I couldn't take any more. I suppose the topic was highly personal for me because my sister's a doctor and I knew how many hours she was putting in ... permanently exhausted, she was. Anyway, within minutes I'd basically accused him of lying, and he quite understandably got angry with me and I retaliated – both of us were literally shouting at one another. I could see my producer going white in horror, but somehow I couldn't stop myself. I refused to apologise and we haven't spoken since.

Speaker 3

Annie? Yes, I know her, she's in my tutorial group. We talk every now and again, but we don't always see eye-to-eye on things. Last seminar, she mentioned she was looking for a part-time job so she could pay off some of her student loan. And I mentioned that the government was thinking about increasing the minimum wage, which I thought she'd be happy about. But no. She went on about how this meant that employers would cut costs by cutting back on the number of people they hired, including her. Actually, her attitude irritated me because she was just thinking of herself, as usual. I mean, she's never been lazy, I'll give her that, but she's from a very wealthy background, it isn't the same for her. If you're a father trying to raise a family – you just can't do it on that kind of income. Anyway, in the end I just gave in. 'I see your point,' I said. Well, I couldn't be bothered to argue any more.

🔊 6.2

/s/	receive ... ceasefire ... associated
/k/	careful ... nuclear ... casualty
/dʒ/	intelligent ... rage ... legitimate
/g/	go ... negotiation ... agreement

Unit 07

🎧 7.1

1 Why on earth do you want to do that?
2 Believe me, you're making a mistake.
3 On the whole, it went very well.
4 It was a disaster, to say the least.
5 What in the world were you thinking of?
6 Funnily enough, the experiment was unsuccessful.

🎧 7.2

P = Professor; V = Dr Vermeulen

P: Please welcome one of the founding members of *Hear-It*, Dr Andrée Vermeulen!

V: Thank you, Professor. For those of you who may not be familiar with *Hear-It*, it's a charity based in Brussels which aims to raise public awareness of hearing impairment. I should make it clear that I'm in the hearing aid business myself, but I take a purely administrative role in the website to avoid bias. Now, to begin ... Can you all hear me?

🎧 7.3

In the mid 90s, there were 400 million hearing-impaired people globally, of which 70 million belonged to the 700 million strong European population, and 25 million to the 300 million people in North America. The European figures are thought to rise to 95 million within the next decade.

Remarkably, only one in five hearing-impaired Europeans uses an aid. There are a number of reasons for this: people may underestimate the severity of their own problem, or they worry that aids will look ugly – this is the biggest issue for newer generations – or perhaps they simply don't realise that help is available.

Hear-It runs an international website that aims to increase public awareness of hearing problems and help those who need it. We regularly publish articles about new products, and allow users to post their own comments about equipment they've used. We also give directions to online shops where people can purchase the products. The main message we try to convey is that, in most cases, problems can be improved by the right equipment.

Let me tell you about Ashkan Tehrani. An Iranian engineer, Ashkan suffered his hearing loss in silence for many years. After coming across our website, he realised it didn't have to be that way. Now, fully kitted out in the latest aids fitted with wi-fi technology, Ashkan not only works in engineering, but also teaches in the subject – and his confidence has taken off, too. Obviously, we can't work miracles – Ashkan needs to use special recording equipment and transmitters in lectures. But this is a comparatively small inconvenience when compared to the gains. You can read more about Ashkan on our homepage. His story is quite inspiring.

Of course, scientists are making breakthroughs in the field of hearing all the time. If you visit our site, you can read about some fascinating new developments in America. There, scientists have discovered that our skin also helps us to listen, by picking up vibrations in sounds. They realised that the full listening process actually involves sight and touch as well as hearing, in order to provide the brain with a full impression of what sounds are being produced. So in the future, we may be able to look forward to a very different range of products developed in response to these findings.

This is just a small selection of the kind of information you can find on our site. It's likely that either you or someone close to you will experience hearing loss at some point, so I'm sure you'll find it an invaluable resource. Now, if I may take a few questions ...

Unit 08

🎧 8.1

P = Presenter; M = Monique

P: Monique, thanks for taking time out of your busy schedule to fit us in. How's it going?

M: Pretty good. I mean, I just got in from Venezuela yesterday, so there's a bit of jet lag, but you know, raring to go for the next climb.

P: Great! So, for anyone thinking about getting into rock-climbing – how do you start? I mean, how did you get into it?

M: Well, my secondary school ran these extra-curricular clubs ... there was football, climbing, music ... I forget. Erm, anyway, most of my friends were keen on footie, so they all opted for that and tried to persuade me, too. I loved football, but there was something about rock-climbing ... I knew I'd have to work at it, that it'd take me out of my comfort zone, and that really appealed. I gave it a go and took to it straight away. The guys training us noticed I seemed to have some natural talent. They put me in for the Junior Nationals and it all took off from there.

P: And you've been winning world-class competitions ever since.

M: Yeah. Well, sometimes! Actually, for me, and probably most other climbers, even when you're not trying to beat someone else, you're trying to beat yourself – do it faster, better ... so the element of competition is permanently there.

P: And what about your training schedule?

M: Well, I train for at least 20 hours a week. Often more. Living where I do, near the mountains, it means the training is largely outdoors. There are times when I use the climbing wall, though, when the weather's dreadful!

P: You're an inspiring figure.

M: Oh, er ...

P: No, really ... Tell me, why does climbing have a particular draw for women?

M: Well with rock-climbing, you're not depending so much on upper body strength, where men usually have the advantage. It's more to do with stamina – how long you can push yourself for. And I think endurance is something we naturally do better.

P: And, er, have you ever noticed any prejudice from male climbers?

M: Hardly any, although sure, there are exceptions – macho idiots! I always enjoy overtaking them! Honestly, though, most serious climbers know what it takes and respect other climbers, whoever they are. Gender doesn't come into it.

P: Will there come a point where you think 'OK, I've accomplished it all. I can slow down now'?

M: I hope not! Look, Lynn Hill, the rock-climbing pioneer, she was still setting new records in her 40s. And I intend to do the same when I'm that age – just get better and better.

P: So what's next?

M: For the moment I'm focused on doing climbs that are completely unfamiliar. Plenty of time to come back and work on improving my time on old climbs later. I'm headed to Austria next week, to do some on-sighting there.

P: Sorry?

M: On-sighting – that's climbing rocks without inspecting them in advance. I'm really looking forward ...

🔊 8.2

1 The mountains are awesome, they really are.
2 It's normally safe but sometimes problems do occur.
3 'Did you see James? Was he on the tour?'
  'He was, but she wasn't.'
4 The scenery can be stunning, it really can.
5 You're not well, are you?

Unit 09

🔊 9.1
Olivia
When I graduated, I found it difficult to get a job, so I started experimenting with ideas I'd had while studying. Having studied industrial design, I was interested in designing something that would be useful to industry, without harming the environment. I was on my way to a job interview, and was walking along a crowded street, when I began thinking about the amount of energy created by people walking every day. What if we could harness at least some of that energy, and use it? This led to experiments with various ideas for controlling and using energy created by everyday human activity, such as workouts in a gym. The challenge was being able to store such energy. I found a way to do this with special batteries. Then I had to patent my design. This was a long process and I wish I'd set it in motion earlier. Funding was another problem. Fortunately, a friend who's a marketing consultant gave me advice on how to sell my ideas. This is really important when you're just starting out. It's still early days yet, but I've been receiving a lot of interest from a number of shopping centres, schools and gyms.

David
When this recession hit, almost everyone around me started talking of growing their own vegetables to save money. So, I decided to create gardening products that were environmentally friendly and ethically produced. One of the difficulties was funding. I experimented in my garden shed, to cut down on costs, and tried to use recycled waste products. I succeeded in ways I never imagined! One of my most successful innovations has been my insect repellent, which contains a secret ingredient from recycled food material. After experimenting, I patented my product, so that no one would be able to copy my ideas. Within weeks, I was selling it on the market. It became popular surprisingly quickly and I suddenly found myself snowed under with orders. My admin skills aren't great, so I had to employ someone to organise files and process orders and deal with the accounts. I worried over this decision for a while, as I wondered whether I'd have enough work to pay them. But in fact, it was the best thing I did. I was able to look more professional to potential customers, and I mean, well ... Lucy's great and I couldn't do without her now. If I'm honest, she's helped to generate business and keep us going.

Rafaela
About a year ago, I lost my job, and I realised I'd have to find alternative ways to make money. I'd begun recycling some of my clothes, partly out of interest and partly to avoid splashing out on new ones. It was fun, and several people remarked on how cool my creations looked. One even suggested I set up a business making ethical fashion and the idea kind of stuck in my head. The thing was to design a series of outfits as a kind of rudimentary collection, then think of a catchy brand name so it would stand out. Once I'd put together a few ideas, I went to a professional for advice on making a business plan – believe me, money well spent – and then designed my website. Your website is like your shop window – presentation is everything. My artistic background helped here and I concentrated on visual impact with minimal text. And well, things suddenly took off! I'm working on some new designs now and am looking for an assistant to help me.

🔊 9.2
1 It was quite nice there.
2 'His behaviour was out of order!' 'Quite.'
3 Have you quite finished? I've had enough of your attitude!
4 This new product's quite amazing!
5 'It was an inspiring performance.' 'Quite.'
6 The presentation was quite interesting, if you like that sort of thing.

Unit 10

🔊 10.1
P = Presenter; I = Iris; B = Brett

P: OK. We've got Iris from Christchurch on the phone. Iris?

I: Good morning, Steve. Look, the thing is, people think that hospitals are there to fix every single thing that's wrong with them, but come on! There are limits, and anyway, hospitals just don't have the funding.

P: I'm with you on that. But isn't that where private health care comes in? Other countries encourage it. Why shouldn't we?

I: Absolutely. Paying for health care ought to be compulsory, I think.

P: Now if that happened, there might be more to spare in the budget for a pay rise for nurses. They deserve it, don't you reckon?

I: Well, nursing is supposed to be a vocational job, isn't it? Not a way to make a fortune. They earn enough for a decent standard of living.

P: Hhmm, I ...

I: Actually, one more point if I may?

P: Go on.

I: If the government really wants to cut costs, they should make smokers responsible for their own hospital bills. I mean, it costs the country millions to look after them.

P: Yeah, I see your point, Iris, but if you're talking about people deliberately putting themselves at risk, then you've got to include anyone that plays sport, anyone working with dangerous machinery ... I don't know where you'd draw the line. Anyway, Iris, you've certainly given us food for thought. Thank you. Right, erm, I think we've got Brett from Mount Roskill waiting to talk to us?

B: Yep, hello.

P: How are you, Brett?

B: Well, better than I was a few weeks ago.

P: What happened?

B: Well, I went to my local doctor ... still only in his 20s ...

P: ... not that that makes any difference.

B: Oh, I think it does. So, anyway, I told him my symptoms and he said it was nothing to worry about. Well, I sort of thought to myself, 'What does he know? He's fresh out of medical school.' So I went up to the hospital, because I thought it would be good to get a second opinion.

P: Well, that's often a sensible idea.

B: And you know what? It was a good thing I did, because it turned out it was serious. Anyway, the hospital doctors sorted me out and I'm still here thanks to them.

P: Glad to hear it ...

B: But some of the hospital policies ...

P: Yeah?

B: Well, I was in a ward, you know, recovering, and what you want is some peace. But no. All these relatives come in and the noise is just terrible. It should be two visitors maximum per day.

P: Yeah, but if Dad's brought the kids to see Mum, you can't just leave some of them in the car. And it's a cultural thing, too, for some communities. Coming along to the hospital shows a bit of respect.

B: But not to the other patients.

P: Mmm, clearly a sore point for you, Brett. But, er, how about the grub? I went to see an uncle of mine recently, and I have to say, the meals they served up looked pretty appetising.

B: Well, all I can say is, I came out a lot thinner than I went in. Hospital catering is years behind the times, if you ask me.

P: All right, Brett. Thanks for calling.

B: Huh, cheers.

🔊 10.2
1 He saw his old doctor.
2 I don't know why he felt unwell.
3 You shouldn't have ignored your injury.
4 I think it was some kind of natural medicine.
5 The doctor asked me to get dressed again.
6 He could have picked up the disease on holiday.
7 I was put on a waiting list for my heart operation.

Unit 11

🔊 11.1
Speaker 1
If you want to be on the podium, you have to give it everything you've got. That means being physically fit – there's a lot of time in the gym and practising out there on the circuit. Saying that, of course, it's not just my performance but the car's that's under test, and the responsibility there is the crew's, of course. It's also a matter of experience. A lot of the new guys know that if they don't get points, their contracts won't get renewed. So they feel obliged to take ridiculous chances to get the edge – that's when you'll see them spinning out of control and taking other drivers out with them.

Speaker 2
Most of the people coming in are older players. Sport's perfectly safe, but you've got to be careful, and they don't make allowances for their age. They think it's just a matter of me prescribing painkillers, but it takes much longer for them to get over injuries than younger players. Oh well. I have to admit to being fairly passive myself – I watch the odd game, but not so much now. It's all about the transfer fees these days. When I was young, a player was with a team for pretty much his whole career, but now the money's just too tempting. It's lost its shine for me – there's no player today who really stands out, keeps the fans on the edge of their seats.

Speaker 3

I've been doing this job for over 20 years and the game's changed, I can tell you. I've always had to put up with abuse from the crowd, but these days the players have a go at you, too. They've played for a season and they think they know it all. But there are very few times my decision hasn't been upheld. Since football became the number one TV sport, egos have grown. Players are only partly in it for the game and the rest is all about the media attention. They spend lots of time on their appearance and making sure they get their photos taken in the right clubs. Pathetic!

Speaker 4

Well, I often work with a person for a year – sometimes longer – until they've got to the point where they can train independently. That's not to say that we don't get some who're back six months later, needing a bit of help sticking to the routines. That's where I come in. I never give up! Anyway, we've often got the sports channel on while people are working out, and it amazes me the range of events you can see nowadays. When I was a kid, it was fairly limited. Now it's stuff like skateboarding, windsurfing – it makes for exciting viewing, which is great. I think a lot more people are drawn to it, to sport generally.

Speaker 5

In my day we got the adulation of the fans, but not the earnings players do nowadays. After I got out of it, I couldn't trade on my looks or celebrity. I wish! I have to say, I wouldn't have minded that kind of money, but I've done all right for myself. One of the things I've always liked about the game is that it doesn't favour the privileged. A kid just needs to know how to kick a ball and get a bit of a lucky break. If he's spotted by a talent scout, then that's it. He's made. I think the same goes for other sports – your natural talent and determination can open up the world.

🔊 11.2

bluff ... tough
coach ... show
court ... pawn
down ... ground
cushion ... football
hurdle ... world

🔊 12.1
R = Radio presenter; P = Penelope

R: So, Penelope, how difficult is it to get started?

P: Well, the golden rule when choosing your subject is to find them fascinating, never mind whether they're historically important or – much worse – fashionable. Then concentrate on the key moments in their life and begin your research by focusing on the details surrounding them. Remember, you've got to win the reader over too, and the scandalous and shocking will attract more than the everyday.

R: What about when the subject's a famous historical figure? Isn't there a danger that it's all been written already?

P: The trick there is to uncover new information or to approach your subject from an original angle. Otherwise, your book will only be of interest to academics rather than booksellers or the general public. This is particularly challenging since you will need to present a different interpretation of what may be already well-documented facts.

R: So, what are the difficulties involved in researching someone's life?

P: Well, the main worry is organisation, although getting funding and especially time are also big concerns! You've got to plan or you'll never succeed. As soon as you can, create digital files of different periods of their life and – sorry, even before that – make a timeline. It's amazing how difficult it is to keep events in order! Finally, sort out any hard copy into similar periods.

R: Hard copy? Do you mean other biographies, history books and the like?

P: No ... sorry! This can mean books, of course, but also things such as letters, diaries – especially those if there are any, photographs, newspaper clippings, and so on. It may be accompanied by transcripts of interviews with people who knew your subject.

R: Ah, I imagine that's very exciting.

P: It can be, yes. But it's also tricky. You'd expect interviewees to feel excited too, or enthusiastic, yet they're actually often very reserved initially, becoming friendlier later. They may not like being recorded and so won't say much during the official interview. You need to be prepared for what they may say afterwards, once they relax. Then they often come out with the really interesting titbits. It's vital to show them respect for their feelings and also gratitude for their time. Remember, you may need to come back to them for more information or to corroborate another person's testimony. It can be a long process!

R: So, what's special about your work, then, Penelope?

P: There's something wonderful about entering the world of an historical great, you know, like Napoleon, Alexander the Great, Genghis Khan. For a while, you are privy to part of the power these great leaders and politicians wielded, and that can be awe-inspiring. Another aspect is the thrill of the chase, as it were. It's almost like you're a detective hunting an elusive suspect, especially when you don't know if he's guilty or not. You might suddenly uncover information about him that completely changes your view and forces you to follow another line of research altogether. I get a real buzz out of that.

R: Penelope Fowles, fascinating, thank you. Now ...

🔊 12.2

uprising ... employer ... employee ... reliable ... evacuee

🔊 12.3

assassinate ... editor ... engineer ... industry ... portrayal ... reflection ... refugee ... scholarship ... validity ... Vietnamese

UNIT 13

🔊 13.1

P = Presenter; M = Marie; A = Araminta; R = Roy

P: With me to discuss the news in the Sunday papers today are Araminta Knowles MP, Marie Brun, journalist for the *World Tribune*, and Roy Vince, novelist. So, Marie, what caught your eye this week?

M: Well, Ewan, one of the biggest stories was the arrest of Liam Degas, the alleged drug lord. The authorities are hailing this as a major step forward in the fight against crime. I'm not so convinced.

A: But it's great news, isn't it? Especially as there've been rumours that some politicians had also got their hands dirty in supporting this evil trade.

P: Allegedly ...

M: Yes, but I question the government's motives here, Araminta. Elections are coming up. They want to convince people they're taking a strong stand.

R: That's quite a cynical view, isn't it? If politicians really were involved in supporting Degas, surely they'd want to cover it up? Especially as he's such a high-profile figure?

M: Oh, his reputation was already on the wane, Roy. Degas was just one small link in the chain. The arrest is of little significance as a crime-fighting gesture, because his second in command will simply take over.

R: I think you're underestimating the power he's wielded for the last ten years! No, I'm looking forward to the positive impact this will have.

P: Definitely a story worth following! Thanks, Marie. Now, Araminta, you've got something of a very different, er, nature, to tell us about, haven't you?

A: Very good! Yes, I was pleased to read that the American author Richard Louv is currently in Britain raising awareness of what he calls the nature deficit disorder.

R: This 'disorder', is it some kind of disease?

A: Not as such, but it's nevertheless a growing problem in today's society. Louv contends that urban parents are turning kids away from the outdoors, which is having a highly detrimental effect. It affects their performance at school, and it could even be a factor in the rise in Attention Deficit Disorder.

R: Well, OK, but isn't he overemphasising a point here? There are parks, school trips – access to nature isn't that limited, surely?

M: I think Louv's got a point. Most parks are largely glorified dog exercising areas, with a bit of grass and a few trees if you're lucky. If kids learn anything about nature, they do it in class or on a screen – in other words, indoors. No, something should be done.

A: What concerns me, Marie, is the nanny state culture at work here. We've become a paranoid society that won't let children outside to play because of the often over-exaggerated or even imaginary risks.

R: With respect, I think you're out of touch here, Araminta. That might have been true a few years ago, but things have moved on since then. People are a lot more health-conscious and you see many more families walking or riding bikes now.

A: Goodness, where do *you* live, Roy? I can't believe it's very typical ...

P: I'm sorry to interrupt, Araminta, but we're running out of time. I'd like us to cover one more story before the news break. Roy?

R: Yeah, thanks, Ewan. Well, I'd like to look at the breaking news about the offshore oil disaster which has polluted the seas in the Atlantic. I can't believe ...

🔊 13.2

1 dealt ... deal
2 natural ... nature
3 society ... social
4 risen ... rise
5 legislation ... legislature
6 advertising ... advertisement
7 station ... statute

UNIT 14

🔊 14.1

Good evening, everyone. It's good to see such a large turnout. Clearly the entrepreneurial spirit is alive and well despite the current economic situation! Now, the first question I have to ask, or rather the question you have to ask yourselves, is 'Why are you starting a company?' If it's because you've carried out a great deal of research, and you've spotted a gap in the market for your product or service, then go ahead. Do it. If, on the other hand, you're fed up with long hours, and you want to free up more time for the kids, think again. A new company will put even greater demands on your time.

Likewise, if you're fed up taking orders from other people, I'd also advise caution. Power-hungry CEOs often struggle to take off! The same goes if profit is all that motivates you. Margins will be low at the start, so you'll probably make very little initially. But if you have a genuine fascination with whatever you're selling, then go for it.

Now, some of you here might be thinking about having your second go at business, because your first attempt was short-lived. Take heart. Some of the world's top entrepreneurs have done exactly the same thing – you can learn a lot from past mistakes.

A word of warning, though. Never try to get a new company going while you're still employed elsewhere. I'll tell you why. If you see your business as a back-up plan or a compensation for your boring regular work, you'll never commit yourself 100% and, no, your new business won't be successful. It's all or nothing. So, what ...

♻ 14.2

It's just as important to know why businesses fail as why they thrive. Many failures occur when entrepreneurs lack sufficient management knowledge. They might be good at dealing with customers, but they lack expertise in handling hard-to-manage employees as well as in financial matters.

The next reason – and you won't believe how often this occurs – but many people have no real idea about how much capital they need. Putting in long hours won't necessarily help you if you sink too far into debt. So you really need to be realistic about this.

People's failure to consider location can also lead to bankruptcy. They haven't thought about how accessible the store or office is, or how close they are to competitors. So don't just choose a location because it doesn't need much renovation, or because it's close to suppliers – or your home!

Now, most businesses these days have the sense to set up a website, with opening hours, addresses and so on. So why do some forget to put up a catalogue, too? If customers can't find one of these, they'll soon look elsewhere. And when times are tough, worry less about promoting your luxury products and services, and more about highlighting your discounts. You'll keep your income up that way. Remember, entrepreneurs who overcharge their customers never see them again.

The final point that I'm going to make is that rather than focusing on short-term business you want to encourage repeat business. That's the way to make your company grow.

♻ 14.3

1   So, how's the family? Tell me all!
2   What are you up to this weekend? I thought you were going camping.
3   So, did you go out? Only, I didn't see you.
4   Did you catch the news this morning? I couldn't believe it.
5   Where are going for your holiday? I can't remember if Clare said Greece or Italy.
6   What're you doing this evening? I fancy going out.
7   How's the house coming along? I'd love to see it!

UNIT 15

♻ 15.1
Speaker 1
There's a definite trend for boys to be more flamboyant in what they wear. I love it! The mainstream doesn't have to be bland – sometimes it's very exciting! In Tokyo, a lot of men, even older men, have started wearing long skirts, or shorter skirts over leggings, like the girls. This is possibly more readily acceptable in Japan, since there's a historical precedent for men to wear robes, called *yukata*. These are also making a comeback, by the way. I try to make my clothes truly unisex, not male, not female ... And it seems to be working, judging by the figures!

Speaker 2
Yeah, well, we just can't cut it like the girls, we just don't get the recognition. So naturally, we don't get the remuneration, either. I did an accessories shoot for a high street chain last month and got €1,000 for it. The girl I was working with – not even that high-profile – took €12,000. That's just the way it is. That said, we guys have it a lot easier in many ways. It's definitely easier to model trousers than dresses or skimpy lingerie! Behind the scenes, male fashion is friendly rather than intimidating. OK, there are pressures at times, but it's generally fun.

Speaker 3
Whenever I go back to India, I try to get to the craft fairs. An outfit is only totally finished when you've added the right shoes, bag, etc. A plain dress can be made into something special by putting a bold necklace with it. Eye-catching jewellery gets you noticed. Most high street shops sell only the same old well-known brands, and the designer labels are too pricey for my budget. The best Indian craft fairs often have innovative products from young designers, and you can sometimes find a bargain that makes you look like a million dollars! I've picked up some exquisite pieces.

Speaker 4
We produce grooming products for men as well as women, and while the market for the latter is definitely larger, our men's range has grown considerably over the last two to three years. Young men are generally keen consumers now, but admittedly they need a slightly different approach in the packaging and marketing. The words 'fashion' and 'cosmetics' sound feminine to most men, and so we use the less off-putting words 'style' and 'grooming'. We're now trying to target *older* men, 35 plus – that's our new target market.

Speaker 5

A lot of people are nervous about clothes shopping – fashion can be unwelcoming, especially if you're a more curvaceous shape or some way past your teens! That's where the web is such a help. By downloading my e-book, users can discover where to find original and affordable items from designer or mainstream brands, or choose accessories which blend subtly with an outfit, and so on. Then they click on a link to find a store that sells their kind of clothes. I've been operating this service for five years now and haven't had a complaint yet!

🔊 15.2

1 A You didn't like him, then?
  B But I did, actually.

2 A So, you liked the show?
  B No, I said I disliked the show.

3 A You must have overslept!
  B No, you're early!

4 A So it's true. You were laughing at me!
  B No, I wasn't laughing. That's not true!

5 A It's your turn to do the shopping.
  B No, it's not my turn. I did it yesterday.

6 A You must have seen her!
  B No, I can't have seen her. I wasn't there!

Unit 16

🔊 16.1

1 P = Presenter; J = Jacek

P: So, um, how often do you get called out, Jacek?

J: Oh, it varies. The majority of visitors have done their homework and have read up on the potential hazards. If you've got the right gear and clothing, you'll usually be fine, so these people rarely need my help. Then you'll get one who sees blue skies in the morning and thinks, 'Right, I'll just go for a little climb,' and up they go in their jeans and sweater, with a little bottle of water, and it comes as a total shock when the clouds suddenly descend.

P: I bet they don't make the same mistake twice.

J: No, but you do get some strange reactions sometimes. There was one English tourist, he was extremely dehydrated and he'd already got frostbite. The next step would've been hypothermia and then … er …. But, erm, unlike other people we've saved, who're usually very grateful and thrilled to be alive, this guy acted like we'd interfered or something, got in his way. At first we wondered if he was suffering from embarrassment – that's quite a common reaction. This guy was far from typical!

2 P = Presenter; G = Geraldine

P: In your latest novel, Geraldine, you've chosen a rather personal theme.

G: Yes, I've based it around the life of my grandparents and the tragedy of the war. After volunteering to fight, my grandfather was briefly sent home to get over a leg wound. During that time, he actually asked my grandmother whether she wanted to call the relationship off, but she wouldn't hear of it. And then my mother was conceived and he was ordered back to his regiment, going with the knowledge he was to be a father. I think they naively thought the war would end and they'd soon be married, but it wasn't to be.

P: So your grandmother never saw him again?

G: Sadly, no. Eventually she heard he'd been killed. And there she was, pregnant and unmarried. There was enormous pressure on her to give the baby up for adoption, particularly from the men in her family. But she refused to give in. She shared my belief that you'll always be sorry for the chance you didn't take, rather than the one you did. Too often people agonise over the possible consequences and let fear get in the way.

3 M = Man; W = Woman

M: Well, I'd been in R&D for, er, going on three years and the guys I'd started out with had moved up, but not me. They were earning more too, I reckon, although that wasn't so much of an issue for me. I wanted people to look up to me, to 'be' someone, whatever that means. Then my sister lent me one of those assertiveness training DVDs.

W: Oh yeah …?

M: Well, it suggested that employers appreciate a direct approach. I was still unsure, but I thought I'd give it a go. I marched into the head of department's office and told her all about the kind of products the company should be developing and all my bright ideas for the future.

W: Hmm, sounds good.

M: You'd think so, wouldn't you? The thing is, once I'd stopped blabbing, I realised she was staring at me, sort of amused. Or maybe it was in confusion. And when I was expecting thanks or encouragement, there was just this silence. I felt *this* big, I tell you. Eventually I stumbled back to my desk and kept my head down for the rest of the day.

🔊 16.2

1 They've come with the right gear.
2 Wait. I'll just catch my breath.
3 'The next step could have been fatal.'
  'Quite.'
4 We're leaving on the first of March.
5 He was sent home to get over a leg wound.
6 I remember quite clearly. I left it there.

ANSWER KEY

UNIT 01

VOCABULARY City life

1

1 congested 2 spotless
3 sprawling 4 run down
5 well-run 6 vibrant

2

1 e 2 g 3 c 4 a 5 h 6 b 7 d
8 f

LISTENING

3

c

4

1 E 2 A+E 3 A 4 – 5 A+E 6 A 7 E

DEVELOPING WRITING
An informal email – writing a reply

5

1 How are you doing? (b)
2 When would be best for you? (a)
3 What's it like? (d)
4 Is there anything good on? (c)

6

nightlife
food
what's on
atmosphere
shopping

7

1 out and about 2 tired
3 miss 4 run down
5 done 6 out

8

1 hit the town
2 be spoilt for choice
3 a (tourist) hot-spot
4 pick (someone) up

VOCABULARY Emphasising and exaggerating

1

1 The room was really, really cold/freezing
2 You could see for miles and miles (around).
3 The way people drive is totally insane/crazy. It's rather like being on a race track.
4 I had to leave the restaurant because it was unbearably hot (inside).

DEVELOPING CONVERSATIONS
Reinforcing and exemplifying a point

2

1 loads and loads 2 literally
3 packed 4 miles and miles
5 totally 6 really, really
7 absolutely 8 spotless

PRONUNCIATION Intonation for emphasis

3

1 I <u>swear</u>, the shop was <u>filthy</u> inside!
2 The woman in the baker's was in<u>credibly</u> <u>helpful</u>.
3 <u>Honestly</u>, the <u>stench</u> was un<u>bearable</u>!
4 It was <u>really</u>, <u>really</u> <u>great</u> to see you again!
5 <u>Seriously</u>, he drove like <u>crazy</u> to get here!
6 Getting across town was a <u>night</u>mare!

READING

5

population increase 5
a method to deal with waste 1
protest against changes 4
the creation of green spaces 2
concerns for the future 6
an idea to improve travel 3

6

1 F 2 T 3 F 4 F 5 T 6 F 7 T
8 T

7

1 with
2 up
3 in
4 over
5 up
6 under

VOCABULARY Recovery and change

1

1 demolished
2 initiating
3 decline
4 neglected
5 soaring
6 undergo
7 flourished
8 poured

GRAMMAR Perfect forms

2

1 She said she ~~hasn't~~ <u>hadn't</u> been to Buenos Aires before last year.
2 My family ~~has lived~~ <u>lived</u> in Milan until 1994.
4 The town hall was reopened last year, ~~had~~ <u>having</u> been completely rebuilt after the fire.
5 It is believed that the number of university graduates will ~~had doubled~~ <u>double</u> / <u>have doubled</u> by 2020.
6 By the time we got there, the concert ~~finished~~ <u>had finished</u>.
7 Where ~~had~~ <u>have</u> you been? We've been waiting here for hours and hours!

3

1 had been destroyed
2 has been developing
3 has been
4 have recovered
5 had been travelling
6 have encouraged
7 Having been done / Done
8 will have been completed / will be completed

VOCABULARY Binomials

4

1 d   2 c   3 f   4 e   5 a   6 b

5

1 on and off   2 sick and tired
3 peace and quiet   4 first and foremost
5 here and there   6 long and hard

6

1 quiet   2 long
3 pieces   4 off
5 now   6 regulations

VOCABULARY BUILDER QUIZ 1

1

1 hard   2 initiated
3 now   4 compelled
5 sick   6 out

2

1 career   2 plans
3 tip   4 a service
5 nerves   6 a crowd

3

1 muggings
2 consumption
3 congestion
4 entitled
5 sprawling
6 thrilled
7 demolition

4

1 underwent
2 downturn
3 run-down
4 spotlessly
5 upturn
6 re-housed

UNIT 02

VOCABULARY Describing people

1

1 snob (c)
2 incompetent (d)
3 bitchy (b)
4 principled (f)
5 pain (e)
6 laid-back (a)

2

1 b   2 a   3 a   4 b   5 b

LISTENING

3

Speaker 1: married couple
Speaker 2: brothers
Speaker 3: grandmother and granddaughter

4

a 3   b 2   c 1   d 2,3   e 1   f 2   g 1

DEVELOPING CONVERSATIONS Giving your impression

5

1 make
2 across
3 the feeling
4 get
5 seemed to
6 strikes

DEVELOPING WRITING

An online comment – giving advice

6

relationships

7

compassionate, forceful, outraged

8

1 to tell
2 shouldn't be treating
3 would have called
4 ask
5 would you rather have
6 were
7 would refuse
8 had better end
9 get hurt
10 Staying

VOCABULARY Phrasal verbs

1

1 away   2 down
3 through   4 on
5 of   6 into
7 out   8 up
9 up   10 down

PRONUNCIATION Contracted forms

2

1 <u>I would</u> have thought <u>you would have been</u> delighted!
2 <u>He will have</u> finished it by tomorrow.
3 She said <u>there would</u> be rain later, but I <u>do not</u> know if there will.
4 She <u>could not have</u> known <u>who would</u> be there.
5 I <u>would not have</u> helped you, even if I could.
6 <u>These are</u> mine, but I <u>do not</u> know whose those are.

READING

4

c

5

1 T   2 F   3 F   4 T   5 T   6 F   7 F
8 T

6

1 point
2 set
3 vain
4 rescue
5 faced
6 action

GRAMMAR *Would*

1
1 e   2 h   3 j   4 f   5 a   6 c   7 b
8 d   9 i   10 g

2
a 4   b 5   c 1,7   d 9   e 6,8   f 2,3,10

3
1 wouldn't pay   2 Would (you) give
3 wouldn't lift   4 wouldn't back
5 would lighten   6 'd have

4
1 He would never mince his words when commenting on their behaviour.
2 I'd say she did that on purpose.
3 Would you mind helping me with this application form?
4 She would get upset over such trivial things!
5 I would have thought that Peter knew all about that!
6 She warned him that she would leave if he didn't stop yelling.
7 I wouldn't have shouted if you hadn't kept interrupting me.
8 I'd go and talk to her if I were you, and try to patch things up. / If I were you, I'd go and talk to her and try to patch things up.

VOCABULARY Relationships

5
1 F   2 T   3 T   4 F   5 F   6 T

6
1 going through a bit of a rough patch
2 be getting on each other's nerves
3 get on
4 a scene
5 ended up
6 been on speaking terms
7 collaborating
8 see eye to eye
9 back down
10 friction
11 confrontation
12 his weight
13 on first name terms
14 makes it so awkward
15 When it comes down to it
16 came as a real shock
17 sparked her interest
18 keeping an eye on him
19 came to his aid
20 put him at his ease

VOCABULARY BUILDER QUIZ 2

1
1 back 2 down 3 out 4 over 5 down 6 out 7 up

2
1 bitchy   2 incompetence
3 snobbish   4 willing
5 intensity

3
1 subjected   2 narrowed
3 determined   4 pull
5 confided   6 slacking
7 draw

4
1 F   2 F   3 T   4 T   5 F   6 T

UNIT 03

VOCABULARY Society and culture

1
1 a   2 b   3 c   4 b   5 a   6 c

2
1 touch   2 superficial
3 revolves   4 outlook
5 let   6 male

LISTENING

3
1 c   2 b   3 a

4
1 H   2 C   3 M   4 H   5 M   6 C

5
1 They take place in springtime.
4 People believe they may bring good luck.

DEVELOPING CONVERSATIONS Challenging overgeneralisations

6
1 about   2 far
3 exaggeration   4 way
5 see   6 harsh
7 overstatement   8 sure

7
a 1,4 b 3,6 c 2,7 d 5,8

PRONUNCIATION
Intonation when agreeing or disagreeing

8
1 down
2 up

GRAMMAR Cleft sentences

10
1 What bothered me was the number of homeless people on the streets.
2 The one thing I found incredible was the lack of crime.
3 The thing that worries me is the amount of money politicians are wasting.
4 What annoys me the most is that no one seems to be listening.
5 One thing that drives me mad is all the red tape.

11
1 What ~~found I~~ I found difficult to cope with were the crowded streets.
2 The thing that amazes me the most ~~are~~ is the strict censorship laws.
5 One thing I hated was ~~that~~ the fact that the officials were so corrupt.
6 The thing that ~~me disturbs~~ disturbs me the most is the fact that everyone seems scared.

VOCABULARY Household objects

1

1 needle	2 dishwasher
3 drill	4 oven
5 cloth	6 tap
7 toilet	8 pin

2

1 brush	2 rope
3 screws	4 stairs
5 pads	6 wires
7 hammer	8 washing-up liquid

READING

3

1 C   2 A   3 B

4

1 a   2 g   3 h   4 f   5 c   6 b   7 d

5

1 f   2 e   3 a   4 d   5 b   6 c

VOCABULARY Words and phrases

1

1 f   2 d   3 c   4 a   5 b   6 g   7 e

DEVELOPING WRITING A description – adding interest

2

The writer is doing 2, 4, 5 and 6

3

1 not to be missed
2 light up the skies
3 electric
4 go wild
5 like there's no tomorrow
6 bring a smile to my face

4

1 warm
2 rule
3 back
4 food
5 showered
6 clockwork

5

a like clockwork
b a warm reception
c like the back of my hand
d as a rule
e showered us with
f provided plenty of food for thought

VOCABULARY BUILDER QUIZ 3

1

1 c   2 f   3 e   4 a   5 d   6 b

2

1 revolves	2 retain
3 stick	4 misinterpret
5 scrubbed	6 conform
7 stained	

3

1 hospitality	2 appliances
3 outlook	4 roots
5 assumption	6 normality

4

1 I   2 C   3 C   4 C   5 I   6 I

UNIT 04

VOCABULARY Politicians

1

1 compassion	2 charismatic
3 communication	4 flexibility
5 self-confident	6 bravery
7 compromise	8 honesty
9 passion	10 ruthlessness

PRONUNCIATION Sound and spelling: /ʃ/, /tʃ/ and /z/

2

1 charisma	2 ruthlessness
3 hasty	4 charming
5 downturn	6 issue

DEVELOPING CONVERSATIONS Giving opinions

4

a 3,5   b 2,6   c 1,4

5

1 some slight reservations
2 completely opposed
3 totally in favour of
4 a good idea in theory
5 totally against
6 far outweigh

6

1 of	2 I stand on
3 to	4 reservations about
5 in, think it's	6 the whole

GRAMMAR Conditionals 1

7

1 c   2 a   3 c   4 c   5 a   6 b

8

1 If ~~you'd be~~ you were elected, what would you do about housing?
2 You're going to get the sack if ~~you'll be~~ you're late again!
4 If they asked for a raise tomorrow, he definitely ~~won't~~ wouldn't give it to them.
5 What if you were unemployed, though, what ~~will~~ would you do then?
6 I would consider running for office, if I were you.
7 If the scandal ~~might break~~ broke, he would lose the election.

VOCABULARY Consequences

9

1 triggered	2 discourage
3 compound	4 undermine
5 benefit	6 reduce

10

1 lead	2 boost
3 triggered	4 devastated
5 compound	6 undermine
7 bankrupt	

LISTENING

1

conservation

2

1 over-exaggerated	2 irreversible
3 idealism	4 politician
5 the economy	6 hospital
7 heavily populated	8 local politics

3

1 d   2 e   3 b   4 f   5 a   6 c

VOCABULARY 'Ways of' verb groups

4

1 giggled
2 raced
3 crept
4 chattered
5 gazed

5

1 muttering	2 staggered
3 gazed	4 giggled
5 grabbed	6 strolled

READING

6

women

7

1 56% = percentage of Rwandan parliamentary seats held by women
2 ⅓ = share of cabinet positions held by women in Rwandan government
3 800,000 = the approximate number of Rwandans killed in the genocide of 1994
4 70% = percentage of females in the population immediately after the genocide
5 30% = approximate percentage of women in parliamentary seats in South Africa and Mozambique

8

1 e   2 h   3 b   4 a   5 g   6 d   7 c

9

1 genocide	2 archaic
3 abolition	4 facilitating
5 detractors	6 hamper

DEVELOPING WRITING A report – evaluating data

1

positive way

2

1 presents	2 overall
3 following	4 forward
5 grows	6 drop
7 However	8 sum

3

1 small	2 more ruthless
3 the most difficult	4 longer / more unhappy
5 so / such	

VOCABULARY Elections and politics

5

1 reached	2 cover up
3 landslide	4 outspoken
5 rigged	6 conducted
7 prominent	8 strike

GRAMMAR Conditionals 2

6

1 If it hadn't been for their support, we would never have won.
2 If she hadn't been in a meeting, she'd have seen you.
3 If I didn't have to finish this report, I'd stop and talk.
4 If we'd been in power, this would never have happened.
5 If she had campaigned longer, she might / would be in office now.

VOCABULARY BUILDER QUIZ 4

1

1 carry on a	2 cover up an
3 set up a	4 an emerging
5 establish an	6 a broad
7 an alleged	8 a narrow

2

1 allegations	2 outweigh
3 satirical	4 representation
5 opposition	6 stance
7 satirical	

3

1 F   2 T   3 F   4 T   5 T

4

1 for	2 about
3 at	4 for
5 to	

UNIT 05

VOCABULARY Nights out

1

1 c   2 e   3 a   4 b   5 f   6 d

2

1 live up to the hype
2 caused a scene
3 was mortified
4 burst into tears
5 was in bits
6 feel / am feeling a bit rough

DEVELOPING WRITING
A review – emphasising your ideas

3

d   **** outstanding

4

1 winning	2 cracking
3 powerful	4 successful
5 fearsome	6 admirable
7 stunning	8 exhilarating

5

1 wooden	2 spectacular
3 disjointed	4 irresistible
5 stilted	6 devastating
7 spine-tingling	

DEVELOPING CONVERSATIONS Commenting on what is said

7

2 that was awkward
3 have been bursting / ready to burst
4 have been pleasant
5 be feeling rough
6 be serious

PRONUNCIATION Intonation in responses

8

1 You <u>must</u> be getting quite <u>good</u> at it.
2 It <u>must</u>'ve been <u>amazing</u>.
3 I <u>bet</u> that was <u>awful</u>.
4 I <u>imagine</u> she was quite re<u>lie</u>ved.
5 I <u>bet</u> she was <u>mor</u>tified.
6 You <u>must</u> be getting pretty <u>tired</u> of it.

VOCABULARY Noun + *of*

1

1 bunch	2 tip
3 pleasure	4 swarm
5 supply	6 sign
7 floods	8 creation

2

1 fraction	2 manner
3 front	4 awkwardness
5 record	6 production
7 thrill	8 pack

READING

3

c a proposal

4

1 e   2 a   3 f   4 b   5 d

5

1 The club is conveniently located.
2 Membership is inexpensive.
3 Chess helps develop prediction skills.
4 Playing helps people to relax.
5 Chess improves ability in certain subjects.
6 The club could create money for the council.

6

1 outwit	2 innumerable
3 disability	4 international
5 unwind	6 aforementioned

GRAMMAR Noun phrases

1

1 a   2 c   3 d   4 b   5 e   6 d

2

Suggested answers:
2 Ken Wilson's talk proved very popular, receiving thunderous applause.
3 *Macbeth* is a gloomy play written by Shakespeare.
4 Look at the actress with the designer dress.
5 The National Theatre Company is producing a number of new plays.
6 The Frankies gave a superb concert, which was watched by millions.

LISTENING

3

Conversation 1 d
Conversation 2 a

4

1 T   2 F   3 F   4 T   5 F   6 F   7 T
8 T

VOCABULARY Describing books

5

1 a   2 c   3 c   4 a   5 b   6 b

6

1 around	2 in
3 to	4 by
5 in	6 on

VOCABULARY BUILDER QUIZ 5

1

1 tale	2 centres
3 stitches	4 bunch
5 yawning	

2

1 dialogue	3 narrator
6 memoir	

3

1 synonymous	2 acceptance
3 oppression	4 creation

4

1 in	2 by
3 into	4 of
5 on	6 At
7 off	

5

1 swarm	2 pleasure
3 hype	

UNIT 06

LISTENING

1

Speaker 1 a
Speaker 2 d
Speaker 3 c

2

Speaker 1 f
Speaker 2 c
Speaker 3 a

3

a Speaker 2
b Speaker 3
c Speaker 3
d Speaker 1
e Speaker 1
f Speaker 2

Vocabulary Arguments and discussions

4

1 f   2 h   3 d   4 c   5 a   6 e   7 b
8 g

5

1 are trying to
2 of taking
3 in discussing
4 prove
5 take
6 are missing

6

1 didn't come out right
2 point in discussing / talking about it now
3 twist my words
4 your point
5 clear the air
6 got our wires crossed

Grammar Wish and if only

7

1 I wish I ~~know~~ knew the answer to these questions.
4 I wish you ~~can~~ could come to support me when I see the boss later.
5 If only I ~~would be~~ were / was better at remembering facts when I'm arguing with someone.
6 I wish I ~~didn't go~~ hadn't gone to class yesterday.

8

1 you'd / would let
2 I could take
3 we hadn't fought
4 tree hadn't been
5 I hadn't yelled
6 you could find

9

1 phone would work properly
2 would stop being late / wouldn't always be late
3 hadn't agreed to help my brother move house
4 I didn't have to go to work today
5 I could come to your party
6 there weren't so many commercials on TV

Developing conversations Defending and excusing

10

1 b   2 e   3 f   4 a   5 c   6 d

Pronunciation Soft and hard c and g

11

1 /s/ re<u>c</u>eive	3 /dʒ/ intelli**g**ent
<u>c</u>easefire asso<u>c</u>iated	ra**g**e le**g**itimate
2 /k/ **c**areful	4 /g/ **g**o
nu<u>c</u>lear <u>c</u>asualty	ne**g**otiation a**g**reement

13

1 a   2 b

Vocabulary Conflict and resolution

1

1 conflict   2 troops
3 invades   4 breaks out
5 defeated   6 negotiating
7 track down   8 join forces
9 violations   10 tension
11 are surrounded   12 seize control

Reading

2

c

3

1 ✗   2 DC   3 ✓   4 DC   5 ✓   6 ✗   7 ✗
8 DC   9 ✓

4

1 civilians
2 casualty rate
3 reconciliation
4 retribution
5 compromises
6 overcome

Developing writing A formal email – complaining

1

to complain about the service of an online DVD rental club

2

1 recently
2 Unfortunately
3 largely
4 desperately
5 evidently
6 extremely

3

1 a   2 a   3 a   4 a   5 a   6 b

4

Suggested answers:
1 In spite of / Despite promising to call us back, he never did.
2 Due to the wrong instructions we couldn't use the product.
3 As there was a fault in the camera, we couldn't take any photos.
4 Due to the casing being cracked, the game didn't work.
5 In spite of / Despite asking for a red model, I was sent a yellow one.
6 I wish to return this camcorder as the lens is scratched.

VOCABULARY Extended metaphors

6

1 launched	2 targets
3 defence	4 guns
5 combat	6 capture
7 bombard	8 invaded
9 challenge	10 aggressive

VOCABULARY BUILDER QUIZ 6

1

1 continuation	2 aggressive
3 notable	4 complexity
5 harassment	6 hostility
7 fatalities	

2

1 d   2 e   3 a   4 b   5 f   6 c

3

1 V+N	2 V
3 V+N	4 V+N
5 V+N	

4

1 made
2 rose / escalated
3 negotiate
4 broke
5 take
6 staged
7 withdraw / recall

UNIT 07

VOCABULARY Talking about science

1

1 created
2 breakthrough
3 negative
4 undertook
5 due to
6 reproduced
7 pave the way

2

1 negative
2 condition
3 down to
4 underlying
5 devised
6 undertake

DEVELOPING CONVERSATIONS
Expressing surprise and disbelief

3

2 How on earth did they manage (to do) that?
3 How on earth do they achieve that?
4 What on earth was it?
5 Why on earth are you going / do you want to do that?
6 But how on earth did they make them? / were they made?
7 How on earth can he / will he be able to afford that?

PRONUNCIATION Expressing opinion and attitude

4

1 <u>Why on earth</u> do you want to do that? (↗)
2 <u>Believe me</u>, you're making a mistake. (↘)
3 <u>On the whole</u>, it went very well. (↗)
4 It was a disaster, <u>to say the least</u>. (↘)
5 <u>What in the world</u> were you thinking of? (↘)
6 <u>Funnily enough</u>, the experiment was unsuccessful. (↘)

DEVELOPING WRITING
A report – making recommendations

6

Suggested answers:
A Introduction
B Course content
C Facilities
D Encouraging participation

7

a 3   b 5   c 8   d 2   e 6   f 1   g 7
h 4

8

1 R   2 A   3 R   4 A   5 R   6 A   7 A
8 R

READING

1

1 an outline of the issue
2 media relations
3 online coverage
4 visual media
5 an idea for the future

2

Suggested answers:

1 communication	2 are employed
3 science blogs	4 liveliness
5 pop musician	6 physicist
7 less	8 videos
9 trained	10 studying

3

1 present
2 inspire
3 estimate
4 stimulate
5 release
6 assess

VOCABULARY Forming nouns and adjectives

4

	adjective	verb	noun
1	exploratory	explore	exploration
2	manipulative	manipulate	manipulation
3	diverse	✗	diversity
4	implied	imply implicate	implication
5	preventative	prevent	prevention
6	abundant	abound	abundance
7	varied	vary	variable variety
8	probable	✗	probability

5
1 cynical　　　　　　2 aggressive
3 capabilities　　　　4 variables
5 fatalities　　　　　6 manipulative

6
1 non-fatal
2 improbable
3 illogical
4 incapable
5 Unfortunately, irreversible
6 unexplored

VOCABULARY Statistics

1
1 e　　2 d　　3 a　　4 f　　5 b　　6 c

2
1 Contrary　　　　　2 up
3 suit　　　　　　　4 interest
5 anomaly　　　　　6 link

LISTENING

3
b　an entrepreneur

4
1 b　　2 a　　3 c　　4 b　　5 c　　6 c

GRAMMAR Passives

5
1 Statistics are twisted by government agencies to suit their own ends.
2 The animals are checked regularly for signs of deterioration in their health.
3 Acoustics can be tested by virtual ears which were invented by a scientist from Cardiff.
4 It is reported that 30,000 elephants have been killed illegally by rangers.
5 The award was given to the scientists in recognition of their work.
6 It is thought that the language barrier will be bridged by online translation services.

6
1 previously thought
2 doubts have been raised
3 bees resemble
4 findings will be presented
5 flower once belonged

VOCABULARY BUILDER QUIZ 7

1
1 C　　2 I　　3 I　　4 C　　5 C　　6 I　　7 I

2
1 with　　　　　2 in
3 for　　　　　　4 of
5 up　　　　　　6 to

3
1 test　　　　　　2 wreaked
3 slope　　　　　4 disorder
5 holes　　　　　6 conclusive

4
1 acceleration　　　2 twisted
3 insertion　　　　4 revelations
5 stimuli　　　　　6 undertaking

UNIT 08

VOCABULARY Describing scenery

1
1 crater　　　　　2 dune
3 plain　　　　　　4 gorge
5 cliff　　　　　　6 glacier

2
1 cliff
2 dunes
3 crater
4 gorge
5 plain
6 glaciers

3
1 c　　2 e　　3 f　　4 b　　5 a　　6 d

LISTENING

4
c　a professional rock climber

5
Monique agrees with 3, 5 and 6

DEVELOPING CONVERSATIONS Emphatic tags

6
a If I were you, I'd move back a bit, I really ~~wouldn't~~ would.
b Mmm. The scenery can be incredibly varied, ~~they~~ it really can.
c Yes. Amazing. I love the sea, I really love it.
e Incredible. I've never seen wildlife like this so close before, I really ~~have never~~ never have / I really haven't.
f That sounds terrifying, it really ~~is~~ does!

7
1 d　　2 e　　3 a　　4 f　　5 c　　6 b

PRONUNCIATION Strong and weak forms

8
1 The mountains are awesome, they really (are).
2 It is normally safe but sometimes problems (do) occur.
3 'Did you see James? Was he on the tour?' (He) was, but (she) wasn't.'
4 The scenery can be stunning, it really (can).
5 You're not well, (are you)?

GRAMMAR Auxiliaries

10
c mountainous

11
1 doesn't   2 did
3 Has / Does   4 do
5 doing   6 would
7 can't   8 do
9 have   10 Is

VOCABULARY Communicating

1
1 butting
2 into your mouth
3 minces
4 struggle
5 bush
6 cry
7 edgeways
8 point

2
1 shoulder to cry on
2 get to the point
3 put words into my mouth
4 me get a word in edgeways
5 mince your words
6 stop beating about the bush
7 it a struggle to express
8 butting in(to our conversation)?

READING

3
a concerned
g fascinated

4
1 e   2 a   3 b   4 h   5 g   6 d   7 c

5
a confounded
b poaching
c alluring
d make way
e vulnerable
f misnomer

VOCABULARY Animals

1
1 claws   2 scales
3 fur   4 horns
5 feelers   6 humps

2
1 leaps – shark   2 withstand – penguin
3 blends – chameleon 4 sense – spider
5 tunnels – mole   6 gnawing – beaver

VOCABULARY Compound adjectives

3
1 d   2 h   3 f   4 i   5 g
6 b   7 e   8 j   9 a   10 c

4
1 tailor-made suit
2 self-help guide
3 award-winning charity
4 water-resistant watch
5 life-threatening disease
6 child-friendly environment
7 long-term unemployment
8 five-mile run

DEVELOPING WRITING
A competition entry – describing a place

5
dolphin-spotting boat trip, excursion to the seal colony

6
1 Wander   2 Gaze
3 Take   4 Sign up
5 Don't forget 6 Avoid
7 Beware, make

7
1 d   2 f   3 a   4 b   5 c   6 e

VOCABULARY BUILDER QUIZ 8

1
1 narrow   2 murky
3 lush   4 sweeping
5 barren

2
1 I hate the way he butts in when we're talking.
2 The beaver gnawed through the wooden fence.
3 Authorities are cracking down on illegal poaching.
4 Stop beating about the bush and just say it!
5 The insect can blend in with its surroundings.
6 He saw the snake and let out a scream!
7 The blow fish will puff up when it is alarmed.
8 Researchers draw on their knowledge of the species' nocturnal habits to locate it.

3
1 scrambled
2 mince
3 dismissed
4 popularise
5 vital
6 defy
7 Predators, prey

4
1 superstitious
2 resistant
3 intuitively
4 extensively
5 ancestral

UNIT 09

VOCABULARY Roles and tasks

1

1 CEO	2 rep
3 PA	4 Admin
5 HR	6 IT
7 R&D	

2

1 liaise	2 oversee
3 troubleshoot	4 input
5 come up with	6 draw up
7 process	8 schedule

3

Suggested answers:

1 HR / PA	2 R&D
3 IT	4 Admin
5 R&D	6 HR
7 HR	8 PA

LISTENING

4

They have b and e in common

5

1 F	2 T	3 F	4 T	5 T	6 F	7 T
8 F						

6

1 harness	2 days
3 patented	4 process
5 generate	6 catchy

DEVELOPING CONVERSATIONS Making deductions

7

2 She doesn't have a lot of free time, then.
3 You must be able to speak Swedish, then.
4 She won't be able to finish that report, then.
5 You must have handed in your notice, then.
6 He must be a good person to talk to about this new product, then.

GRAMMAR Continuous forms

8

2 A number of new colleagues will be ~~join~~ joining us over the next couple of weeks.
3 I ~~work~~ have been working for the same pharmaceutical company for 15 years.
5 We'll have ~~been finishing~~ finished the project by next week.
7 This time next week we're supposed to ~~celebrate~~ be celebrating the book launch, but I'm not sure it'll be ready in time.
8 I've been having a lot of trouble with that photocopier ~~before~~ since it broke down.

9

1 broken	2 've been
3 been looking	4 'd left
5 contained	6 's been
7 'd been	8 was
9 have felt	10 was going

VOCABULARY Adverb–adjective collocations

1

1 Advertising is fiercely competitive and can be quite stressful.
2 I'm not remotely interested in working with children because I have no patience with them!
3 Caring for people with Alzheimer's can be emotionally draining, so I try to remain detached.
4 Factory workers should take reasonably frequent breaks to stay alert.
5 Accountancy was financially rewarding, but I hated it.
6 I'm blissfully content with my present job and have no plans to retire.
7 Working as a receptionist is technically straightforward, although problems occasionally arise.
8 I'm utterly exhausted by the work and really need a break.

PRONUNCIATION quite

2

1 F	2 A	3 C	4 C	5 A	6 F

READING

4

1 d	2 a	3 b

5

They'd generally agree with 2, 3 and 6

6

1 makes mistakes
2 Think, tell
3 blame
4 make amends
5 Avoid
6 trust
7 learning, improve

7

1 T	2 T	3 F	4 T	5 T

VOCABULARY The world of work

1

1 industrial	2 voluntary
3 unfair	4 subsidised
5 compassionate	6 minimum
7 early	8 state

2

1 early retirement
2 industrial tribunal
3 state pension
4 minimum wage
5 voluntary redundancy
6 compassionate leave

3

1 perks
2 subsidised
3 creche
4 childcare
5 opposition
6 crackdown
7 absenteeism
8 grateful

DEVELOPING WRITING
A job application – making a positive impression

4
Suggested answer: a, b, d and f

5
a, b, d and f

6

1 demonstrated	2 developed
3 awarded	4 impressed
5 realise	6 relish

VOCABULARY BUILDER QUIZ 9

1
1 d　2 a　3 c　4 e　5 b

2

1 tribunal	2 condemn
3 liaise	4 inherently
5 enthusiastically	6 screw

3
1 inevitability
2 blissfully
3 fiercely
4 mind-numbingly
5 dismissal
6 redundancy
7 technical

4
1 set
2 troubleshoot
3 Pull
4 mind-numbingly

5
1 back
2 perk
3 screw

UNIT 10

VOCABULARY Operations

1
1 f　2 c　3 g　4 d　5 a　6 e　7 h
8 b

2

1 undergo	2 fast
3 insert	4 swelled
5 scan	6 take part
7 stitches	8 broke

DEVELOPING CONVERSATIONS Vague language

3
1 It may take a few years so until they find a cure.
2 When Martin was in a coma, I knew he could hear somehow me hear me somehow / somehow hear me.
3 He made a kind of bandage or somehow something.
4 I knew I needed to do some sort of exercise but I wasn't sure what type.
6 He somehow managed to mix up the children's medical records.

4
1 kind of / somehow
2 or so
3 something
4 some kind of
5 somehow
6 kind of
7 or so

DEVELOPING WRITING A story – describing events

5
Juri cut his head badly and had to go to hospital.

6

1	introducing the story; setting the scene	*Have I ever told you about the time …?* *It all started when …* *It was (back) in … when …*
2	moving from one event to the next; re-establishing the situation	*But the … part of … was yet to come …* *In the middle of all this,* *So there we were, …* *While all this was going on, …*
3	concluding the story; giving the outcome of an event	*After all that, …* *I ended up …* *One thing it's taught me is …*

7
1 It was at this point that I did notice noticed my foot was bleeding quite badly.
2 It was wasn't until we had been walking for a couple of hours that we remembered our flashlights.
3 It was only when Lois reached the village that felt she she felt a sense of relief that the trip was over.
4 Not until midnight we could could we find our way back. / It was not until midnight that we could find our way back.
5 Only after standing up did I realise how much I have had hurt myself.

VOCABULARY Mind and body

1
1 mind / drift
2 clench / fist
3 flutter / eyelashes
4 raise / eyebrows
5 shrug / shoulders
6 stretch / legs

2

1 pat	2 shrug
3 spit	4 hug
5 sniff	6 wipe

3
1 stretched fluttered
2 glared blinked
3 raised clutched
4 support stretch
5 fluttered crouched
6 blinked raised
7 crouch support
8 clutched glared

READING

4

She has cyberchondria.

5

1 b   2 c   3 a   4 c   5 b   6 a

6

1 turned out   2 headed off to
3 clear up   4 come up with
5 taken up

LISTENING

1

a to discuss ways in which hospital services could be improved

2

1 I   2 B   3 B   4 I   5 I   6 B   7 B
8 I

3

1 A   2 D   3 A   4 D   5 A   6 D   7 D
8 D

VOCABULARY Nouns based on phrasal verbs

4

1 c   2 g   3 e   4 b   5 f   6 a   7 d

5

1 breakthrough
2 upbringing
3 dropouts
4 runup
5 outbreak
6 shakeup
7 workout

GRAMMAR Modal auxiliaries

6

1 b   2 a   3 c   4 d   5 e   6 h   7 f
8 g

7

1 must be feeling
2 can't possibly have seen
3 shouldn't have been driving
4 could have had a vaccination if
5 might / may / could have been the hamburger that
   gave me
6 should have told / ought to have told your parents
   about not

PRONUNCIATION Linking sounds

8

2 I don't know why he felt unwell.
3 You shouldn't have ignored your injury.
4 I think it was some kind of natural medicine.
5 The doctor asked me to get dressed again.
6 He could have picked up the disease on holiday.
7 I was put on a waiting list for my heart operation.

VOCABULARY BUILDER QUIZ 10

1

1 swollen
2 dietary
3 eradication
4 anaesthetised
5 underpinned
6 extensive

2

1 write-off
2 walkout
3 falling-out
4 bypass
5 break-in
6 shake-up

3

2, 5 & 6 describe a form of treatment

4

1 mortality
2 cure
3 aftercare
4 disease
5 your fingers
6 remission
7 head

UNIT 11

VOCABULARY Sports and events

1

1 sponsoring
2 sending
3 fading
4 challenging
5 substituting
6 doping
7 thrashing
8 blowing

2

1 out
2 underdog
3 overturned
4 fading
5 scrape
6 close
7 suspended
8 fixed

LISTENING

3

1 a current sportsperson
2 a doctor
3 a referee
4 a fitness instructor
5 a retired sportsperson

4

a 3   b 1   c 2   d 5   f 4

5

1 a   2 b   3 b   4 a   5 a   6 b

DEVELOPING CONVERSATIONS Irony and humour

6
1 b   2 a   3 b   4 a+b 5 b   6 a

VOCABULARY Talking about gaming

7
1 f   2 d   3 b   4 a   5 e   6 c

8
1 engrossed
2 confronted
3 grasped
4 informed
5 attached

9
1 ~~with~~ **in** moderation
2 universal ~~fact~~ **truth**
3 ~~true~~ **pure** and simple
4 ~~cooperative~~ **collaborative** games
5 Multi-~~tasking~~ **player**

GRAMMAR Linking words and phrases

1
1 even though
2 otherwise
3 Although / Even though
4 whether
5 in order to / so as to
6 Provided / So long as

2
1 c   2 b   3 a   4 e   5 d   6 f   7 i
8 h   9 g

3
1 Johnson's taking some rest so he can recover from his injury.
2 You won't improve unless you train more.
3 Marc was disqualified, even though he protested.
4 You must have cheated, otherwise you wouldn't have won.
5 I'm unable to give up my job in order to train professionally.

READING

4
a a concerned parent

5
1 F   2 T   3 F   4 DS   5 F   6 T   7 F
8 F

6
1 of   2 in
3 between   4 to
5 of   6 with
7 to   8 in

DEVELOPING WRITING
An essay – expressing personal opinion

1
a

2
1 The question is
2 in two respects
3 In other words
4 Moreover
5 On the other hand
6 In summary

3
1 belief
2 ability / abilities
3 participation
4 comparison
5 determination
6 Resentment
7 development
8 freedom

4
1 b   2 a   3 a   4 a   5 a   6 b   7 b
8 b

VOCABULARY Alliteration

6
1 marriage   2 lost
3 family   4 bred
5 nothing   6 kith
7 disappointed

7
Love's Lesson Learned, Rob and Rose, far from

8
Accept all answers. Suggested answer:
'Rose and I are head over heels,
And despite what you may think
Our love will stand the test of time,
We'll battle through thick and thin
Inseparable.'

PRONUNCIATION Different spelling, same sound

9
bluff / tough, coach / show, court / pawn, down / ground,
cushion / football, hurdle / world

VOCABULARY BUILDER QUIZ 11

1
1 chanted   3 substitutes
2 chants   4 substitute

2
1 bite
2 flies
3 let
4 fosters
5 dragged
6 jump
7 nodded
8 stop

3

1 moderation
2 suspension
3 abusive
4 simulation
5 traumatic
6 attentive

4

1 I   2 C   3 I   4 C   5 I   6 C   7 C

UNIT 12

VOCABULARY Personal histories

1

1 flee, coup
2 radical
3 deprived
4 orphaned
5 saw active service
6 broken home

2

1 deprived
2 sheltered
3 knit
4 scholarship
5 privileged
6 evacuated
7 fled
8 scratch

LISTENING

3

b   historical biographer

4

1 fascinating
2 scandalous
3 the general public
4 organisation
5 timeline
6 diaries
7 reserved
8 detective

VOCABULARY Similes

5

1 like a fish ~~in a sieve~~ out of water
2 as hard as ~~a dodo~~ nails
3 as old as the ~~plague~~ hills
4 smokes like ~~mud~~ a chimney
5 as clear as ~~a chimney~~ mud
6 like chalk and ~~nails~~ cheese
7 avoid ... like ~~mud~~ the plague
8 a memory like a ~~sheet~~ sieve

DEVELOPING WRITING
Contribution to a longer piece – a profile

6

Your profile should include b and e

7

Paragraph 1: b, e
Paragraph 2: a, f
Paragraph 3: c, d

8

Suggested answers:
a The recession brought a time of great hardship.
b She was arrested on suspicion of theft.
c For many years, we were consumed by guilt.
d She struggled to make sense of it all.
e Her book is a very moving account of the events.
f It pays tribute to the bravery of / shown by some of
the people.

READING

1

a

2

1 F   2 T   3 T   4 T   5 F   6 T   7 F
8 F

3

1 Cleopatra
2 Sir Francis Drake
3 Alexander the Great
4 Alexander the Great
5 Marie Antoinette
6 Alexander the Great, Sir Francis Drake

4

1 manipulate
2 portrayed
3 condemn
4 maligned
5 contended

DEVELOPING CONVERSATIONS Contextualised
questions

5

2 You cited ...
3 You suggested that ...
4 be arguing that ...
5 You made the point that ...
6 You referred to ...
7 You claimed that ...

6

1 d   2 a   3 b   4 f   5 g   6 e   7 c

VOCABULARY Historical events

1

1 e   2 g   3 i   4 a   5 j
6 c   7 f   8 b   9 d   10 h

PRONUNCIATION Stressed and unstressed suffixes

3

1 ●○○	uprising editor industry scholarship
2 ○●○	employer portrayal reflection
3 ○○●	employee engineer refugee
4 ○●○○	reliable assassinate validity
5 ○○○●	evacuee Vietnamese

VOCABULARY Discussing arguments and theories

5
1 establishing
2 put
3 played
4 stemmed
5 challenged
6 claimed
7 gave
8 cast

6
1 Sirimavo R. D. Bandaranaike
2 Marie Curie
3 Virginia Apgar
4 Anna Akhmatova
5 Corazon Aquino
6 Fanny Blankers-Koen
7 Gabrielle Chanel
8 Shirley Chisholm

GRAMMAR Dramatic inversion

7
1 At no time
2 No sooner
3 Not only
4 Nowhere else
5 Not until
6 Only after

8
1 Never before had I seen such a huge crowd of people gathered in one place.
2 Only when the police fired tear gas at them did the crowd disperse.
3 Not only did the tsunami kill eleven villagers, but it also destroyed nearly all of the fishing boats in the area.
4 Two people signed the Declaration of Independence on 4 July, but not until five years later was the last signature added.
5 No sooner had war been declared between Britain and Zanzibar in 1896 than the latter surrendered.
6 Despite being afraid, at no time during the earthquake did the little boy cry.

VOCABULARY BUILDER QUIZ 12

1
1 evacuation
2 declaration
3 intervention
4 nationalised
5 overstatement
6 crippling

2
1 cheese
2 sheet
3 sieve
4 plague
5 mud
6 chimney

3
1 to
2 up
3 out
4 from
5 on
6 on
7 over
8 round

4
1 massacred
2 privileged
3 challenged
4 nails
5 upbringing

UNIT 13

VOCABULARY Newspaper headlines

1
1 a   2 h   3 d   4 f   5 c   6 e   7 g
8 b

2
Suggested answers:
2 Cole to pull out of Arsenal contract / Cole pulls out of Arsenal contract
3 Chancellor rules out tax increase / Tax increase ruled out by Chancellor
4 President Carver to slash / slashes arms spending / Arms spending slashed by President Carver
5 Drugs seized in warehouse raid / Police seize drugs in warehouse raid
6 Landlords vow to bar hooligans from city centre pubs / Hooligans will be barred from pubs, vow landlords

DEVELOPING CONVERSATIONS
Rhetorical questions and common opinions

3
1 g   2 e   3 a   4 f   5 c   6 b

DEVELOPING WRITING A proposal – being persuasive

4
B Appeal of the station
C Types of programme
D Community

5
1 attract
2 encourage
3 broad
4 appeal
5 generate
6 allow
7 an asset
8 improve

6

1 A review supplement would make the paper appeal to a wider readership.
2 Clear headings would make the web page more accessible to users.
3 Colourful images would make the page more attractive to a broad readership. / Colourful images would attract a broader readership to the page.
4 A careers supplement would encourage more advertisers / more businesses to advertise.

VOCABULARY Common sayings

1

1 Don't count your chickens before they hatch.
2 The grass is always greener on the other side.
3 Every cloud has a silver lining.
4 It takes all sorts to make a world.
5 too many cooks spoil(ing) the broth.
6 the early bird catches the worm.
7 when in Rome, do as the Romans do.
8 When the going gets tough, the tough get going.

READING

2

A 3   B 5   C 1   D 2

3

1 c   2 d   3 a   4 c   5 d   6 d

4

1 circulation
2 discerning
3 took
4 narrow
5 isolated
6 detriment

LISTENING

1

1 d
2 b
3 a

2

1 A
2 M
3 R
4 A
5 M
6 A
7 R

PRONUNCIATION Short and long vowel sounds

3

2 na̲tural
3 so̲ciety
4 ri̲sen
5 legisla̲ture
6 adverti̲sing
7 sta̲tute

GRAMMAR Patterns after reporting verbs

5

reporting verb pattern	verbs
1 verb + (*that*) clause	acknowledge, claim, confirm
2 verb + object + (*that*) clause	assure, confirm, express, reject
3 verb + *to*-infinitive	refuse, vow
4 verb + object + *to*-infinitive	urge
5 verb + noun phrase	acknowledge, deny, reject
6 verb (+ object) + preposition	blame, praise

6

1 expressed
2 acknowledged
3 assured
4 praising
5 claimed
6 confirmed

7

1 The Prime Minister vowed to cut taxes in the next six months.
2 The speaker urged the crowd to sign the petition and make the outcry too loud to be ignored.
3 Gerard rejected the committee's offer.
4 The physicist acknowledged that s/he had been misguided in his / her calculations.
5 The company spokesperson denied that the company / they had tried to play down the importance of the problem.
6 Marie blames the nanny state for children's loss of contact with nature.
7 The minister confirmed that Parliament is / was going to pass the new education bill this / that year.
8 The MP refused to discuss the issue with the press until the next day.

VOCABULARY BUILDER QUIZ 13

1

1 pulls
2 hails
3 clash
4 slash
5 raid

2

1 denied
2 tipped
3 join
4 thrown
5 slash

3
1 profits
2 cover up
3 praise
4 rise

4
1 of
2 to
3 on
4 of
5 in
6 to
7 for

5
2 ✓   4 ✓

UNIT 14

VOCABULARY How's business?

1
1 flooded
2 taken on
3 picked up
4 relocating
5 making
6 hanging in
7 downturn
8 client base
9 overheads

DEVELOPING CONVERSATIONS Small talk

2
1 c   2 e   3 g   4 b   5 f   6 a   7 d

DEVELOPING WRITING
An information sheet – making suggestions

3
1 d
2 c
3 a

4
1 c   2 a   3 e   4 d   5 f   6 b

5
1 action plan
2 job satisfaction
3 rest break
4 work-life balance
5 time management
6 to-do list

6
1 a checking
   b to have
2 a putting
   b to do
3 a to leave
   b reading
4 a to inform
   b spending
5 a to eat
   b getting

LISTENING

8
c a business advisor

9
1 ✗   2 ✓   3 ✗   4 ✗   5 ✓   6 ✓   7 ✗

10
1 employees
2 capital
3 competitors
4 catalogue
5 discounts
6 repeat

VOCABULARY Loanwords

1
1 c   2 a   3 c   4 b   5 a   6 c   7 a
8 b

PRONUNCIATION Intonation in questions

2
1 FSO
2 MS
3 MS
4 FSO
5 MS
6 FSO
7 FSO

READING

4
A Jason

5
1 B   2 C,D   3 A   4 B   5 A   6 D   7 C
8 C   9 D

6
1 spin
2 grey area
3 buzz word
4 Plan A
5 agenda
6 do-gooder
7 undercut
8 give it a go

GRAMMAR Relative clauses

1
2 which
3 (which)
4 (where)
5 when / that
6 in which / that
7 which
8 (that / which)
9 to whom / to who
10 (that)
11 (that)
12 whose / for whom / for who
13 what

2

2 (d) , whose policy of employing experienced staff was very successful.

3 (a) , when / whereupon a number of changes to company policy were made.

4 (f) , none of which were of good quality / which were all of poor quality / , all of which were of poor quality.

5 (c) that / which described how profits had plummeted.

6 (b) by which time / point it was too late to win back their solid customer base / when it was already too late to win back a solid customer base.

Vocabulary Business situations

3

1 gap
2 stakes
3 deal
4 meeting
5 line
6 concessions

4

1 exceeded
2 seal
3 bid
4 recommend
5 undertake
6 ongoing
7 conduct
8 demands

5

1 competitive
2 lobby
3 scale
4 drop
5 outsource
6 upped
7 threat
8 make

Vocabulary builder quiz 14

1

Sentences 1, 2, 4 and 6 relate to money

2

1 served time
2 weathering the storm
3 won (mining) concessions
4 sealed the deal
5 bottom line

3

1 flotation
2 relocating
3 diversifying
4 ongoing
5 termination
6 upturn

4

1 in	2 to
3 on	4 out
5 through	6 under
7 with	8 to

UNIT 15

Vocabulary Style and fashion

1

1 scruffy
2 high heels
3 revealing
4 split
5 beads
6 linen
7 collar
8 a ponytail

2

1 e   2 c   3 a   4 f   5 d   6 b

3

1 silk, knee-length
2 conventional, formal
3 worn out, trainers
4 checked, spotted
5 bob, shades
6 lining, ripped

Listening

4

Speaker 1: g fashion designer
Speaker 2: f male model
Speaker 3: d consumer
Speaker 4: c manufacturer of beauty products
Speaker 5: a online shopping consultant

5

1 India, Speaker 3
2 Japan, Speaker 1

6

a 4   b 3   c 1   d 2   e 2   f 4   g 3
h 5

7

1 skimpy
2 flamboyant
3 eye-catching
4 feminine
5 bland

Developing conversations
Backtracking and correcting

8

1 then
2 lose
3 wrong
4 clash
5 Are you saying
6 on

9

a 4   b 3   c 1   d 6   e 2   f 5

DEVELOPING CONVERSATIONS Defining yourself

10

1 c   2 a   3 d   4 e   5 f   6 b

PRONUNCIATION
Stress in corrections and contradictions

11

1 A: You didn't like him, then?
   B: But I <u>did</u>, actually.
2 A: So, you liked the show?
   B: No, I said I <u>dis</u>liked the show.
3 A: You must have overslept!
   B: No, <u>you're early</u>!
4 A: So it's true. You were laughing at me!
   B: No, I <u>wasn't</u> laughing. That's <u>not</u> true!
5 A: It's your turn to do the shopping.
   B: No, it's <u>not</u> my turn. I did it <u>yesterday</u>.
6 A: You must have seen her!
   B: No, I <u>can't</u> have seen her. I <u>wasn't there</u>!

READING

1
b

2

1 g   2 h   3 d   4 b   5 e   6 a   7 c

3

1 speaks volumes
2 dragged around
3 do the leg work
4 ripped off
5 go about
6 build a rapport with

GRAMMAR Prepositions

4

1 in	2 to
3 At	4 in
5 from	6 with
7 from	8 by
9 into	

VOCABULARY Snowclones

5

1 not as we know it
2 the flatmate from hell
3 my middle name
4 It was the mother of all
5 of whom you speak?
6 the word 'mutt' in the dictionary
7 the new 'speak'
8 life's too short

VOCABULARY Verb forms and word families

1

verb	noun	adjective
simplify	simplification	simple / simplified
(de)mystify	mystery	mysterious / mystifying / mystified
commercialise	commercialisation	commercial / commercialised
lighten	lightening	lightening / lightened
authorise	authority	(un)authorised
justify	justification	(un)justified / (un)justifiable
idealise	ideal / idealisation	ideal
widen	width	wide / widening

2

1 unjustified	2 mystified
3 Self-objectification	4 over-simplification
5 lightening	6 disheartened

DEVELOPING WRITING
An informal letter – using input material

3
Yes

5

1 tricky	2 How's it going?
3 stuff like that	4 pay was pretty good
5 Let me know	6 full-on
7 beyond my reach	8 About

VOCABULARY BUILDER QUIZ 15

1

1 stuck out like a sore thumb
2 opted for
3 pulled it off
4 is set to
5 take new fashion items on board
6 on the wane

2

1 incidence
2 traits
3 masculinity
4 pinpoint
5 profound
6 endorsements
7 disorientated

3
1 seam
2 laces
3 flares
4 shades
5 zip
6 bushy

4
1 (set) to (top)
2 (take) on (board)
3 (opted) to
4 (on) the (wane)
5 (shield their children) from
6 (hair) in (a ponytail)

UNIT 16

LISTENING

1
Speaker 1: d member of a rescue team
Speaker 2: b writer
Speaker 3: c office worker

2
1 a   2 b   3 b   4 a   5 a   6 b

PRONUNCIATION Final /t/

3
1 They've come with the <u>right</u> gear.
2 Wait. I'll <u>just</u> catch my breath.
3 'The <u>next</u> step could have been fatal.' 'Quite.'
4 We're leaving on the first of March.
5 He was sent home to get over a leg wound.
6 I remember <u>quite</u> clearly. I left it there.

DEVELOPING CONVERSATIONS Interjections

5
1 b   2 a   3 c   4 c   5 c

6
1 Whoa! / Oh! / Yuck!
2 Oops!
3 Wow! / Gosh!
4 Oi! / Whoa!
5 Sshhh! / Umm ...

VOCABULARY Accidents and injuries

7
1 tearing
2 came to
3 banging
4 consciousness
5 burn
6 deeply
7 sliced
8 whacked

VOCABULARY Laws and regulations

8
1 dismissed, grounds
2 awarded, damages
3 conviction, overturned
4 sued, libel
5 set, precedent
6 opposed, legislation

READING

1
c

2
1 C   2 A   3 B   4 A   5 D   6 B   7 A
8 D   9 C   10 B   11 C

3
1 churn
2 draw
3 conjure
4 head
5 rush
6 word

VOCABULARY Synonyms

4
1 threat
2 peril
3 hazards
4 menace
5 risk
6 danger
7 threat
8 risk

5
1 menace
2 hazard
3 threat
4 danger

DEVELOPING WRITING
An online comment – linking ideas

1
1 it: the government
2 this: the intention to get tough on crime
3 these: adolescent road accidents, drink- and drug-driving, illegal drag racing
4 What: the facts about the dangers of driving
5 so: taking driving courses to keep skills current

2
a But still
b therefore
c Indeed
d As for
e As well as this
f in order to

3
a Nevertheless
b consequently
c In fact
d With respect to
e On top of this
f so as to

4
1 As well as this / On top of this
2 Indeed / In fact
3 in order to / so as to
4 As for / With respect to
5 But still / Nevertheless
6 therefore / consequently

GRAMMAR Talking about the future

6
1 for
2 bound
3 In
4 possibility
5 to
6 chances

7
1 The President is set to meet the Prime Minister in December.
2 Your contract is due for renewal next month.
3 Logan is bound to have an accident.
4 The odds are that we'll reach the summit within a couple of days.
5 The researchers believe that they are on the verge of finding a cure.
6 I think there's a slim chance that Nathan's plan will work.
7 In all likelihood, Prash won't survive the operation.
8 The search party has just announced that they are on the point of quitting.

VOCABULARY BUILDER QUIZ 16

1
1 to
2 off
3 with
4 off
5 to
6 against

2
1 d   2 e   3 g   4 c   5 b   6 a   7 f

3
1 verge
2 confiscated
3 peril
4 scalded
5 absurd

4
1 plagiarism
2 unprecedented
3 Menacing
4 appraisal
5 disruption
6 negligence
7 liability

TRACK	ITEM	
1	titles	
2	1.1	
3	1.2	
4		Speaker 1
5	2.1	Speaker 2
6		Speaker 3
7	2.2	
8		Speaker 1
9	3.1	Speaker 2
10		Speaker 3
11	3.2	
12	4.1	
13	4.2	
14	4.3	
15	5.1	
16	5.2	Conversation 1
17		Conversation 2
18		Speaker 1
19	6.1	Speaker 2
20		Speaker 3
21	6.2	
22	7.1	
23	7.2	
24	7.3	
25	8.1	
26	8.2	
27		Speaker 1
28	9.1	Speaker 2
29		Speaker 3
30	9.2	
31	10.1	
32	10.2	
33		Speaker 1
34		Speaker 2
35	11.1	Speaker 3
36		Speaker 4
37		Speaker 5
38	11.2	
39	12.1	
40	12.2	
41	12.3	
42	13.1	
43	13.2	
44	14.1	
45	14.2	
46	14.3	
47		Speaker 1
48		Speaker 2
49	15.1	Speaker 3
50		Speaker 4
51		Speaker 5
52	15.2	

TRACK	ITEM	
53		Extract 1
54	16.1	Extract 2
55		Extract 3
56	16.2	